The Gulf Cooperation Council

About the Book and Editor

The Gulf Cooperation Council represents both a model of development and unity in the Arab world and a working example of interstate cooperation to other nations. In this volume, contributors describe the rationale for Gulf unity and cooperation and analyze the financial, economic, and legal institutions of the GCC member states (Saudi Arabia, Kuwait, the United Arab Emirates, Oman, Bahrain, and Qatar). They focus on the GCC's role in maintaining stability in the Arabian peninsula, an area that is clearly vital to U.S. interests.

Contributors pinpoint the essential elements of GCC unity, including its efforts to obtain optimum economic self-sufficiency, to maximize market share and revenue from oil production, and to establish an integrated legal framework. The GCC's unique security needs, given the member states' vast combined area and thinly spread populations, are also discussed. An overview of the strategic interests and policies of both superpowers toward the region reveals a history of decline in their influence and prestige that is a result, it is argued, of misperceptions and misguided policies. Finally, documentation and bibliographic sections enhance the book's usefulness as a handbook on the GCC and the Arabian Gulf states.

John A. Sandwick is director of development at the American-Arab Affairs Council.

The Gulf Cooperation Council

Moderation and Stability
in an Interdependent World

edited by John A. Sandwick

Foreword by George McGovern

Westview Press • Boulder, Colorado

**American-Arab Affairs Council
Washington, D.C.**

Published in 1987 in the United States of America by Westview Press, Inc., Frederick A. Praeger, Publisher, 5500 Central Avenue, Boulder, Colorado 80301; and by the American-Arab Affairs Council, 1730 M Street, N.W., Suite 512, Washington, D.C. 20036

Library of Congress Cataloging-in-Publication Data
The Gulf Cooperation Council.
  Bibliography: p.
  Includes index.
  1. Majlis al-Taᶜawun li-Duwal al-Kaltj al-ᶜArabīyah.
I. Sandwick, John A.
DS201.G85 1987   953'.6   86-34003
ISBN: 0-8133-0475-X
ISBN: 0-8133-0476-8 (pbk.)

Composition for this book was provided by the American-Arab Affairs Council.
This book was produced without formal editing by Westview Press.

Printed and bound in the United States of America

10   9   8   7   6   5   4   3   2   1

CONTENTS

FOREWORD

George McGovern

The Hon. George McGovern served as a U.S. Senator from 1963 to 1981. He served on the Senate Foreign Relations Committee and was chairman of its sub-committees on African Affairs and the Middle East. In 1972, Senator McGovern was the Democratic nominee for President.

The mere attempt at close cooperation between states is a difficult and remarkable undertaking which deserves respectful consideration, as the obstacles are so often insurmountable. The strength born of unity is a concept the founders of the United States of America set forth in documents which have become sacred texts. Begun in revolution and tested in the crucible of an agonizing civil war, the idea of union became the core of American historical experience. Few would deny the benefits which such unity has spawned.

The recent cooperative effort among sovereign states to which this book is devoted involves Saudi Arabia, Kuwait, the United Arab Emirates, Oman, Bahrain and Qatar, which in 1981 formed the Cooperation Council for the Arab States of the Gulf, the GCC. They have a natural affinity, sharing close proximity and a common language and religion. With combined resources perhaps unique in the world, they should be able to expect a bright future of economic and political success. They are located, however, in an area where conflicts begun in the distant past as well as those of contemporary origin continue to play themselves out, threatening the stability of the entire region.

There is every reason for the United States to support and encourage moderating and stabilizing influences in the Middle East. American national interests coincide in this instance with the cause of peace and justice as defined by international consensus. Primary U.S. policy goals include ensuring open exchange of goods and services and limiting the intrusion into the affairs of the region by coercive power, from whatever source. The Gulf countries' unity enables them to take more responsibility for the political arrangements in the region.

It was thought by many analysts when the Iranian revolution began that it would spread throughout the Middle East, destabilizing the Gulf region. This worst-case outcome did not materialize, in large part due to the stability of states thought to be internally divided and weak. That Iraq and the Gulf states did not roll over when faced with Islamic fundamentalism indicates a vigor of national resolve and a resistance to extremism for which they were given little credit in 1979 and which their unity helped them achieve.

The governments of the moderate states of the Gulf have responded to challenges of leadership much as have the industrialized democracies—through commonly agreed-upon principles, traditional practice and continuous reassessment of national interests. The evolution of thought that has taken place over the past decade among Gulf leaders in light of changed economic and political circumstances has been achieved through a consensus which has fostered legitimacy and stability.

It is clear that the interests of the GCC countries largely coincide with those of the United States. Paradoxically, U.S. reluctance to continue to sell defensive weapons to these states implies a naive belief that Arab countries should forego basic efforts to protect their own sovereignty. It is the strength and autonomy which have sustained the GCC since its inception at the beginning of the Gulf war that make possible the free flow of commerce and the resistance to outside intervention which are the minimal objectives of U.S. policy in the region.

The GCC states' desire for independence should strike a responsive chord among Americans, former colonials who have revered the idea of freedom for more than 200 years. But another idea whose time has finally come in the small, tightly integrated world of the late twentieth century is that of interdependence, whereby members of the international system all play essential roles. This book provides a basis for understanding the role of the GCC in that system. It is to be hoped that American leaders, aware of their own fundamental interests in the Middle East, will act to formulate rational policies to ensure those interests before the leaders of the area, in frustration, become disillusioned with their natural ally and look elsewhere for more productive relationships.

The Gulf Cooperation Council

INTRODUCTION

John A. Sandwick

Mr. Sandwick is the Director of Development at the American-Arab Affairs Council.

That many American policymakers, strategists and corporate planners have not yet had access to any single collection of analyses and resource material on the GCC states contributes to a general misunderstanding of the region. In the interest of filling this gap, the American-Arab Affairs Council and Westview Press have published *The Gulf Cooperation Council: Moderation and Stability in an Interdependent World*. As the title implies, the purpose of the book is to examine the GCC's contribution to a region clearly vital to U.S. interests. In many ways, its member states' interests frequently coincide with those of the United States in the international system.

An additional purpose of the book is to examine the financial, economic, legal and security institutions of the GCC member states and the complementary role Americans have played in their development. Recognizing the long history of and contemporary interest in U.S.-GCC cooperation and interdependence is key to a progressive approach to future U.S.-GCC relations.

This is the first book of its kind to organize many of the basic elements necessary to any thorough examination of the GCC and U.S.-Arabian Gulf relations. To date, there has been no single author that has discussed all GCC-related subjects included in this book. The multiauthor approach, with each writer selected for his consummate knowledge of a specific field, is the most effective method of analyzing in depth the various elements of Arabian Gulf and U.S.-GCC issues. Additionally, there has to date been no attempt to compile GCC documentary and bibliographic material for further research on GCC subjects. As much of the relevant material on the GCC as possible is presented in the Documentation and Bibliography sections of this book. It is hoped that these sections will enhance its value as a "handbook" on the Arabian

1

Gulf states, their efforts toward integration and long-term U.S. interests in the region.

The initial two articles trace the history of the GCC. John Christie's chapter, "History and Development of the Gulf Cooperation Council: A Brief Overview," explains the historical precedents for Gulf cooperation and eventual union. By describing the similarities of the social and governmental systems of the member nations, Christie establishes the rationale for Gulf unity and cooperation. As a coda to his chapter, Christie envisages that the GCC's success might provide a "blueprint" for successive Arab unity efforts, an elusive but almost universal objective in the Arab world.

Joseph Twinam's chapter, "Reflections on Gulf Cooperation, with Focus on Bahrain, Qatar and Oman," is based on his many years as a U.S. diplomat in the region. By assessing the value of cooperation and union to the smaller states of the GCC, Ambassador Twinam clearly defines the positive and progressive nature of GCC integration to all its members. Parallel to Twinam's conclusions, social commentators in the Gulf believe that GCC political, economic and security integration at the state level is stimulating an even greater degree of kinship and shared values among all levels of their respective societies. Through the GCC, the aspirations of both the common man and the elite are bound together, thus further encouraging cooperation and development in the region.

Following the general history and overview section are several articles that provide description and analysis of GCC financial, economic, petroleum and legal institutions and their contribution to GCC integration. "The GCC and Economic Development" section begins with Bruce Henderson's chapter on U.S.-GCC financial interdependence. Emphasizing the mutually beneficial contributions each side has made to the other's economy, Henderson outlines the history of American finance and investment in the GCC area as well as the arrival of GCC-based or GCC-owned financial institutions in the United States and in the international banking arena. The relationship between the United States and the GCC states in this industry is an example of how American and Gulf interests can best work together in the pursuit of shared objectives.

Abdullah El-Kuwaiz's chapter on achievements and outlook for GCC economic integration outlines the specific goals that have been established by the GCC for economic integration and the degree to which these objectives have been realized. In his analysis El-Kuwaiz argues that, while a considerable amount of integration can and will be maintained through the GCC's present structure, the organization needs additional autonomy and authority to appropriate factors of production

2

among the GCC member nations in order to obtain an optimum level of GCC self-sufficiency through complementarity.

Hossein Askari and Babak Dastmaltschi take the issue of GCC decision making over national sovereignty an additional step. They argue in their chapter that for the best interests of the GCC states' long-term economic development and integration, oil-pricing and production strategies should be devised by the GCC states as a unit within OPEC and not independently, as is now the case. GCC combined oil reserves, as near-limitless as any nation's on earth, have created a situation where the objectives for pricing and production are almost the opposite of those of the non-GCC members of OPEC, the authors state, thereby justifying a common GCC oil policy that will maximize market share and revenue over the life span of oil production in the Gulf.

The GCC economic integration section concludes with Nicholas Angell's "The Impact of the GCC on Developing Legal Systems in the Gulf Countries." In a uniquely comprehensive study of the legal systems of the Gulf, Angell outlines the institutionalized framework within which the social, economic and security integration of the Gulf states will occur. Describing the legal systems by state and field, and then offering a prognosis as to how these systems may develop and unify under the aegis of the GCC, the author illustrates a framework which the member states may establish to overcome the very real barriers to integration at the institutional and bureaucratic levels.

The book concludes with a section of articles that discuss the security imperatives of the Arabian Gulf states. While it is commonly accepted that in order to defend themselves from threats of external aggression the GCC states will find it necessary to increase cooperation and integration among their various defensive units, it has not been frequently or widely accepted among Western military strategists where the Gulf Arabs perceive their greatest security threat.

In his article on the Soviet Union's policies toward the Gulf, Stephen Page observes this seemingly formidable foe to U.S. interests in the region. However, he unveils a history of decline in influence and prestige which both superpowers have experienced in the region as a result of misguided policies and misperceptions. The Soviets, Page states, have lost for many reasons, including the basic incompatability between communism and traditional Islamic societies. America, on the other hand, has been victimized not by the Soviet Union but by its own policies. By an uncompromising and unquestioned support for Israel, the United States has created an environment of greatly diminished confidence and respect among the GCC leadership and people.

In the final article in the series, J.E. Peterson assesses GCC military capabilities and U.S. preparedness for interdiction in the Gulf and agrees with many of Page's conclusions. The GCC, Peterson writes, comprises six separate nations in a vast area with thinly spread populations, thereby necessitating unique security measures and defense-force integration. While there may be an ancillary role for the United States and the West in providing for its defense, the GCC will accept only an "over-the-horizon" approach to U.S. involvement. The GCC is only hindered, not enhanced, by pre-positioned and pre-staged American defense capabilities and therefore needs to be able to rely on the United States only in a worst-case scenario, and then by invitation only.

Concluding the book is an essay by the noted Arabian and Islamic scholar, Ralph Braibanti, in which he briefly ties together the essential elements brought forth in the preceding chapters and arrives at conclusions relating to the GCC's integration efforts. The GCC, Braibanti states, is not just serving as a model for development and cooperation in the Arabian peninsula region and the Arab world generally. It also provides a working example of interstate cooperation to the larger structure known as *ummah*, the commonwealth of 45 Islamic nations, and to the even broader global system of nations.

At this juncture it is important to mention other relevant works on the Arabian Gulf and the GCC. An indication of the newness of studies in this field is that all books cited below were published in 1986.

Emile Nakhleh's *The Gulf Cooperation Council*, the first book devoted to the topic, is to be praised for the comprehensive manner in which the author has treated the GCC and its development. In the security field, two excellent works stand out: J.E. Peterson's *Defending Arabia* and Mazher Hameed's *Arabia Imperilled: The Security Imperatives of the Arabian Gulf States*. No single work on the economies of the GCC states has recently been completed that we are aware of, yet *The Saudi Arabian Economy* by Ali D. Johany, Michel Berne and J. Wilson Mixon, Jr. is an excellent examination of the largest GCC economy, and many parallels can be drawn with the economies of the kingdom's neighbors. Finally, the recent work of Muhammad Rumaihi, *Beyond Oil*, offers a unique Gulf perspective of the future for the GCC states, and what they can expect to encounter socially, politically and economically when oil resources begin to diminish.

This book could not have been completed without the valuable assistance of a number of individuals and institutions. The editor owes a great debt of appreciation to Joyce Bouvier, who served as both production assistant and assistant editor, roles in which she displayed great skill and expertise in preparing the manuscripts. Anne Joyce, Editor of *American-Arab Affairs* and Director of Publications at the Council, added her objective review of each of the authors' works, always with an eye for conciseness and objectivity.

In the early stages of preparation, Sabra Purtill, a graduate student in Arab studies at Georgetown University, helped compile the book's

Bibliography. David Partington, Middle East Librarian at Harvard College, was also very helpful in assembling a large part of the Bibliography. I wish to give special thanks to Abdullah El-Kuwaiz for the substantive support he gave in supplying GCC documents. These materials provide the foundation of GCC integration efforts and record the primary examples of cooperation among the GCC states.

Finally, a great deal of appreciation is due to the authors themselves. All have worked laboriously to produce chapters of outstanding content and given the reader a close examination of the Gulf states' efforts toward integration and cooperation. As a model for further Arab and non-Arab cooperative efforts, the GCC plays an ever-important role by illustrating successful interstate cooperation through reason and moderation.

Chapter 1

HISTORY AND DEVELOPMENT OF THE GULF COOPERATION COUNCIL: A BRIEF OVERVIEW

John Christie

Mr. Christie is editor of the London-based Middle East Newsletters, *one of which covers Saudi Arabia, the other, the Gulf States.*

Any alliance or close combination of countries is founded, in the first instance, on the perceived identity of interests among the parties involved and on an assessment that there is more to be gained in association than there is to be had from isolation. The identities of interest may be of almost any kind; political, economic, military or cultural; but a common denominator is essential if a coalition of states is to have real substance and explicit purpose. The many existing international groupings, such as the Arab League, the Warsaw Pact, the European Economic Community, the Islamic Conference Organization, may be disparate in constitution and differ widely in their objectives, yet they all possess the thread of commonality that binds together their members into an organizational fabric.

The Gulf Cooperation Council (GCC), formed by six nations of the Arabian peninsula—Bahrain, Kuwait, Oman, Qatar, Saudi Arabia and the United Arab Emirates—is no exception to the general rule. Where practically all other alliances of separate countries must absorb different languages, cultures and political systems, the GCC can—and does— emphasize the close similarities the GCC countries enjoy. There is the common language—Arabic, a common religion—Islam, closely comparable social structures, roughly the same standards of economic development, very similar systems of government, a collective culture and a shared geography. And, perhaps among the more important factors in the composition of the GCC, the people of the six nations

7

recognize and understand their fraternity in the wider implications of Arab nationality.

All these common qualities had been in existence for centuries, yet, despite the apparent advantage they brought to ideas of coalition and coordination among the Gulf Arab states, the past levels of official cooperation among the six countries were so slight as to be of little effect and without lasting importance. Under the previous umbrella of British political and military suzerainty, the sheikhdoms of the Gulf littoral kept to their separate and largely independent ways and the contacts between them of a cooperative nature were desultory and inconsequential. Saudi Arabia, outside the direct British orbit, followed its national preoccupations and policies with only a passing regard to the regional reference. Although Saudi Arabia was a fully independent state and the Gulf countries had, technically at least, the responsibility for their own internal affairs, there was neither political nor popular enthusiasm for moves towards closer ties. As long as Britain remained in effective control of all the larger and wider issues affecting the region, there was no necessity or incentive for the individual states to take any initiatives in the field of cooperation.

But by the early 1960s the course of events had begun to sharpen Gulf perceptions of the possible political future unfolding before them. The accession of Kuwait to full independence in 1961 was a watershed in the political development of the Gulf, serving as it did a tacit notice that Britain would eventually relinquish its overall authority in the rest of the area. Around this time, the British began to give mild encouragement to the smaller sheikhdoms of the so-called Trucial States to consider some forms of greater cooperation and integration among themselves. The development of the oil industry in the Gulf was also having its marked effect, bringing economic independence in place of former financial subservience and offering a proper economic support to independent statehood. By the late 1960s, the British were telling the Gulf rulers of their intention to withdraw entirely from the Gulf and were urging specific measures of cooperation and association upon them. The forewarnings of the British were met, in some instances, with incredulity mixed with alarm; a not entirely surprising reaction to the impending end of a dominant foreign presence stretching back almost 150 years. However, when it was clear that the British did mean to go, the prospect wonderfully concentrated minds on the practical aspects of life in an independent and unsupported state.

In 1971 the Dubai Agreement was reached, under which Bahrain, Qatar and the seven Trucial Sheikhdoms of Abu Dhabi, Dubai, Sharjah, Ajman, Ras al Khaimah, Fujairah and Umm al Quwain were to consider joining together in some kind of federation or union. The following year, after Britain had made its official announcement that it was withdrawing from its bases and colonies east of Suez including the Arabian Gulf, the nine emirs and sheikhs signed an agreement to form the United Arab Emirates (UAE). But it took three more years of negotiation before the UAE came into being, and then it was without Bahrain and Qatar, who both decided against joining the federation and opted for independence on their own. Nevertheless, with the former British-protected states fully independent and with Oman having ended its era of isolation with the accession to power of Sultan Qaboos, by the 1970s all the countries of the region were in a position (if not then ready) to forge closer links in a common unity.

In 1976, from an initiative by Sultan Qaboos of Oman, the foreign ministers of Iran, Iraq, Kuwait, Bahrain, Qatar, the UAE, Saudi Arabia and Oman met in Muscat to discuss the Omani suggestion that a coordinated regional security and defense policy be established. But the ministers were not able to agree on a common position and the conference came to an end without any conclusions reached. The issue was never followed up and no further action took place on the Omani initiative. Then, also in 1976, another effort was made to arrive at an Arab regional consensus. Sheikh Jaber al Ahmad al Sabah, the present amir of Kuwait and at that time crown prince and prime minister, toured the Gulf countries to discuss joint action to "preserve the region's security and stability in the face of political, economic and security challenges threatening this strategic area." Sheikh Jaber formally proposed the establishment of a Gulf union as a vehicle for this joint action, with the objective "of realizing cooperation in all economic, political, educational and informational fields."

As much as anywhere, the genesis of the GCC lay in the Kuwaiti proposal although it was another five years before the idea became a reality. However, Kuwait's exploratory talks with the UAE led to the establishment of a joint ministerial council of the respective prime ministers of the two countries. The consultations with Saudi Arabia, Bahrain, Qatar and Oman were fairly successful and all officially endorsed the concept of a Gulf union.

Over the following five years a series of meetings and discussions took place on the subject of a regional grouping, now refined in concept to include only the six countries which eventually did form the GCC. But the pace of negotiation was leisurely. To the six governments concerned there was no difficulty in agreeing on the virtues of cooperation or, indeed, to practice it in certain fields; but the necessary impetus to action was lacking. Had it not been for outside events, the agreeable discussions on the shape and substance of a formal association among the six states might have continued interminably. Then, a real and alarming urgency was brought to the deliberations of the six by major developments involving other powers.   The overthrow of the shah of

9

Iran in 1979 and the establishment of the revolutionary regime of Aya- tollah Ruhollah Khomeini totally changed the security picture of the Gulf region. The apparent power vacuum created by the British with- drawal was supposed—in some eyes—to be filled by Iran. With strong U.S. support, especially in the defense field, the shah had happily accepted the role of Iran as "policeman of the Gulf." The acquiescence if not the approval of the Gulf Arab states to this arrangement was assumed, although the lukewarm reception the Arabs gave to it sug- gested considerably less than enthusiasm for Iran being cast as the prime regional power. However, the plan had its *de facto* advantages, at least as far as maintaining a desired level of security in the area was concerned. But, the change in nature and character of the new regime in Tehran quickly dispelled any sense of comfort or complacency in the Gulf Arab states about regional security.

Next, in December 1979 the Soviet Union invaded Afghanistan and the area's defenses began to look very thin indeed. Also, by this time, the worsening relations between Iran and Iraq were apparent. In Sep- tember 1980, after border clashes and artillery exchanges, Iran and Iraq became locked in open war. The vulnerability of the countries of the Arabian peninsula was chillingly exposed and the six countries of the embryonic Gulf union needed no further spurs to action.

In early February 1981 the foreign ministers of the UAE, Bahrain, Kuwait, Qatar, Oman and Saudi Arabia met in Riyadh and unanimously agreed on the establishment of a Gulf Cooperation Council (GCC), aimed at fostering cooperation and coordination among the member states "in all walks of life" and intended to present a unified Gulf position on major political, economic and social issues. A GCC charter was quickly drawn up and the basic structure of the Council agreed upon. Three months later, on May 25, 1981, the six heads of state met in Abu Dhabi and signed the Charter and the GCC came into formal existence.

The terms of the GCC's constitution are both comprehensive and far- reaching. It speaks (Article 4) of "the ultimate aim of unity" and an eventual confederal union emerging from the GCC framework. How- ever, the Charter was carefully worded to take account of the larger Arab canvas and to mollify potential Arab opposition to the new orga- nization. The GCC, the Charter states, "conforms with the national aims of the Arab Nation as expressed in the Charter of the Arab League . . . .The GCC can be seen as confirming the support of these states for the Arab League, its Charter and objective, and Islam as a whole."

From the outset the GCC took pains to emphasize its economic and social aims and, other than affirming the members' determination to defend their independence and territorial integrity, any suggestion that a military alliance was in the making was studiously avoided. Nevertheless, beyond the agreeable premises of kinship, fellow feeling and shared values, the GCC states were fully aware of the implicit threat to their survival from the overall situation in the Gulf. If the press releases were about economic cooperation, the urgent discussions within the GCC were about defense and internal security.

The organizational structure of the GCC reflected the Council's collective view of the best means and methods for the new body to function to its maximum advantage. The collective view involved, inevitably, some areas of compromise. When the Charter was being drawn up the ministers had before them two working papers, one submitted by Kuwait and the other by Oman. The Kuwaiti paper suggested the administrative constitution of the proposed organization and the broad outlines of the policies it might follow. With only minor alterations, the Kuwaiti paper was accepted and became the blueprint on which the Charter was based.

Oman's written proposals were concerned with the extremely sensitive issues of defense and security. The Omani paper said, in essence, that there should be the closest military cooperation among the member states, leading to an eventual objective of full military integration in command, communications, supply and strategy. More significantly, the Omani paper pointed out that the six GCC states, even at the point of full military integration, were inadequate by themselves to ensure the successful defense of the region against a substantial external attack. Therefore, the Omani paper maintained, the GCC should plan its combined military defense in open cooperation with a major friendly power whose security perceptions were close, if not identical, with those of the GCC. The only friendly power with the required viable military strength and with the desired political profile was, the Omani working paper propounded, the United States. Whether the ministers accepted or rejected the military analysis put forward by Oman, they preferred to delay any decisions—even in private—concerning the military and defensive strategies the Council should adopt. The Omani paper was shelved and the foreign ministers drafting the Charter said the time was not ripe to come to conclusions on the question of defense.

The makeup of the GCC owes much to the forms of other supranational and international organizations. The GCC's highest authority consists of a Supreme Council composed of the heads of state of the six member countries. When required, the Supreme Council can constitute itself as the Disputes Settlement Board. In the Council each country has a single, equal vote, and a unanimous vote is required to approve any substantive measure or policy. The Council lays down the guidelines of the higher policy objectives of the GCC and its approval is necessary to implement proposed executive action. The chairmanship of the Supreme Council is held for one year by each country in alphabetical order; currently (1986) the chairman is Oman. Succession to the chairmanship is made at the regular annual meeting of the Supreme Council, usually in November of each year when the GCC summit takes place.

Below the Supreme Council comes the Ministerial Council, made up of the foreign ministers of the six member states. The Ministerial Council is the working policy group of the GCC. It considers the proposals, policies and projects, winnows the recommendations and suggestions put forward by other GCC ministerial and expert-level committees and formulates the final proposals put forward to the Supreme Council for its approval.

If the Supreme Council is the captain and the Ministerial Council the officers on the bridge, then the Secretariat is the engine room of the GCC ship. The GCC Secretariat General, headquartered in Riyadh, plays a significant and influential role in the GCC scheme of things; it has much of the power and style of the United Nations Secretariat-General. In addition to its expected administrative functions, the GCC Secretariat initiates in its own right many studies and reviews of actual and potential cooperation and integration among the member states; it commissions outside feasibility studies on suggested and potential projects; it creates committees and subcommittees to look into the prospects of new or possible fields of GCC action; and it drafts the legislation required to implement agreed GCC policies. The secretary-general, H.E. Dr. Abdulla Yacoub Bishara, is the first and, so far, only holder of the office. Bishara, an articulate and energetic former diplomat, was Kuwait's ambassador to the United Nations for many years. His two associate secretaries-general are H.E. Ibrahim Subhi, an Omani, who is responsible for political affairs, and H.E. Dr. Abdullah El-Kuwaiz of Saudi Arabia, who oversees economic affairs at the GCC headquarters. With the Supreme Council meeting but once a year and the Ministerial Council at three-month intervals, the importance of the GCC Secretariat is not to be underestimated.

There are over 60 official pan-Arab and inter-Arab organizations currently in existence, covering almost every kind of political, technical, economic, social and cultural field known. This multitude of associated entities, all officially sponsored, paid for, and manned by the Arab countries has—in common with other similar international and national combinations—a varied record of success and a largely unquantifiable measure of value to the Arab nation.

Among the burgeoning bureaucracies of the Arab world, does the GCC have a justified place and a commendable role? The question is neither unfair nor superfluous, when the recent history of previous creations of Arab unity is considered. Egypt, Syria and North Yemen as the United Arab Republic, a brief confederation of Jordan and Iraq in the 1950s, the short-lived unities of Libya and Sudan, Tunisia and

Libya, and Sudan and Egypt—none of which survived or developed into a marriage of political or economic substance—were all fatally flawed in conception or execution. Is the GCC any different from these? And does it have a genuine and viable future?

The GCC itself will give a stout affirmative to the questions and point to a dozen or more kindred characteristics of the peoples of the GCC states. But the GCC's credibility and its likely durability rest heavily on a factor which the GCC itself chooses not to make too public. With only parochial differences of a minor nature, the systems and forms of the governments of the six GCC member states are consistently alike in style, principle and circumstance. Throughout the GCC-member nations one finds an easy familiarity in the uniformity of government and the application of its rule. Common language, religion and culture may be the bricks of the GCC edifice; the coincidence of matching government rule is the cement that binds them together.

This unity of form in government is both an advantage and a disadvantage to the GCC. In one sense, it allows the GCC to operate on a set of basic domestic assumptions which, if workable in one member country, should be equally valid in any other of the member states. New ideas and developments acceptable in one member country should find a ready approval in another. But the look-alike systems of government of the GCC six have few parallels in the wider international scene—and none at all in the rest of the Arab world. It is difficult to imagine another Arab government, outside the GCC, being entirely comfortable within as closely knit an organization as the GCC. A few years ago Yousuf Shirawi, Bahrain's minister of development, gave a talk in London in which he suggested that there was nothing to prevent the enlargement of the GCC group by allowing other Arab states—by invitation—to join the association. Shirawi cited the Yemen Arab Republic (North Yemen) and Iraq as two potential member candidates; the first on the grounds that the Yemen has at least a geographical linkage with the rest of the peninsula countries, and the second on the basis that Iraq is, in maritime terms, a Gulf state. The other conforming Arab characteristics of Yemen and Iraq were, reasonably enough, assumed by Shirawi to be self-evident. However, such suggestions have not been heard again from the GCC. In fact, the tacit current premise from the GCC itself, made in its official statements and comments, is that membership in the GCC is not really open to other Arab states. Moreover, it is a reasonable conclusion that the GCC's composition as an exclusive club of traditional and benevolent autocracies is a fairly permanent condition, and not unless and until the GCC governments and their systems of rule change very radically could an Arab state with a markedly different political pattern qualify for entry into the GCC.

Still, exclusivity has its virtues and values in the political field and the GCC uses its unique characteristics skillfully and to advantage. Some sections of Arab opinion have a somewhat critical view of the GCC, seeing in its separation and distinction a detraction from the struggle for the goal of Arab unity. The GCC is also sometimes regarded as having walled itself off from the Arab League, the main organizational body in which all Arab countries are represented. Responding to such criticism, the GCC says that its formation fully complies with the objectives of the Arab League charter, which specifically encourages regional cooperation as a means of strengthening the Arab nation. The GCC, it says, is a "confirmation of these states' support for the Arab League and a promotion of their role in realizing the objectives of its charter, which serves Arab and Islamic causes equally."

Within the general frame of the Arab world, the GCC has been a force of moderation, conciliation and mediation. Its overt essays into inter-Arab affairs have been few and far between, although its private collective voice has undoubtedly carried weight in Arab councils. In November 1983, when the GCC was holding its fourth summit conference in Qatar, an envoy from the Palestine Liberation Organization appeared in Doha and appealed to the GCC leaders to mediate in the factional fighting that had broken out among PLO groups in Lebanon. After several hours of deliberation and debate, the GCC decided to send the foreign ministers of Kuwait and Qatar to Damascus to try to negotiate an end to the internecine fighting. The two ministers were partially successful in that they persuaded the two PLO factions to call a cease-fire and sit down to discuss their differences. The cease-fire did not last very long, it is true, but at least the GCC had tried and managed to achieve something.

The GCC was also active in helping to end the longstanding hostility between the Sultanate of Oman and the Peoples Democratic Republic of Yemen (PDRY). Through the good offices of the UAE and Kuwait acting at the behest of the GCC, the two disputing sides were brought together in a series of formal and informal meetings. Eventually, in 1983, after two years of negotiations, Oman and the PDRY agreed to the "normalization" of their diplomatic and political relations. The GCC can claim some credit for this modest improvement in the regional security situation.

In other purely Arab affairs, the GCC usually adopts the "consensus position," a policy exemplified by the Council's stated attitude to the convening of the frequently postponed Arab summit meeting. The GCC was, is, and will be willing to attend an Arab summit wherever and whenever there is a large official Arab agreement to do so; lacking such agreement, the GCC endorses the majority view that a continued delay is the wisest course. This nimble negotiation of the tightrope of inter-

Arab politics is typical of the GCC's skill—and desire—to be, politically, all things to all men. Given the limitations of the GCC's power and influence and remembering that the Council's first responsibility is to its own membership, the GCC's usually cautious and uncontroversial approach to Arab political matters is understandable.

On the international front the GCC has, to some extent, an easier task. Only rarely does the GCC present itself as a formal league of states; more commonly, the international relations of the constituent members are their own individual business. However, in the economic field the GCC does act as a single entity, particularly over the question of the GCC countries' present and future exports of petrochemical products to the United States, Europe and Japan. The GCC has been in continuing negotiation with the European Economic Community (EEC) for a long time on this issue. The secretary-general, Dr. Bishara, has several times visited Europe on these negotiations and a senior Saudi Arabian diplomat, Ambassador Mamun Kurdi, has been delegated as the GCC chief negotiator at the international level on GCC petrochemical exports. The negotiations over the GCC's petrochemical products are mainly concerned with tariffs, trade barriers and market access. However, on a broader canvas, the GCC is also seeking a formal trade-cooperation agreement with the EEC to cover the whole range of trade and economic cooperation on a regional basis.

One of the more notable GCC forays into the international arena took place in 1984. Then, extremely concerned about the increasing number of Iranian attacks on oil shipping in the Gulf and alarmed by the new Iranian tactic of "stop and search" of civilian shipping bound for Gulf Arab ports, the GCC sponsored a resolution at the United Nations which, with only a few revisions of the text, was approved by the Security Council. By thirteen votes and two abstentions, the 15-member Security Council voted in favor of a revised GCC resolution calling on "all states to respect the right of free navigation in the Gulf and refrain from any act which may lead to further escalation and widening of the conflict." To have the U.N. Security Council agree on a resolution is no mean political feat; it requires the United States and the Soviet Union to vote in agreement and it entails the extremely judicious expenditure of political capital on the part of the sponsors. In that episode, the GCC's main spokesman at the U.N. was Kuwaiti Foreign Minister Sheikh Sabah al Ahmad, and he was supported by his Bahraini and Qatari counterparts.

The Iraq-Iran war has been, and still is, one of the constant and primary concerns of the GCC since the organization was founded. As Kuwait's foreign minister said, in reference to a recent (June 1986) meeting of the GCC Ministerial Council, "There never has been a meeting [of the Ministerial Council] at which the Iran-Iraq war has not figured on the agenda." The Gulf war epitomizes the difficulties the GCC faces in reconciling its stated aims and objectives with the practical dictates of inescapable political and military developments. The GCC emphasizes the importance of its nonaligned position "to all countries" and its exclusive collective responsibility for stability in the GCC region. Much is made of the doctrine of self-reliance and an insistence that no other power—especially superpowers—has any right of intervention in the area. At the same time, there is an ample awareness among the GCC leadership that their collective military capabilities may not be quite sufficient for their strategic needs. It is for this reason the GCC makes such fine technical distinctions about their regional sovereignty and other nations' responsibilities where the Gulf waters are concerned. Freedom of navigation in the Gulf and the region's neutrality are cardinal tenets of the GCC's position. Yet, the GCC emphasizes that this does not absolve the international community from *its* obligation to ensure the safety and freedom of navigation in Gulf waters. The GCC's distinction is legally correct and politically justified and blends both international responsibility for peace and security in this vital region with the GCC's role as guarantor and motivator of regional stability in the Gulf.

The political philosophies and attitudes of the GCC are not based on merely a series of intellectual conceptions and doctrinaire conclusions. They are grounded in hard, material fact which, in turn, creates many of the GCC's strategic and geopolitical policies. A key element in the facts of the GCC's life is the members' awareness that only in combination do they possess a proper viability as a political and demographic independent entity in today's world. Individually, four of the six GCC countries are, in population and territory, extremely limited. Only Saudi Arabia and the Sultanate of Oman have a sizable land mass on a world scale and none of the six has, individually, a population of any magnitude.

But, together, the six nations add up to a respectable compass. In the mid-1980s the best official and expert estimates give the GCC a population of over 13,600,000, and all the constituent countries have a high rate of population growth. The total land area of the GCC group is substantial by any standards: about 2,600,000 square kilometers. But more important than its mass, the GCC territory occupies a crucial strategic position on a global level. Flanking the vital sea-lanes of the Red Sea and the Gulf—the one a doorway to the Suez Canal and the other including the critical Strait of Hormuz through which passes some 40 percent of the non-communist world's oil supplies—the geographical connotations of the GCC are immense. The strategic implications of its territorial presence are of paramount significance to all nations.

The military assets the GCC commands in the service of its geopolitical position and the furtherance of its political objectives are easy enough to quantify but considerably more difficult to evaluate. Among them the GCC countries have some of the most sophisticated weapons available, some of the best the superpowers and major powers can supply. The total regular military manpower of the six GCC states adds up to around 140,000 men. Saudi Arabia, the largest in all respects of the GCC partners, has approximately 35,000 in its regular army and about the same number in its national guard and other defense units. The kingdom has a fair-sized air force, with some 180 modern U.S., and now European, fighter and intercept aircraft, as well as the formidable AWACS (Airborne Warning and Control System aircraft). Saudi Arabia's defense expenditure dwarfs the military outlays of its fellow members in the GCC: $27 billion or so of total GCC defense spending of $34 billion. Among the GCC's armed forces, only the Sultanate of Oman has had fairly recent experience in modern warfare, in the campaign in Dhofar in the 1970s, and even there the sultanate's regular forces of 20,000 in the army and 5,000 in the air force and navy needed outside help (from Iran) to bring the foreign-supported rebellion to an end. A little surprisingly, the UAE has the biggest single army in the GCC—46,000 regular soldiers. However, many of the rank and file are foreigners and the federation's true military strength is much diluted by each of the component emirates having its own individual military force, which as a group are referred to as a "regional" command.

Much of the military capacity and potential effectiveness of the GCC rests on extremely sophisticated high technology weaponry, all of it bought from outside non-Arab powers. The GCC states have no indigenous arms industry, although discussions have taken place among them on setting up a regional arms manufacturing facility. The GCC's reliance on sophisticated armaments is compounded by the necessity to have outside skilled assistance—usually from the country of supply—to operate the equipment obtained. The U.S.-supplied AWACS aircraft are a case in point. Although Saudi Arabian aircrews will fly the aircraft, the operation requires a civilian maintenance team of 450 men from the aircraft makers, Boeing, and a technical assistance contingent of 21 uniformed men from the U.S. Air Force, who will be needed at their posts in the kingdom for at least two years. In the same way, a recent (1986) purchase from the Soviet Union by Kuwait of ground-to-air missiles brought a Soviet military training team to Kuwait.

The GCC is sufficiently flexible and pragmatic not to make too much of an issue about the various defense arrangements its members have. Saudi Arabia's close links with the United States in the defense field are politically played down in a regional context, yet the kingdom is not backward in praising the high quality of the military equipment it receives from the United States. Oman's separate arrangements with the United States are also accommodated by the GCC without difficulty. The United States is improving and upgrading certain military facilities in Oman, especially on the Omani island of Masirah in the Indian Ocean, which could—by Omani invitation only—serve an American Central Command force. The GCC, as such, has no overriding authority whatsoever over its member states; the independence and sovereignty of the individual states remain intact within the organization.

While in the early days of its existence the GCC stressed the economic side of its cooperative efforts, since about 1983 the Council has allowed military coordination and GCC defense matters to assume a higher public profile. In 1984 the first GCC joint military exercises were held. These, under the title "Peninsula Shield," were largely command and communication exercises, but they were a beginning toward the establishment of a credible GCC military response capacity. The GCC secretary-general openly admits that the GCC has a long road to travel before the Council can claim to dispose a coherent and united military capability. However, as he frequently points out, the GCC is not to be equated with, say, NATO, which is purely a military association of countries. The military cooperation in the GCC is, Bishara says, only one aspect of the many dynamics of change the Council seeks to promote. However, the continuation of the Iran-Iraq war and the escalation of the conflict to include attacks on civilian shipping in Gulf waters, thrust defense and security matters into the forefront of GCC affairs.

At the fifth GCC summit meeting in Kuwait in November 1984, the Council approved the formation of a GCC Joint Strike Force. At the time, Abdulla Bishara described the establishment of the force as "symbolic" and commented that its military effectiveness should not be exaggerated. The Council nevertheless set out the basic structure for the Joint Strike Force—subsequently renamed the "Peninsula Shield force." It was, and still is, commanded by a Saudi Arabian general and composed of some 6,000 or 7,000 men from designated units of the armed forces of the GCC member states. Its base is at Hafr al Batin, in northeast Saudi Arabia not far from the border of Kuwait, and its operational employment and deployment require the unanimous decision of the GCC Supreme Council. Seven thousand or so men might not be much of a military deterrent in the scale of a modern war, but the GCC's joint force has a powerful political strength to a potential aggressor.

The very existence of a combined military force confirms the GCC's oft-stated position: that an attack on any one GCC state will be regarded as an attack on all. None of the GCC countries deludes itself that the Peninsula Shield force is a viable military counter to large-scale external aggression and all realize that, in the last analysis, they would have to commit their national armed forces in any large-scale and substantial conflict in which they became involved. Depending on the scope and dimension of such a conflict, the GCC is also aware that its military capacity may not be sufficient in every possible case and an eventual recourse to outside assistance might have to be made. But these speculative military disadvantages do not signify that the GCC countries could not give an adequately good military account of themselves if they were required to do so. There is ample evidence throughout the region of popular and official determination to preserve the independence and integrity of the GCC states. As military coordination improves and integration comes closer, so the GCC's policy of self-reliance edges all the time to a more valid premise.

If there is sometimes some uncertainty among the GCC countries about the many military problems and the numerous strategic difficulties before them, singly or jointly, a far more comfortable certitude exists about the GCC's economic affairs. When the GCC stresses the importance of the Council's moves to economic cooperation and unification, it does so with a probable realization that it is in this field, rather than in the defense and political areas, that a likely majority of the GCC populace will be able to identify with the aims and objectives of the GCC. Despite its careful and cautious approach to all proposed changes, its very conservative reactions to new measures and its painstaking concern to ensure that all substantive initiatives are acceptable to the general public in all the member states, the GCC knows that its creation was a wholly executive action of governments. Leaving aside the untested questions of public enthusiasm for the GCC and what it stands for, the mechanics of its functions and the machinery of its operation, the GCC owes its existence solely to the national leadership in the region. Its formation may have filled a proper need, it might even have anticipated a popular desire, but no popular vote was cast for its establishment, no opinion polls were conducted to endorse the leadership decision and no widespread consultations were held to approve its genesis. All the governments of the region, from long practice and proved experience, were adept in the art of consensus politics, and it was a rare event for a government initiative or action to run into a hostile popular reception. The establishment of the GCC proved the point. Once propounded, the idea of a cooperative common effort, aimed to enhance an already-approved lifestyle and intended to embellish recognized indigenous strength, had a ready, popular acceptance among the people of the Arabian Gulf. And that essential public acceptance was made more sure by the emphasis on the economic modalities of the new framework.

Hence, economic integration rather than military unification was the keynote for the Council. And within two weeks of the signing of the GCC Charter, the Council's Unified Economic Agreement was announced. The Agreement has been described as the backbone of the GCC and its activities, the basic foundation on which all the rest of the GCC's cooperative and integrative endeavors are built. If the GCC looks anywhere for a model for its aims and objectives, it is to the Common Market of the EEC rather than the military alliances of the Warsaw Pact or NATO. The 28 articles of the Unified Economic Agreement (see p. 239 for the text of the Unified Economic Agreement) shifted the countries' approach in all economic sectors from the individual to the collective.

Not every clause of the Economic Agreement has been implemented, but the GCC is consistent and firm in its prediction that the GCC region will have an operable and properly functioning common market by 1990. For those who like to note such coincidences, most experts predict that 1990 will mark the end of the present depressed state of the world oil market and the return to oil-boom days for the major oil exporters, especially the Arab Gulf GCC nations.

The choice of trade, industry and economy as the areas of the thrust of the GCC was made that much easier—and eminently more sensible— by the amount of economic muscle the six nations possess among them. Indicative of the GCC's financial strength was the establishment of the Gulf Investment Corporation with a capital of $2 billion, later increased to $3 billion, as the GCC's main vehicle for financing joint ventures set up by member states and as the investment agency for the six Gulf states. Externally, the GCC has taken the lead in conducting negotiations at the international level on behalf of all six member states, especially over the question of access to European, Japanese and American markets for GCC-produced petrochemical products.

The GCC has now been around long enough and has made sufficient progress towards its objectives to substantiate its actual and promised regional significance. On a wider stage, the GCC is bound to have an increasing international importance and a weightier voice in world affairs as the political and economic integration of the six countries proceeds. If and when the GCC attains the confederal status envisaged for it, some significant and positive prospects could lie ahead. Disproving past failures at Arab regional cooperation, the GCC might offer the blueprint for a general Arab unity—something the Arab League has, for whatever reason, failed to do. Short of some unforeseen change, the GCC should continue to be able to deploy its favored economic circumstances in pursuit of its own policies. If they remain as sober and as sensible as those in force today, the conceptions of the GCC should find a receptive audience even beyond those with a common heritage whom the GCC originally addressed and encompassed just over five years ago. It is not only the Arab world which would be bettered with the conversion of the principle of cooperation into the reality of current practice, but the interests of the United States and the Western world as well.

Chapter 2

REFLECTIONS ON GULF COOPERATION, WITH FOCUS ON BAHRAIN, QATAR AND OMAN

Joseph Wright Twinam

The Hon. Joseph W. Twinam, John C. West visiting professor at The Citadel, Charleston, South Carolina, was formerly dean of the Executive Seminar and Professional Studies at the Foreign Service Institute. He served as the first resident U.S. ambassador to Bahrain and as deputy assistant secretary of state for Near Eastern and South Asian Affairs.

I f there is strength in unity, then the weaker must benefit. If there is prosperity in cooperation, then surely it serves the less affluent well. As a broad proposition Bahrain, Oman and Qatar, as the "smaller," that is, the less populous and less affluent of the six member states of the Gulf Cooperation Council (GCC), stand to gain much from the sort of cooperation which the Council symbolizes and stimulates.

At the outset, however, we should note the artificiality of treating these three smaller members as a group and thus implying that they have a significant set of characteristics setting them apart from Saudi Arabia, Kuwait and the United Arab Emirates, the three "larger" GCC members. Overall, all the GCC states, including the relative colossus Saudi Arabia, have very much in common. That is what the GCC is all about. Spokesmen for the GCC concept have always been quick to point out the peculiarly common characteristics of the member countries in justifying why these six states came into association to the exclusion of other Arab countries.

Within this general similarity, however, each of the Six has its own special situations, potentials and needs. The smaller members are no more identical to one another than they are different from the larger.

Each of the Six finds certain aspects of Gulf cooperation particularly to its liking. Each has peculiar hesitations about certain other aspects of abandoning particular interests in pursuit of a common good. But this is not really the main point. The main point is that cooperation among GCC states is not a zero-sum game in which some benefit and others sacrifice. The whole idea of such cooperation is that all are stronger for it. To the extent that the Council is an effective instrument for such mutual benefit, the larger gain along with the smaller. To judge the effectiveness of the Council one must first look at whence it came and what it is all about.

THE ROAD TO THE GCC

Much of the limited Western writing on the GCC tends to stress the Iranian revolution and the Iran-Iraq war as the forces driving the six Gulf Arab monarchies to come together in the Council. Certainly both events were catalysts, and the entanglement of the larger Gulf neighbors in hostilities presented a unique opportunity for the six Gulf nonbelligerents to form an institution which excludes Iraq. But concentrating on the impact of the revolution and the war puts too much weight on the security aspects of the GCC, while ignoring its economic and, even more important, political significance. Moreover, the focus on events since the fall of the shah ignores a substantial earlier history of Gulf Arab yearning for unity and groping toward cooperation.

A diplomat from a GCC country has recently asserted that the origins of the movement toward Gulf Arab cooperation reach back to 550 B.C.[1] On the basis of my own experience in Gulf matters, I am unable either to challenge or support this claim. But certainly for two decades prior to the establishment of the GCC there was a strong sense, particularly in the Gulf emirates, of the need for cooperation among Gulf Arab states and perhaps even unity of at least the smaller ones. A driving concern was the gut feeling that entities as small in population as the emirates could not easily make their way independently. When Qatar became fully independent in 1971, there was some initial opposition to that state's admission to the United Nations. The hesitation, which was quickly overcome by the efforts of the United States, the United Kingdom and other friendly U.N. members, rested solely on a general concern about the proliferation of ministates. Should a political entity with perhaps less than 100,000 citizens properly take a place among nation-states?

Given the striking success which all GCC members have achieved in nation building, developing modern societies and playing a constructive

---

[1] An interview with Ambassador Abdul Kader B. al-Ameri, *American-Arab Affairs*, No. 15 (Winter 1985-86).

role in the international community, it is today hard to appreciate how bleak their prospects appeared a quarter century ago when Kuwait achieved full independence. The nationalist fervor sweeping the Arab world was revolutionary in thrust. Hereditary rulers of the Gulf Arab variety, including—indeed most particularly—the House of Saud, were branded by most Arab nationalists as headed for the dustheap of history. The chaos of Aden was a frightening omen of how the British retreat from empire might end in the small states of the Gulf. While oil wealth assured a certain prosperity, there was no inkling of the enormous income and influence which oil would bring the Gulf Arabs by the 1970s.

Certainly the GCC states have done well in making their way in the world. But for all their progress, these nations—with the exception of Saudi Arabia—still suffer from a weakness beyond remedy, tininess. Of course, populations have grown rapidly over the last two decades, but largely through the rapid increase of unassimilated resident alien communities which pose a further question about the long-term viability of such small nations.

The issue was not simply a question of survival. It also involved the aspiration for identification with a psychologically satisfying political community. Twenty years ago a Kuwaiti trying to explain to me the appeal of Arab nationalism put it in words to this effect: "It's fine to be a Kuwaiti, but we need a larger political identity. After all, how would you like to have to say, in making a point in good company, 'Well, we Liechtensteiners think . . . .' "

Citizens of the GCC states embrace Arab nationalism in its broader meaning and find satisfaction in dedication to the Arab cause. But by the early 1960s it was fairly clear that the Arab League was about as far as "Arab unity" was likely to go in creating all-inclusive political institutions. Moreover the most vocal advocates of Arab unity at that time—Nasserists, Baathists and the Arab Nationalist Movement—were painting a vision of a new social order which was hardly inspiring to conservative and prosperous citizens of the Arab states of the Gulf— particularly the hereditary ruling families. Thus the search by Gulf leaders for a political identification more intense than that offered by membership in the Arab nation began to focus close to home. From the beginning, however, the quest for the sort of cooperation represented by the GCC has been perceived by the questers as compatible with and complementary to a dedication to Arab nationalism.

KUWAIT AND THE LOWER GULF

The active search for Gulf cooperation began with the Kuwaitis, who remain among its strongest advocates. Shortly after full independence, Kuwait was embarked on a special economic and technical assistance program for the lower Gulf states and the Yemens, featuring the establishment of schools and hospitals. The concept of a federation of the nine lower Gulf sheikhdoms sprang to life in the wake of the United Kingdom's announcement in 1968 that it would relinquish its remaining protective treaty relationships by the end of 1971. When the movement for federation faltered, the Kuwaitis took the initiative among neighboring Arab states in trying to urge the nine sheikhdoms toward a viable federation. They also, at least in the view of Western observers, galvanized the Saudis into action in support of the "greater federation."

Once the composition of the independent lower Gulf emerged—Bahrain and Qatar as separate nation-states and the seven Trucial Sheikhdoms laced into the United Arab Emirates (UAE), with Oman under new management finally tuning into the neighborhood—the Kuwaitis by the mid-1970s were back on the search for at least structured cooperation among the Gulf Arabs and perhaps even some form of unity. Kuwait's various efforts to push the broad concept of a Gulf union, to establish a Gulf monetary regime and to promote a successful regional security conference were not blessed with immediate payoff. Part of the problem that the smaller Gulf states had in following the Kuwaiti lead—a problem always carefully unstated—was that of recognizing another emirate as leader rather than equal, when the alternative of being led by a kingdom of even greater wealth and potential beneficence loomed on the horizon. To some extent the smaller states were waiting for the natural leader, Saudi Arabia, to bestir itself. Another hesitation on the part of the smaller states—still somewhat evident today—had to do with why Kuwait was no longer an "equal." The widely acknowledged traditional dynamism of the Kuwaiti merchant had been combined with enormous oil wealth and a new tradition of progressive society. In the economic sphere the Kuwaitis were the "go-go" entrepreneurs of the Gulf. In the smaller states there was—and to some degree remains—concern that somewhere between cooperation and union lay the opening through which Kuwaiti capital and commercial daring would leap, to the potential detriment of local interests.

In addition, more conservative elements in the lower Gulf undoubtedly had another concern about following the Kuwaiti lead. Much to its credit in the eyes of Western observers, at home Kuwait was well launched on a progressive course, exhibiting serious dedication to such concepts as constitutional monarchy, parliamentary democracy, women's rights and press freedom. Such notions promised to be highly appealing to many down the Gulf, and this gave pause to those whom some would call behind the times and others label as prudent.

THE NOT-SO-SLEEPING GIANT

If the Kuwaitis were first off the mark in pushing for Gulf Arab coordination, it should not be assumed that Saudi Arabia was either dormant or indifferent. The Saudis had quite another role to play. They were the "superpower" of what would become the Six, with more people and wealth than their five colleagues put together. They also occupied a vast kingdom which influenced their early attention to Gulf affairs in two ways. First, there was an overwhelming amount of work to do at home, in applying oil wealth to economic development and nation building. Second, the Saudis, in the third of a century before the Iranian revolution, had less to worry about on their Gulf flank than elsewhere. Conflict, revolution and hostility came from a true "arc of crisis" centered in the Palestine problem but stretching eventually as far east as revolutionary Iraq and as far south by west as Nasser's Egypt and the turmoil of the Yemen. The Gulf Arab region, first under British control and then a collection of small but prospering states facing a seemingly stable giant neighbor ruled by the shah of shahs, seemed a sea of tranquility compared to tempests elsewhere around the king-dom's vast domain.

Moreover, from the standpoint of the smaller states, as the quest for Gulf cooperation began there was some historic precedent for concern about how honorable long-term Saudi intentions toward at least some of them might be. In their history was resistance, with British support, against Wahhabi expansion. Even by the late 1960s some Saudis would acknowledge in private the inevitability of a Saudi "manifest destiny" along the Arab shore of the Gulf. Western observers know little for sure about the precise nature of Saudi dialogue with smaller neighbors in the two decades before the GCC was launched. It is hard to believe, however, that the smaller Gulf states saw the Saudi Arabia of Kings Faisal and Khalid as harboring grand plans of expansion toward fully independent neighbors. The Saudi bitterness about territorial problems with Abu Dhabi and Oman over Buraimi had been, after all, largely driven by resentment of the "outside" intervention of the United King-dom in that matter. Yet this difficult boundary issue remained as the British prepared to withdraw.

However reassuring the concern of well-intentioned Saudi leaders about the security and welfare of the smaller states may have been, leaders in at least four of the states had a modern-day reason for pause about slipping firmly into the grasp of Saudi cooperation. Saudi Arabia was not only a giant in resources, people and potential compared to their states, the Saudi kingdom also had displayed some quite firm convictions on religion, the social order and the philosophy of gover-nance which were uncomfortably conservative for significant elements of the societies in the smaller states. The Saudis were not insensitive to these concerns; indeed their actions for some time suggested a hes-itancy about asserting a role of leadership which might not meet universal welcome when the need for strong leadership did not seem critical.

Early on, however, Saudi Arabia worked hard at establishing an environment in which Gulf cooperation might flourish by doing some things it alone could do. Foremost, in anticipation of British withdrawal, Saudi Arabia established a good working relationship with the shah's Iran. In addition, it finally came into harmony with republican Egypt, in ways that caused the Nasserist revolutionary force to withdraw from the Gulf before the British military forces did. More broadly, and for wider reasons, the Saudis set about building a position of influence in the Arab and Islamic worlds and the international community generally which made it prudent for any country ambitious to influence events in the Gulf to consider how its designs squared with Saudi interests in the region. Thus the stage was set for the smaller Gulf countries to establish their modern nation-states and pursue cooperation with each other in a somewhat protected regional environment.

More directly, the Saudis took steps to ease longstanding tensions with Abu Dhabi and Oman over Buraimi, thus fostering the viability of the fledgling UAE and facilitating Oman's entry into the Arab political community. A steadying Saudi hand was evident in assuring that newly independent Qatar would be tranquil in the wake of the bloodless 1971 family coup bringing Amir Khalifa to power. By the mid-1970s the Saudi defense umbrella was clearly cast around Bahrain. Also by the mid-1970s the two least affluent Gulf states, Oman and particularly Bahrain, were significantly benefiting from a variety of supportive Saudi acts in the economic sphere. As the 1970s drew toward a close, all of the smaller states were much more comfortable with the Saudi connection than some perhaps would have been a decade earlier. Moreover, from their perspective, a structure like the GCC had the potential benefit of channeling the force of the Saudi link in ways that might be less over-powering than sole reliance on a bilateral relationship with the kingdom.

THE SEARCH FOR THE GREATER FEDERATION

Particularly for the smaller states the vain quest for a nine-state federation was a formative and instructive milestone on the path to cooperation. The British decision to end by 1971 longstanding protective treaty relations with Bahrain, Qatar and the seven sheikhdoms of the Trucial Coast sparked concern and diplomatic action in the Gulf and beyond. In addition to the tough problems of trying to resolve Iranian claims to Bahrain and the tiny islands of Abu Musa, Greater Tunbs and Lesser Tunbs, and to settle the vestiges of the Buraimi issue, the British and anyone else who would help had to cope with assisting the nine sheikhdoms to form a union.

A lot of countries wanted to help—Kuwait, Saudi Arabia, the United States, even Sadat's Egypt, to name a few. Once the Bahrain issue was resolved, the shah was not unhelpful. Governments interested in the stability of the Gulf were keen on seeing the nine sheikhdoms form some kind of workable entity. We must recall that in 1970 all nine could not put together populations—including foreign residents—nearing one million. Under the circumstances the "greater federation" seemed to have a lot going for it. Bahrain, the most populous potential member, could bring much-needed human resources to compensate for its relative lack of mineral resources. Qatar and particularly Abu Dhabi could bring impressive oil wealth to make up for shortages of technocrats. Dubai could throw in a certain entrepreneurial flair. The other five sorely needed to be in union with some source of wealth, talent and protection. Together they had difficulty assembling a population large enough to rival Gulfport, Mississippi.

Inspired to face the outside world by the January 1968 British announcement of withdrawal, the nine lower Gulf rulers declared at their late February meeting in Dubai the establishment of a Federation of Arab Emirates effective March 30. The basic structure of the initial concept was not unlike that of the GCC, with revolving chairmanship of the Supreme Council of Rulers. Things slipped, but a lower Gulf tour by the Kuwaiti foreign minister in late May got the Supreme Council back in session in July to appoint a Provisional Council to flesh out the federation's organization. The Provisional Council's recommendations were ratified at a third Supreme Council meeting in Doha in October.[2]

As the nine sheikhdoms got down to serious business, however, the ideal of unity fell victim to particular interests. Bahrain's enthusiasm for union so long as the shadow of Iran's claim lay over it seemed matched by the zeal of potential partners not to get involved in that issue. Once the Iranian claim was abandoned, Bahrain got more particular about the weight it would be accorded in the councils of a federation with less populous and advanced neighbors. Old Bahraini-Qatari and Abu Dhabi-Dubai rivalries took on new life, leading in the view of Western observers to the formation of Bahrain-Abu Dhabi and Qatar-Dubai axes in the haggling over relative influence in the proposed union.

In the end, the "greater federation" effort failed. Several months before the self-imposed British deadline for withdrawal, Bahrain announced its full independence. Predictably, if Bahrain were to join the family of nations on its own, Qatar would not be far behind. The British, and their helpers, were left with the task of lashing together the

---

[2]For a discussion of the early progress toward establishing the Federation of Arab Emirates, see William Brewer's "Yesterday and Tomorrow in the Persian Gulf," *Middle East Journal*, Spring 1969.

minimum goal of lower Gulf union, a loose structure called the United Arab Emirates, which would at least permit the descendants of the Trucial Oman Scouts to roam the former Trucial Coast in quest of order. The stitching together of seven was hard enough. Ras al Khaimah, proud in heritage and desperately hoping for the fabulous Union Oil gusher that would restore its place in the pecking order with Abu Dhabi and Dubai, held out from joining up until somewhat after the British threw their hand in and the United Arab Emirates—short both the Greater and Lesser Tunbs—stepped on the world stage.

Some British observers considered the lesser federation, which British diplomacy had sweated hard enough to achieve, as a stop-gap measure. In time, Oman, finally headed into the twentieth century, would absorb this collection of less than a third of a million souls in what was, after all, known as Trucial Oman. This viewpoint, strong in its emphasis on the past, apparently assumed that Abu Dhabi's growing treasure of proven oil reserves would forever sell for around $3 per barrel.

With outside supporters of Gulf cooperation the idea of the "greater federation" died hard. The United States, in recognizing the independence of Bahrain and Qatar, specifically expressed the hope that each would eventually find its way to join the larger federation. Had that happened, there would have emerged on the Arab side of the Gulf three entities of roughly equal population and all with very substantial natural resources—Kuwait, the "greater federation" and Oman. In that situation, a close if informal cooperation among these entities and between them and Saudi Arabia would surely have emerged. But when it shortly became clear that the three survivors of the quest for the "greater federation" would not shift focus from making it alone to getting it all together, the problem of tininess began once again to haunt the Gulf Arabs. In this concern was born the seed of the GCC.

In the decade between the failure of the "greater federation" and the establishment of the GCC, the six members learned a lot about what would and would not work in terms of structured association and about the paths to pursuing it. They also in time got on with a significant collection of cooperative efforts, most of which involved bilateral or trilateral undertakings or ventures including not just all or some of the six but other countries as well. The result was a broad context of cooperation of which the GCC would be but part and symbol.

Those who by the mid-1970s despaired over the prospects for structured cooperation had missed a lot of what was going on. In the first place, once the British withdrew there was a necessary period of acquaintance building among the states involved. Certainly there were strong cultural bonds and important family and commercial ties among the countries that were to form the GCC. But given the external orientation of the oil-based economies and the British protective role, there had been little for Gulf Arab leaders to cooperate about. Insofar as the nine sheikhdoms of the lower Gulf—and until 1961 Kuwait—were concerned, there had been a *rais* (leader) for security and political cooperation. He was *rais al khalij* (leader of the Gulf), the British political resident in the Gulf. Oman was also clearly in this orbit of British coordination, and Saudi leaders had perhaps more contact with British officials than with their Gulf neighbors. Thus in the first half of the 1970s there was a necessary and ever-broader process of getting to know and to get on with one another, launched usually at the head of state and cabinet levels and then filtering down into burgeoning bureaucracies with a growing agenda of problems requiring consultation and coordination with Gulf neighbors.

One day in the mid-1970s Bahrain television suddenly went off the air—not because of political trouble but because a key part of the transmitting equipment blew out. As the result of a few quick telephone calls, within hours a young Saudi official, an American-trained doctor of engineering as I recall, arrived in Bahrain with the only spare within several thousand miles, donned white overalls and personally made the repair. Within little more than a day the citizens of Bahrain—for better or worse—were once more glued to the tube. The event was perhaps totally unnoticed by world leaders, but it was very much the stuff on which solid Gulf cooperation was being built.

THE STRATEGY FOR GULF COOPERATION

Through trial and error and serious thinking Gulf leaders began to see a way to more structured cooperation. The main goals were both a more secure strategic environment for the GCC states and meeting the aspirations of their citizens for a closer Gulf identity. The "greater federation" effort—and numerous examples from the wider Arab world—taught that attempts to proclaim political "unions" without careful nurturing of common interests were doomed to failure. How then to get to closer political cooperation?

Cooperation in the security field certainly had a catchy glamour to it. None of the Gulf governments ever tired of proclaiming that the security of this critically strategic region should be solely the responsibility of the Gulf states themselves. But there were more than six Gulf states. There were also Iran and Iraq. Therein lay a major obstacle to formalizing cooperation among the six.

How could one talk about "Gulf cooperation" without including the power of the Gulf, the shah's Iran? How could one think of "Gulf Arab cooperation" without including Iraq, with a population equal to that of the other six Gulf Arab countries put together? The abortive Gulf Security Conference of 1976 proved the point. Iran under the shah, though quick to assert its own interests in the Gulf, seemed by the mid-

70s quite relaxed about, if not positively supportive of, closer cooperation of the Six under Saudi leadership. The shah had come to recognize that Saudi Arabia had an important political role on the Arab side of the Gulf which Iran was not capable of playing and that, in any event, the Iranian-Saudi relationship was the key to Iran's relations across the Gulf. But for Iran, even after the 1975 Algiers accord, an Iraqi leadership role was an entirely different matter. Iraq reciprocated in concern about Iranian leadership in the region.

The Six, of course, had their own good reasons for pause about letting Iraq into the club. It was not just that Iraq's elite wore trousers instead of robes and were republicans rather than monarchists. They also were Baathist revolutionaries with territorial claims on Kuwait and documented—and subversive—political ambitions down the Gulf. Let us recall that during its major 1978 effort to get the Congress to accept selling F-15s to Saudi Arabia, the Carter administration publicly described Iraq as the principal military threat to Saudi Arabia. The Saudis were uncomfortable with this but did not dispute it. Reports were that the Iraqi leadership could not decide whether to be insulted as Arabs or flattered as Baathists in being so described.

The balance in which Iran was a check against Iraqi ambitions down the Gulf was shattered by the Iranian revolution. This precipitated a readjustment of attitudes—or at least in conduct and rhetoric—in both Iraq and the Six. The rapprochement did not solve the problem of how the latter could formally get together to the exclusion of Iraq—indeed it complicated it. But the outbreak of the Iran-Iraq war would provide a way around this obstacle. The GCC is an exclusive grouping of Gulf nonbelligerents.

Even among the Six there were difficulties in pursuing security cooperation in the 1970s. One was differing views about the extent to which they would welcome or, more accurately, acknowledge the significant Western role in the security of the region. Although all were to a striking degree dependent on the West—specifically the United Kingdom, France and the United States—in this regard there was a broad spectrum of policy stances, ranging from Kuwait to Oman, on the political acceptability of the Western connection. In short, the security road to Gulf cooperation was strewn with political landmines.

Advocates of cooperation, therefore, chose a safer if less spectacular route—political harmony through economic cooperation. Not knee-jerk Arab attempts at unity but the solid progress of the European Community would be the guide. Indeed, by the mid-1970s Western observers had reason to suspect that their contacts in Gulf governments were faithfully studying the Arabic version of the "Jean Monnet Handbook."

The economic road to political association was difficult enough. Unlike the industrial countries of the European Community, the Gulf Six were externally oriented oil economies with little potential for the sort of complementarity that gives dynamic to a common market. For them the main benefit of a common market would be to make import substitution industries of marginal viability in narrow domestic markets somewhat more viable in a regional one. While this is clearly beneficial, it is by no means critical to economies that invariably will rise and fall not on the basis of producing for each other's consumption but on the tides of the world oil market.

In short, the Gulf Six were fairly hard put to find economic activities in which they could all cooperate. Moreover, they needed big and dramatic ventures if economic cooperation were to sustain the spirit of political unity. The Kuwaiti proposal for a currency union fell short of acceptance. The strong common currency that the oil-exporting economies would inevitably maintain was too rich for Bahrain, which had to sell services and aluminum in competitive world markets. Prospects for rationalizing or apportioning development projects among the Six looked bleak as several scrambled to force-feed domestic industrialization. The Western press made much of the proliferation of "international" airports in the UAE. The most striking example of going it alone was Dubai's building a major drydock to compete with the one that the Organization of Arab Petroleum Exporting Countries (OAPEC)—including the UAE—had built in Bahrain.

Some major progress was made, however, in cooperative ventures among several of the Six. The participation of Bahrain, Qatar, the UAE and Oman in Gulf Air was perhaps the most striking example. Gulf Air is not only a successful venture but also a facilitator and symbol of cooperation among the four lower Gulf states. It soon became apparent, however, that Saudia and Kuwait Airlines would not fly united.

In the period 1976-78, Gulf Arab governments got together to launch various commercial, industrial or financial joint ventures. Membership in two of them, the United Arab Shipping Company and the Gulf International Bank, included Iraq but not Oman. All six plus Iraq participated in the Gulf Ports Union, the Gulf Organization for Industrial Consulting and the Gulf News Agency. Saudi Arabia agreed with both Kuwait and Bahrain to establish jointly owned cement companies.

As early as 1977 the first general conference of Gulf Arab trade ministers was held, and it proposed the creation of a common market among the represented states. By 1980 Gulf Arab planning ministers had met twice, and the Gulf Federation of Chambers of Commerce and Industry had been established.

For Bahrain economic cooperation paid off in a big way when Saudi Arabia and Kuwait decided to back the development of Bahrain as the regional banking center and when, during King Khalid's 1976 visit,

Saudi Arabia agreed to invest in Bahrain's aluminum industry rather than develop competing plants.

Thus, major steps toward economic cooperation were achieved well before the GCC's Unified Economic Agreement was approved in 1983. Through these proofs of the benefits of working together an important foundation was laid on which the GCC could be rapidly erected once revolution and war prompted Saudi Arabia and its nonbelligerent Gulf neighbors into greater activity in 1981.

THE GCC BECOMES A REALITY

Advocates of Gulf cooperation could thus be confident, when the six heads of state signed the GCC Charter in Abu Dhabi on May 25, 1981, that this was a carefully prepared and serious venture, "based on their faith in the common destiny and destination that link their peoples," which would "complement efforts already begun."[3] The appointment as secretary-general of an energetic and skilled diplomat, Dr. Abdulla Bishara, who had built a strong reputation for effectiveness as Kuwait's permanent representative to the United Nations, augured well for the Council's getting quickly down to business.

ECONOMIC COOPERATION

Initially, member governments commenting on the purpose of the GCC tended to stress its economic role, but it is significant that Secretary General Bishara has stated that "economic integration is not a goal in itself, but merely a means for the attainment of the final objective, . . . which is the unity of the Gulf."[4] Thus the integrationists were steady on their strategy, which had long found particular favor in Kuwait and Bahrain.

Even outsiders impressed by the purposefulness of the cooperative venture, however, were struck by the ambitious sweep of the Unified Economic Agreement which the Supreme Council soon approved. One wondered if members more interested in the security than in the economic aspects of cooperation, notably Oman, were ready to accept that "by the end of the 1980's the Gulf will be one common market, with all the obligations and privileges which that step entails."[5] For six chapters the Economic Agreement sketches goals for freedom of trade, for freedom of movement of capital, citizens and economic activities, for coordination of development, for technical cooperation, for freedom of transport and communications and for financial and monetary cooper-

---

[3]Preamble of Charter, Cooperation Council for the Arab States of the Gulf.
[4]H.E. Dr. Abdulla Yacoub Bishara, "The Gulf Cooperation Council: Achievements and Challenges," *American-Arab Affairs*, No. 7 (Winter 1983-84).
[5]Ibid.

ation, which might well give pause to those concerned with protecting domestic interests in the smaller states. They outline a spectrum of economic integration which raises the obvious question whether the larger and more sophisticated economies, notably Saudi Arabia and Kuwait, will overwhelm the smaller and less developed as integration proceeds. But there is an artful escape clause, for those who feel threatened, in Article 24 in the seventh chapter, which begins "In the execution of the Agreement . . . consideration shall be given to differences in the levels of development between the member states and the local development priorities of each."[6]

In strictly economic and human terms, will progress toward economic integration benefit the smaller GCC members? There are several aspects and interests to be considered, including those of consumers, the private sectors and governments.

Certainly the efforts of the GCC to standardize various technical regulations or practices in commerce and communications, such as the Transit System Regulations approved by the Financial and Economic Cooperation Committee in June 1982, are beneficial to all, including outsiders conducting commerce with the Six. So obviously are arrangements for free movement of citizens within the Six.

The freedom of GCC citizens to practice their professions throughout the grouping should cause little concern and might present some useful opportunities. Most professional activities, like some wines, do not travel well in a marketing sense. Most of the dentists of Riyadh will continue to practice close to home. But in highly specialized professional areas or for the exceptionally talented professional the wider scope of the Six will present new worlds to conquer. Here the larger countries have no real advantage over the small. An expert in maritime law or a brilliant consulting engineer can come just as easily from Salalah as Kuwait. From the consumer standpoint, a Qatari undergoing surgery will want the best surgeon in the region, even if he comes from Medina rather than Doha.

In general, consumers throughout the Six will benefit from economic integration. Efforts to make combined purchases of foreign-origin commodities and thus obtain more favorable prices—assuming the Council carries this off efficiently—should be of general advantage and, in theory, most beneficial to the smaller countries. Consumers in the Six have, since the oil booms began, endured significant disadvantages of scale. The prevailing pattern was for local merchants to collect a bunch of distributorships for foreign products to protect themselves against the thinness of the market for any particular line. The results were

---

[6]The Unified Economic Agreement, GCC. See p. 239 for text.

inadequate specialization and service and high prices through inefficiencies in distribution. If economic integration in the commercial sphere leads to more efficient distribution, better servicing of products and more competition within similar product lines, the consumers throughout the Six will be better off, again, in theory, particularly in the smaller states. Insofar as these potential benefits become tangible, popular support for economic integration, and more broadly for Gulf unity, is likely to grow.

It could be argued that such a trend would in the long run be generally beneficial to distributor merchants in all the states, as they eventually sorted themselves out to do one or a few things efficiently in a wider market rather than lots of things less well in a smaller one. But there is perhaps more risk in the practice than in the theory, and herein lies some of the private-sector concern in the smaller states about real integration of the common market. The concern applies as well to the industrial sector. Since all GCC governments are themselves directly involved in industry and are sensitive to the views of politically influential business communities, it is sometimes difficult to sort out where the government's interest ends and the private sector's begins.

It is clear, however, that each of the three smaller economies of the Six sees the risks and benefits of integration from different perspectives.

Bahrain thrives on Gulf economic integration, indeed virtually survives on it. Most of the crude oil for its refinery comes from Saudi Arabia. Almost half its oil revenue comes from a field shared with the Saudis. Its major banking industry depends on the support of the regional financial powers—Saudi Arabia and Kuwait. Its aluminum industry benefits from Saudi and Kuwaiti participation. In April 1986 the Gulf Organization for Industrial Consulting, implementing the GCC industrial strategy, opened its $100 million Gulf Aluminum Rolling Mill in Bahrain. The tiny island state is a service center for the region. Gulf Air is headquartered there. The OAPEC-owned ASRY drydock is a major feature on the industrial-service landscape. Bahrain has over a decade of experience with the mixed blessings of private Kuwaiti investment. With the recently built causeway open to the public, Bahrain will become inextricably linked with the industrial and commercial life of Saudi Arabia's Eastern Province. Bahrain has a relatively sophisticated private sector which long has found opportunity beyond the narrow confines of the island. In short, Bahrain's economy was "integrated" well before the GCC was established. Of all the Six, Bahrain is the biggest winner from the economic cooperation symbolized and driven by the GCC. If the new Gulf University, established in Bahrain, develops into a significant research institution encouraging the creation of the Gulf version of Silicon Valley, Bahrain may enter yet another dimension of benefit from Gulf cooperation.

Qatar is in some ways at the other extreme, a truly independently wealthy country with sufficient oil and gas wealth to keep its small citizen population in style for many years to come. Qatar has developed at a steady, sensible pace with heavy government participation in industry and infrastructure and no need for foreign capital except for the early oil concessions. Its private sector has not had market scope to develop the aggressiveness and sophistication characteristic of the larger contractors, distributors and investors in neighboring countries. Qatari businessmen have some reason for caution about the impact of Gulf economic integration. But in another sense both government and private sectors have much to gain from such industrial and commercial opportunities as a Gulf common market will offer. Qatar on its own is a market so small as to make efficiency in commerce and viability in import-substitution industries hard to come by. Thus those Qataris of commercial and industrial daring—including the government as industrial investor—need the wider stage of a Gulf common market. One of the jewels in the GCC crown, the Gulf Organization for Industrial Consulting, is based in Doha.

Oman has exhibited particular hesitation about economic integration because of its special circumstances. Considerably more populous and much larger in territory than the other "smaller" states, Oman is still new to oil wealth and well behind the rest of the Six in economic development. Its merchant class, although boasting a proud history of commerce in the traditional era, still needs time to catch up with neighbors in both capital formation and modern business skills. There is some scope for developing "infant industry" in a society which is but now acquiring the capital to launch such ventures. Therefore, Oman has reasons to restrict the inflow of venture capital from elsewhere in the Gulf, to protect its market from less expensive regional products such as cement, and to insure that Omani ownership dominates in industries such as fisheries which have interesting prospects. Oman wants to go slow on integration. Yet Oman as well can find certain unique opportunities in a wider Gulf market, in such areas as development of its potential to process asbestos and marble and provide agricultural crops in which it alone has economic prospects for commercial-scale production. Additionally, Oman will get the proposed GCC tire factory.

While the GCC does not have the industrial might on which the European Community built unity, its search for integration is at least essentially free of the agricultural problems which have plagued the development of the European Common Market. Notwithstanding the clinging to subsistence agriculture here and there—and the emergence of Saudi agribusinesses which produce history's most expensive wheat— GCC statesmen really do not have a "farm vote" to contend with.

What they do have to reckon with is the addiction of Gulf private capital to real estate. The hesitation in the smaller states about the free movement of capital is to some good degree based on the fear that the main thrust of such movement will be an onslaught of Saudi, Kuwaiti and Abu Dhabi real estate speculation, distorting local land values without lasting benefit to the domestic economy.

In other areas, the governments of Bahrain, Qatar and Oman have much to gain from the economic goals of the Council. Certainly the creation of the Gulf Investment Corporation gives them a chance to participate in industrial ventures within and beyond the region which might be beyond their capacity acting alone. Rationalization or coordination of industrial development within the Six makes special sense for the smaller economies which can least afford launching unviable undertakings. GCC coordination of foreign-investment and foreign-aid policies might give the smaller countries' views some airing in areas in which they are not, except Qatar to a degree, significant participants. The meetings of GCC oil ministers, such as the extraordinary session in January 1983 in preparation for a critical OPEC ministerial meeting, presumably permit Bahrain and Oman, neither of which belongs to OPEC, to express views about a world market which determines their prosperity but on which they have scant individual influence.

In sum, all three smaller states of the GCC have something to gain in economic integration, and at little significant sacrifice. It is important to stress, however, that the success or failure of GCC economic integration will not have a critical impact on any of the economies, except perhaps that of Bahrain. For the foreseeable future, there is nothing the others can do with one another that will compare, in economic importance, with how their petroleum sectors fare in the market beyond the Gulf. What is critical about the pace of economic integration is whether it will maintain sufficient momentum to sustain the vision of Gulf unity.

SECURITY COOPERATION

Upon the launching of the GCC, while members stressed its economic role, Western observers tended to focus on its significance in the security area. This was an understandable reaction. Within the Gulf and beyond, it had always been understood that security in the broadest sense—that is, the creation of a more stable strategic environment in the region—was much of what the quest for Gulf cooperation was all about. Moreover, in the crisis days of the early 1980s it was not the economies of the Six that the West was worried about. What bothered the West, and what certainly prompted the Saudis to finally lead the Six into the Council, was fear of the threats to the Gulf monarchies posed by the hostility of revolutionary Iran and the potential spread of the Iran-Iraq war.

From the beginning, Oman was the strongest advocate of defense cooperation in the GCC structure. Oman's interest in defense was understandable. A unique strategic role was the main asset Oman had to offer its new partners. With the collapse of order in Iran, Oman had assumed the lead responsibility for freedom of navigation in the Strait of Hormuz. The Omani leadership had long been concerned about the strategic environment in the region. Once the shah had fallen and Egypt had become ostracized in the Arab world for making peace with Israel, Oman not only sought a close strategic relationship with the United States to complement its strong military relationship with the United Kingdom but also tried to get its new Gulf partners more interested in the common defense.

At the beginning of the 1980s, Oman was still short on cash and long on defense spending. It felt threatened by South Yemen, which had supported the Dhofar insurrection. The small but proficient, largely British-officered, Omani air and naval forces were protecting the vital oil lifeline of the other members of the Six. Oman saw in the GCC a chance to get the beneficiaries to bear a good share of the cost of keeping Hormuz open. Indeed as early as 1979, Oman had vainly pushed Gulf neighbors to establish a $100 million common defense fund to improve the security of the Gulf sea-lanes.

Initially the other GCC members held back on pushing security aspects at the pace Oman would have preferred. Possibly they were a bit shy about Oman's strong Western connections at a time when the GCC was emphasizing the need to keep superpower rivalry out of the Gulf. More likely was a concern to play the delicate and dangerous game with Iran as subtly as possible. It was important to keep the GCC from appearing as a defense pact aimed against Khomeini's revolution. Moreover, to the Saudis the military threat posed by the Iran-Iraq war looked much more serious up the Gulf than toward Hormuz, and they were already deeply engaged outside the GCC context in developing an air defense perimeter in the region closer to hostilities.

The December 1981 discovery of an attempt by Iranian-backed terrorists to assassinate Bahraini leaders sharply refocused the GCC on security cooperation. It certainly made the Bahrainis, long devout disciples of the political and economic aspects of Gulf cooperation, "reborn" in their enthusiasm for the security aspects. Earlier dialogue among Gulf interior ministers had laid a basis for an urgent Saudi proposal for a GCC internal security agreement. In fact, the Kuwaitis opted out, but Saudi Arabia quickly concluded bilateral agreements with the other four states for cooperation in internal security. The net effect was a working GCC internal security arrangement, with a Kuwaiti reservation as to making it formal. The smaller states could rest easier knowing that the sort of informal cooperation Bahrain had received from Dubai security forces in exposing the 1981 plot would henceforth work on an institutionalized basis. After the 1985 assassination attempt against the amir of Kuwait, the Kuwaiti government was emphasizing a coordinated GCC approach to internal security.[7]

The GCC also pushed forward on the defense front. Chiefs of staff and defense ministers met. By mid-1983 the GCC had agreed to establish a joint defense industry. The November 1984 Council summit meeting announced plans to create a joint "rapid-deployment force" to help deter military threats to the Six.

There has been considerable Western comment about the inadequacy of the GCC as a defense alliance. In the broad sense the military potential—standing forces and population base to maintain them—of all the GCC states does not match that of Iraq—to say nothing of Iran.[8] There are indeed major problems of coordination of mission and standardization of equipment, as well as the formidable "command and control" challenges inherent in any alliance. But excessive focus on these difficulties misses three salient points. First, the GCC countries are highly unlikely to have to fight a "total war" with anyone. What they are aiming for, beyond assurance of internal security, is "deterrence," with a special focus on air defense and protection of sea-lanes. They have at their disposal in pursuit of this objective a variety of economic and political assets in addition to strictly military ones. In addition, they have the firm knowledge that the strategic importance of Gulf oil reserves assures them the concern of the international community, especially the industrial democracies. Thus, well before a military threat of potentially unsustainable damage is likely to get beyond the capability of the Six to cope, a variety of interested "outsiders" can be expected to exert efforts to restore tranquility. This consideration should be kept in mind in judging the tendency of the GCC states to buy arms from a variety of sources, rather than stressing standardization of equipment. Finally, there is the sort of question that Benjamin Franklin posed when the American colonies were about to plunge into the dangerous business of hanging together in pursuit of a common independent destiny: "We must all hang together or assuredly we shall all hang separately." If the GCC united is still vulnerable in a military sense, would its members be any more secure in isolation?

The emphasis of the GCC on defense coordination is, of course, very much in Oman's interest. Oman has a critical flank of the GCC territory

---

[7]"Kuwait," Embassy of Kuwait in Washington, No. 49, August 1985.

[8]For a thorough discussion of the military capabilities of the GCC states, see Anthony H. Cordesman, *The Gulf and the Search for Strategic Stability* (Boulder, CO: Westview Press, 1984) and Thomas L. McNaugher, *Arms and Oil: U.S. Military Strategy and the Persian Gulf* (Washington, DC: The Brookings Institution, 1985).

to defend. It has air, land and sea forces of some significance, particularly in terms of quality and experience. Oman provides an important component of the Council's "rapid-deployment force." Within the GCC context a generous amount of Saudi funding, perhaps $2 billion worth, has been pledged to upgrading the equipment of the Omani forces. With both Oman and Saudi Arabia acquiring the British Tornado aircraft, there are possibilities of Oman's having access to the elaborate and expensive training and maintenance infrastructure which the Saudis will acquire. Most important, GCC military cooperation gives Oman, once isolated in dependence on the United Kingdom and, more recently, on both the United States and United Kingdom for security support, a firm link to the Arab world in providing for its defense.

The military role of the GCC as an institution is perhaps less critical to Bahrain and Qatar. Long before the Council came into being, geography had dictated that these states would be included in Saudi Arabia's eastern defense perimeter.

This is particularly true of Bahrain, which is within eyesight of the vital Dhahran area, where so much of the Saudi air and sea defense capability is based. As a senior Saudi official told U.S. Senate staff members: "We consider the defense of Bahrain to be the defense of Saudi Arabia."[9] Bahrain's small defense force, while carefully organized and trained, has always been so light on modern equipment as to offer only token resistance to an outside military threat. Wisely the government has seen the nation's security in a broad diplomatic and social context and has been averse to spending much of the relatively modest public treasure on arms.

Saudi Arabia has also not been keen on spending money on Bahrain's independent defense capability, apparently feeling that its own massive expenditure to defend its Gulf shore automatically covered Bahrain's real defense needs. Now, however, the Saudis are supporting Bahrain's acquisition of 12 F-5 aircraft. By tying into Saudi Arabia's extensive support facilities for this weapons system, Bahrain would be able to avoid much of the heavy cost of independent maintenance capability. The addition of Bahrain-based F-5s will, of course, improve and extend eastward the Saudi air defense network. Already Bahrain is an important radar surveillance segment of the common defense zone.

For Bahrain the GCC provides an important institutionalization and broadening of an existing informal defense alliance. The GCC system assures periodic Bahraini-Saudi consultation on defense matters and probably reinforces Bahraini prospects for Saudi (or GCC-wide) funding of its defense buildup.

---

[9]"War in the Gulf," Staff Report, Committee on Foreign Relations, United States Senate, August 1984.

This same formalization of cooperation is important to Qatar, which also lies snugly under the Saudi defense umbrella. Qatar's armed forces are almost as modest as Bahrain's, reflecting a sensible view that all the guns that big money can buy are of limited benefit if there are too few troops to man them. Qatar, like Bahrain, has but a limited capability to contribute to the common GCC defense. It clearly benefits, however, from being "in the loop" as the Council's defense planning moves forward.

There is a final point about the importance of defense cooperation among the GCC members, one perhaps of particular note to the smaller states. Historically the military threats to the GCC states have by and large come from one another. Happily the tradition of conflict among Gulf principalities had passed into history well before the Council sprang to life. The quest for Gulf cooperation, unlike the pursuit of a European Community, was not seriously motivated by a felt need to prevent the partners from ever again fighting one another. But against the historic backdrop it is reassuring that GCC defense ministers are planning how to protect one another rather than plotting border raids on neighbors.

POLITICAL COOPERATION

The essence of the association among the Six is neither economic nor security measures but a broader, somewhat intangible thing which we might call political cooperation. This is both the real goal of the Council and the context in which specific economic or defense steps are possible. The main events of Gulf cooperation are the meetings of the Ministerial Council, the foreign ministers, and the Supreme Council, the heads of state. These are the fora for broad consultation on a range of issues affecting the welfare of the Six and for hammering out common positions with which to face the world beyond.

In its brief history the GCC has accomplished some specific things on the political and diplomatic fronts. The Fahd Plan was vetted by the Council on its way to becoming the Arab position on Middle East peace at the 1982 Fez Summit. Additionally, under the banner of the GCC, members were successful in easing, perhaps ending, longstanding tensions between Oman and South Yemen.

Of course, the main diplomatic preoccupation of the Council since its inception has been how to end the Iran-Iraq war. The Six have consulted frequently on this problem, and the Council has repeatedly put forth mediation initiatives. To date, however, the GCC, like so many other states and institutions in the world community, has been unable to persuade Iran to cease hostilities or to restrain Iraq from actions which dangerously increase the threat which the conflict poses to the region and to freedom of navigation. Yet the Council's efforts have been useful in keeping international attention focused on the dangers of this conflict. The GCC has carefully asserted its members' rights as nonbelligerents. Most important, the common stand of the Six has helped ease the enormous pressures which the conflict brings on individual member states. If the day ever comes when this tragic struggle is ripe for the ending, the GCC can be expected to play an effective, perhaps essential, role in bringing about a workable peace.

Obviously, such political cooperation among the Six is of benefit to the smaller states. In the 1970s it was often said of at least two of the talented members of Bahrain's cabinet that they had a personal influence which extended beyond the limited range of Bahrain's power in the world. But what did that really mean? Where was a Bahraini—or Qatari or Omani—statesman of particular distinction to exercise his talents? In Arab League councils, for instance, were Algerian or Egyptian delegates likely to hang on the every word of a Bahraini representative while the Saudi was preparing to speak?

The Council creates an important forum for the leaders of the smaller states to have their say. Here the influence of the Bahraini or Qatari or Omani is limited only by his own wisdom and eloquence, not by the wealth, landmass or population of his homeland. The smaller states have much good sense to contribute to the deliberations of the GCC. They also, of course, have much of value to learn from the experiences and perspectives of the larger member states. A particular benefit is that close consultation among the Six permits the smaller states a keener view of something which they lose sight of at their peril—the exact location and movement of the political currents in the Gulf region and the wider Arab world. The GCC thus opens new horizons of understanding and problem solving for its members.

Much of the quality of cooperation among the Six existed before the GCC was created, and informal political consultation among them undoubtedly would have expanded even without the GCC structure. But the formality of the GCC mechanism provides something of special value to the busy leaders of the Six: a discipline of focus. With periodic Council meetings coming up, it is no longer so easy to let hard issues slip. All must focus on cooperation. Even disputes which have long been intractable, such as that between Qatar and Bahrain over islands and offshore boundaries, become embarrassments in the context of having to gather with Gulf peers to discuss how to work together to deal with obviously more significant issues.

The real essence, however, of what GCC political cooperation is all about is a set of perceptions. It is the perception of the peoples of each of the member states that they belong to a larger union of real purpose and influence in the world. It is the perception of the outside world that each of the Six is stronger and more to be heeded for the cooperation among them. It is the perception among them that they are more secure for their togetherness and able in union to influence in constructive ways problems which might be beyond their reach individually. The Gulf is a safer place for the efforts of the Council.

PROSPECTS FOR THE GCC

The Council has cut out a lot of ambitious tasks for itself. One might well ask whether it can accomplish all of its goals—including the ultimate one of true political union. Obviously the jury will long be out. In the meantime considerable progress has been made—and in difficult times. It is noteworthy that the Council came to life at a highwater mark of prosperity in the Gulf. Since 1981 the economic trends in the six states have been downward in the face of an oil glut that appears to be with us for some years more. In a time of belt tightening in the Gulf economies, the environment is difficult for furthering GCC goals which involve more industrial investment, more foreign aid and larger defense spending. A recessionary mood in the individual markets makes their opening to business interests from other GCC countries particularly hard to achieve, just as it is difficult to induce a private sector struggling with recession at home to take further risk abroad to achieve the GCC common market.

Clearly there will be weighty obstacles and causes for delay on the GCC's path to union. But the advocates of Gulf cooperation can take considerable pride in what has been accomplished to date. In the broadest sense, moreover, perhaps nothing the GCC will accomplish in the future can ever match the deed of May 25, 1981. Given the unique nature of the GCC economies, the strategic importance of the territory and the subtle environment in which the Six must seek their survival, the most important thing about the GCC is not what specific things it does but simply that it exists and inspires the allegiance of its member states and their peoples.

THE UNITED STATES AND THE GULF COOPERATION COUNCIL

The establishment of the GCC was sharply attacked by the Soviet Union as an American initiative designed to bring Gulf states under greater U.S. influence. Despite the absurdity of this charge, the initial public U.S. reaction to the Council was restrained in deference to the sensitivities of the Six, who were, after all, busy describing what was very much their own doing as, among other things, an effort to keep superpower rivalry out of the region. Since the United States had long urged Gulf cooperation and had stressed its support for the security and progress of each of the Six, the favorable U.S. attitude toward the Council was not in question. The negative Soviet reaction made it clear that the Council was a good thing for all nations with an interest in tranquility and orderly progress in the region.

In congressional testimony on U.S. policy toward the region, the U.S. assistant secretary of state for Near Eastern and South Asian Affairs in May 1982 noted that the establishment of the Council was an "important step in the sustained search for cooperation." He added that "this is an objective which the peoples of the region cherish, and which we welcome and support, for such cooperation is central to building prospects for peace and orderly progress."[10]

The U.S. view of the merits of Gulf cooperation has reflected a range of interests which are among the objectives of the GCC itself. It is in the U.S. interest that the Six be secure and in harmony, that their economic growth be rational and orderly and that they work in common purpose as important donors of economic assistance and consistent advocates of moderate policies in the Middle East and beyond. Thus the Council in a broad sense furthers U.S. objectives in the region precisely because it furthers the interests of six countries whose welfare is important to the United States.

In the political-diplomatic sphere, the Council is compatible with U.S. interests because it strengthens the voice of what Westerners persist in describing as "moderate Arabs." To some degree, moreover, the functioning of the Council gives an additional dimension to U.S. diplomatic relations with the smaller states. U.S. relations with Bahrain, Qatar and Oman have been consistently cordial—notwithstanding significant disagreement on how to deal with the Arab-Israeli issue. American officials have listened carefully to the views of these states on a range of issues, just as officials of these countries have heard America out with unfailing courtesy and frequent sympathy. But there has been a certain passivity to the dialogue, simply because none of the three states acting alone was capable of exerting major influence on most regional and international issues of mutual concern. The Council permits each of the three governments a role upon a wider stage. As they become more participants in, rather than observers of, events around them, the relevance of their diplomatic dialogue with the United States, and the industrial alliance generally, is bound to increase, adding texture to already sound relationships.

The point is well illustrated by the quite successful visit of Bahrain's foreign minister to Washington in July 1982. Given the relationship, any Bahraini official is going to be welcome in Washington. Given the foreign minister's superb reputation, he is assured a careful hearing

---

[10]Nicholas A. Veliotes, Statement before the European and Middle East Subcommittee of the House Foreign Affairs Committee and the Joint Economic Committee, May 10, 1982.

wherever he goes. But on this occasion the minister did something notably skillful. Having consulted with GCC counterparts on certain issues prior to his visit, he was careful to point out to senior U.S. officials when he was expressing the individual view of the government of Bahrain and when he was setting forth a GCC consensus. When he spoke for Bahrain he certainly held everyone's attention. But when he spoke for the GCC, things took on something of the quality of "and E.F. Hutton says. . . ."

In the economic sphere the Council is not likely to affect U.S. interests strongly one way or another. Insofar as cooperative industrial ventures become a significant aspect of GCC activities and a dynamic common market develops, U.S. interests will to some degree be served. Over the years a major inhibition on the transfer of American technology and the flow of American commerce to the smaller Gulf states has been the thinness of the markets. Frequently there simply was not enough to do in Bahrain, Qatar or Oman to entice American firms to undertake the considerable effort required to compete in the market. Both private and public American technical assistance to the three has been fairly limited, not for want of political will to build this important aspect of the relationships but simply because opportunities to be of real help were limited. The creation of a GCC-wide market for both goods and services should be significant incentive for increased American economic activity in the smaller states, particularly once the market doldrums caused by the drop in oil revenue end.

A notably promising recent development has been the initiation of an economic dialogue between the GCC and the U.S. government. Over the years official American economic dialogue with the governments of the Six has not been as sustained as the importance of the economic relationships warrants. The new initiative will help solve this problem. Hopefully it will lead to a truly constructive and ongoing discussion of such key issues of mutual concern as world energy and petrochemical markets, the international investment climate and the economic assistance needs of developing countries.

In contemplating the defense role of the GCC, some American observers saw opportunities while others saw problems. To the degree that the GCC moved to standardize its military equipment, there were perhaps opportunities, building on the Saudi base, to increase the supply of U.S. military equipment to the region. To date the theory has hardly been tested. GCC members have not demonstrated great zeal for standardizing equipment. In any event, it serves U.S. interests well to have them continue to rely on the United Kingdom, France and other Western allies as additional sources of military supply. What has happened, of course, is a decline in the U.S. position as arms supplier to the Gulf states through no fault of either the GCC member nations or the Europeans. The problem has been political opposition in the United States to providing certain weaponry to the region, a problem that has seriously undercut the U.S. reputation as a reliable partner in security.

In some quarters in the United States there was concern that the GCC would be an obstacle to the prospects for U.S. "strategic cooperation" with member states. The fear was of a sort of lowest-common-denominator effect in which the zeal of an Oman for close security cooperation with the United States would be tempered by association with members less keen on this sort of thing. Certainly GCC rhetoric about keeping the superpowers out of the Gulf gave a superficial plausibility to this concern. There is no evidence, however, that these fears were well founded.

In the first place, the most powerful and influential member of the GCC, Saudi Arabia, was the one with the strongest overall relationship with the United States. Therefore the Council was just as capable of facilitating as of hindering the American connection. In the second place, this concern reflected a lack of realism about how far "strategic cooperation" with the Six would go even under the most favorable political circumstances. What has happened, or not happened, in the Middle East peace process since the Council was established has not, of course, created very favorable political circumstances. Insofar as the realistic prospects for a growth in the U.S. security relationship with the Six have been thwarted, one should look elsewhere than the councils of the GCC to find the culprits, including perhaps along the Potomac.

There is another aspect of this that U.S. policymakers might well heed. If the overriding U.S. interest is in the orderly progress and stability of the GCC states, then the United States should refrain from pushing military relationships which are beyond the long-term political tolerance of the country concerned. To the extent that association with the GCC keeps member states well in the political mainstream of the region, it lessens the risk that Gulf states will get into military relationships with the United States or others which in the long term might fuel the very political instability that U.S. policy has so long sought to prevent.

The principal benefit of the GCC to U.S. interests, however, is akin to the main significance of the Council to its members. Because there is a GCC, six small states friendly to the United States are more secure. Because Gulf cooperation is flourishing, a region of critical importance to the United States is safer. Therein lies the overriding American interest in seeing the Council make sound and steady progress toward reaching its ambitious goals.

Chapter 3

A HISTORICAL PERSPECTIVE OF U.S.-GCC ECONOMIC AND FINANCIAL INTERDEPENDENCE

Bruce F. Henderson

Mr. Henderson is President and CEO of UBAF Arab American Bank, New York.

The birth of the Gulf Cooperation Council in May 1981 initiated an era of regional unity and cooperation among the six member countries which has already been marked by considerable progress in the quest for economic integration. Established more as a defense pact against the threat of the Khomeini revolution in Iran and Soviet aggression in Afghanistan, the concept of forming a cohesive Gulf-nation alliance had already existed prior to the fall of the shah and the decline of Iran's powerful position in the area. But there were other prompting political factors that spurred the formation of the GCC and the rapid implementation of its precepts.

SECURITY AND ECONOMIC FORERUNNERS TO GULF INTEGRATION

One of these political factors was the onset of the Iran-Iraq war on September 26, 1980, culminating with Iran's shelling of Iraq's southern terminals at Khor Al-Amaya and Mina Bakr, which exacerbated the political tensions already existing in the area by casting an umbrageous pall over the Gulf. It is well acknowledged at this juncture that both protagonists in the conflict had economic and military objectives, for the destruction of Iraq's terminals over the Shatt Al-Arab territorial dispute prevented the tanker shipment of approximately 70 percent of Iraqi oil exports through the Gulf. The strategic importance of the Arab Gulf and the Strait of Hormuz suddenly crystalized. The GCC states became a focal point of international significance due to the dependence of the industrialized Western world and Japan on oil from the Arab Gulf. Iraq became solely dependent upon the Turkish and Syrian pipelines for oil exports, and the focus on Gulf petroleum resources increased when Syria closed its Iraqi oil pipeline in April 1982, further inciting tension in the region.

Simultaneous to these events, in the late 1970s Kuwaiti foreign policy under the leadership of Foreign Minister Sheikh Sabah Al-Ahmad emphasized two basic tenets that helped in the initial structuring of the GCC: first, that the Gulf should be kept free of superpower involvement and second, that the Gulf states themselves should be responsible for the security of the Gulf. This "hands off" policy clearly outlined for the GCC founders the flexibility of negotiating security and arms arrangements with a variety of alternatives and was formulated so as not to restrict either the acquisition or use of arms to binding political coalitions with outside powers.

Finally, another political factor leading to the integration of the Arab Gulf states was the 1973 oil embargo. The Arab members of OPEC experimented with oil as a political weapon in October 1973 when the oil embargo was invoked to pressure the United States into taking a more ameliorative position concerning the Palestinian situation. Although the action did not have the desired political impact on the peace process, the cohesive implementation of a unified economic policy underscored the relative ease in accomplishing an Arabian Gulf cooperative effort when there was unanimity in the objective.

With this brief history as a backdrop, it becomes more evident that there was not only an inherent desire but a need for the Gulf states to reaffirm their existing bonds of unity. The Gulf Arabs had always shared feelings of heritage and common destiny and thus the consensus for formalization of a unifying organization culminating in the establishment of the GCC. Furthermore, in conceiving the GCC one of the principal objectives of the founding fathers was to create a community of nations similar in scope to the European Community generally and the European Economic Community (EEC) specifically, thereby establishing a common, unified approach to economic affairs, defense and foreign policy.

While the intention was to develop an organization based on the successful EEC, the founders fully understood that there were certain factors existent within the EEC that were missing in the Gulf states, i.e., developed member-country markets and sophisticated communications, the lack of which would impede duplication of the EEC structure in the Gulf. Certainly, the common language and similarity in the cultural and ethnic origin of the Gulf member states would facilitate the process of integration. Furthermore, there was a greater nucleus of the most strategic area of the world, and thus the destiny of the founders was to enhance the structure of the existing EEC to enable adaptations of additional principles of cooperation and unification.

HISTORICAL BACKGROUND TO ARAB GULF ECONOMIC DEVELOPMENT AND AMERICAN INTERESTS IN THE REGION

In August 1922, U.S. corporate oil interests negotiated their first concessions in the Middle East by obtaining first 12 percent and eventually 20 percent of the Turkish Petroleum Company, the predecessor of the Iraq Petroleum Company. Exxon, Gulf, Texaco and Mobil were encouraged by the U.S. State Department and Washington to make the investment; and Standard Oil of California (SOCAL), excluded from the famous Gulbenkian Red Line Agreement of July 1928, which prevented the partners of the Iraq Petroleum Company from seeking concessions within the bodies of the original Ottoman Empire, subsequently obtained the first foreign oil concession in Bahrain. Following Bahrain's oil discoveries in 1931, Saudi King Ibn Saud was anxious to obtain for his nation an alternative source of income and eagerly sought a concessionaire for the Saudi Arabian oil potential. SOCAL was the likely candidate since they were already producing and exporting from Bahrain and were exempted from the restrictions of the Red Line Agreement. In August 1933, SOCAL and Saudi Arabia entered into an historic agreement, and six years later, in May 1939, production was initiated.

It is little wonder that U.S. interest and trade activity with the Arabian Gulf region accelerated as the years progressed. By 1985 the Arabian Gulf market represented the fifth largest export market for the United States after Canada, Japan, Mexico and the United Kingdom. Because of its oil production and consequent infrastructural and developmental requirements, Saudi Arabia quickly became the largest single importer of foreign products during the decade 1974-84, and U.S. exports to Saudi Arabia increased from less than $300 million per annum in pre-oil boom 1973 to $9 billion in 1982. Trade figures between the United States and the other Gulf states are equally impressive, but EEC market penetration of the Gulf was also strong. By 1984 European products accounted for approximately 37 percent of the Gulf states' import market, while absorbing 20 percent of its exports, and thus, suddenly, the Gulf market became a prime target for European exporters. Therefore, it was logical for the founders of the GCC to maintain a dialogue with the EEC to discuss a strategy for on-going collaboration, and the extent to which this initiative was welcomed by the Europeans is obvious. The continuing infrastructural development of the Gulf states and prosperity of its citizens and other residents represented a lucrative potential for increased EEC exports of capital and consumer goods. The EEC quickly recognized this as an opportunity to expand cooperative efforts in order to secure an even larger market share of such an important new economic community.

However, as the Gulf states emerged into the 1980s from a decade of infrastructural development and began to industrialize in order to provide alternative sources of foreign currency income, the export of their petrochemical as well as other products met competitive pressure from EEC, U.S. and Japanese petrochemical and other commodity producers. Whether or not the EEC and other Western nations will adopt a protectionist position to defend their aging industrial sectors remains to be seen, but the lagging economies of all three major trading partners portends a necessity for the Arabian Gulf industrial sector to develop with the maximum technological efficiency. This technological efficiency is being enhanced and developed by central, coordinated planning by the GCC. Despite a trend toward protectionism, the U.S. Congress should make every effort to alleviate the growing pains of the Arabian Gulf industrial sector, for it is certainly in the best interests of the United States to have the Gulf states develop a more balanced economy rather than be totally dependent on oil exports as an earner of foreign exchange.

Initially, the Japanese displayed a reluctance to accede to the GCC's petrochemical export campaign, but having emerged as the area's favored trading partner and, more important, willing to make internal sacrifices in order to develop long-term cooperation with the GCC states, they have undergone a certain accommodative process which has strengthened their status in the Gulf area. As a result, the Japanese have reportedly established over 50 joint ventures with Gulf partners and there will probably be additional investment. The American partners in Aramco, desirous of maintaining, if not strengthening, their own corporate interests in the area, will be reviewing investment opportunities in Saudi Arabia as will EEC corporate investors, but given the extent to which their own petrochemical and refining sectors have been developed and represent a significant lobbying factor with their respective governments, it is doubtful that substantial new investment in the petroleum sector will be forthcoming from either the United States or Western Europe with the GCC states.

U.S. PRIVATE SECTOR PETROLEUM JOINT VENTURES: THE FIRST LINK IN U.S.-GULF ECONOMIC INTERDEPENDENCE

The petroleum-related joint ventures that have been consummated between private U.S. business interests and public- and private-sector GCC parties have been substantial and represent the initial link in establishing an economic interdependence between the United States and the Arabian Gulf. It is interesting to note that U.S. oil involvement in the Gulf is still in the hands of U.S. private corporate interests, and one can only speculate whether the oil decade of the seventies and consequences of the eighties would have been different if President Franklin D. Roosevelt's secretary of the interior, Harold Ickes, had been able to involve the U.S. government as a partner of Aramco in negotiations that occurred in 1943 with some of the Aramco partners. The vehicle designated to make the investment on behalf of the U.S. government, the Petroleum Reserve Corporation, was actually established and several meetings were held before policy differences between U.S. public- and private-sector participants sealed the fate of the idea. The U.S. corporate partners in Aramco would thus play the unique role of both defending U.S. government interests in the Saudi oil patch and protecting their shareholders for the foreseeable future. Some of the more noted U.S.-GCC joint ventures are described in the following paragraphs.

To date, Texaco has established two joint ventures with private Saudi interests. The first was established in December 1977 in which Texaco Marine, a wholly owned subsidiary, invested 49 percent with three Saudi individuals (51 percent) to form Saudi International Petroleum Carriers Ltd., a company engaged in the transport of crude oil from the Gulf to foreign importers. The second company, SAPTEX, was established in 1982 and is a joint venture between Texaco (40 percent) and Saudi Plastic Products, Ltd. (60 percent), a private Saudi company. SAPTEX manufactures and markets urethane insulation panel board for use in the construction of Saudi industrial, commercial and institutional buildings. Chevron has a private sector investment in the Saudi Cable Company which manufactures and markets electric steel cable products. Exxon has a 50 percent investment with the Saudi Arabian Basic Industries Corp. (SABIC), in the Jubail Petrochemical Company (KEMYA), a joint venture with the private sector Kanoo Group in Saudi Arabian Lubricating Additive Company (SALACO) located in Yanbu, and a lube oil marketing operation with the same Kanoo Group. On the other hand, Mobil, the largest foreign investor in Saudi Arabia, has the following joint-venture investments:

—*Petroleum-Mobil Yanbu Refining Company, Ltd.* (PEMREF)
A 50-50 joint venture with Petromin in an export fuel refinery at Yanbu with a capacity of 250,000 barrels per day, it has been operational since August 1984.
—*Saudi Yanbu Petrochemical Co.* (YANPET)
A 50-50 joint venture with SABIC in a petrochemical plant at Yanbu producing polyethylene and glycol since December 1984.

—Petromin Lubricating Oil Refining Company (LUBEREF)
A Petromin (70 percent)-Mobil (30 percent) joint-venture lubricating-oil refinery in Jeddah with a capacity of 1.6 million barrels per year. LUBEREF is the sole supplier of domestically produced feed stocks for the lube blending and automotive oils.
—Petromin Lubricating Oil Company (PETROLUBE)
Two joint-venture lube-blending plants with Petromin in Jeddah and Riyadh. Ownership shared by Petromin (71 percent) and Mobil (29 percent).

In addition to the aforementioned, Mobil has a private joint-venture lube-marketing operation with the Alireza family, known as Arabian Petroleum Supply Company, and a host of other private-investor joint ventures.

These many joint-venture operations constitute an investment of several billion dollars and guarantee that U.S. firms will continue to participate as partners with the Gulf Arab nations in their long-term economic development. GCC authorities acknowledge that the private sector in the Gulf has become very receptive to the joint-venture concept as a means of attracting both foreign investment and technology. However, the current recession in the area has prompted the private sector to reassess market strategies and seek a longer-term business approach rather than pursue the short-term tactics of the past. Instead of initiating protectionism in industries the Gulf Arabs are developing, the United States should wholeheartedly support more joint-venture relationships in the Gulf. In the long-term, the price of oil will in all probability increase, and since the GCC states control approximately 50 percent of the world's proven reserves, its availability outside the Gulf area will continue to be subject to not only supply and demand but the producing states' restrictive policies, thereby necessitating expanded U.S. interest in the GCC. This will provide a strong rationale for the American government to fully cooperate with the GCC nations as economic partners and not adversaries. And with almost 27 percent of global oil reserves located in Saudi Arabia (the combined reserves of North and South America, Western Europe and Africa are approximately the same as Saudi Arabia) having a life span exceeding 100 years, it becomes the obvious country for American business interests to seek investment opportunities in. It is important for American corporate oil interests to establish good long-term relations and product availability, and their participation in well-conceived joint-venture projects is an attempt to accomplish these objectives. While long-term access to crude oil and petroleum by-products is an essential element in the success of any fully integrated oil company, their ability to facilitate the transfer of technology to GCC joint-venture parties actually accelerates the process of industrialization in the Arabian Gulf. The training of personnel in the West enables the GCC to become active participants in the up-lifting and manufacture of petroleum products which, over the long term, is beneficial to both joint-venture parties.

U.S.-GULF BANKING AND INVESTMENT: THE SECOND LINK IN U.S.-GULF ECONOMIC INTERDEPENDENCE

Prior to the oil price revolution of October 16, 1973, the importance of the Gulf states' petroleum resources was not widely recognized and greatly underestimated. But when the representatives of the six Gulf-state members of OPEC met in Kuwait on October 16 and voted to increase the posted price of crude oil by 70 percent, the impact of OPEC had a resounding effect throughout the world. Suddenly the hegemony of the major international oil companies was being boldly challenged, and not since the formation of OPEC in 1960 had the role of the producing members become so dominant. Heretofore, oil prices were largely controlled by the international oil companies, and only in 1960, when excess production caused crude prices to decline, was OPEC established as a defensive measure to stabilize the price trend.

Immediately following the October 1973 price hike, the Arab members of OPEC voted an embargo of oil exports to the United States, and then on January 1, 1974, the ten Arab constituents of OPEC doubled the price of oil to $11.65 per barrel, causing a global economic upheaval. Oil production had suddenly become both an important political weapon and an economic windfall, especially to the GCC member nations.

Who could have envisioned the impact that greatly increased OPEC dollar reserves would have on the world economic system in 1974 when OPEC countries received $95 billion in oil revenue and spent only $35 billion of that sum on imports? Approximately $10 billion in oil revenues was retained to fund internal requirements. When the remaining $50 billion available in disposable income was suddenly deposited in European ($28 billion), U.S. ($10 billion) and various international financial institutions ($12 billion), the balance of the international economic system was clearly being jeopardized. Such threats had unimaginable implications and consequences at that time. The foremost concern of the placing power was safety and liquidity. Almost $6 billion of the $10 billion invested in the United States in 1974 was used to purchase U.S. government securities, an alternative which was subsequently to play a major role in America's financing of the nation's budget deficits over the next decade. By the end of 1975 approximately $55 billion in GCC reserves were invested in the government securities of the United States, the United Kingdom, Germany and Japan, of which $33 billion was reportedly in U.S. government securities alone.

53

Another $3.5 billion flowed into the U.S. banking system in 1974 in the form of direct deposits in banks domiciled in the United States, while actually, a substantial part of the $28 billion placed in Europe also flowed into the U.S. banking system. Regrettably, a misuse of these deposits in the international banking system was their enthusiastic, but sometimes indiscriminate, recycling to fund syndicated term loans to the lesser-developed countries (LDCs). It was the rapid accumulation of OPEC wealth in the Gulf states and the aggressive determination of the U.S. banks to compete for petrodollar deposits that galvanized the interdependence of the Gulf states and the U.S. banking system.

The initial accumulation of wealth and subsequent recycling to U.S. banks occurred in the mid-1970s when U.S. banks were facing a liquidity squeeze due to a plethora of nonperforming loans in real estate and shipping. The sudden inflow of petrodollars provided Western banks with a large pool of new funds, and it was only when their existing funding requirements were satisfied that they turned to the needs of the LDCs and became major lenders to a capital-starved Third World. There have been varying estimates of the extent of accumulated GCC net foreign investment, but, according to the official records of the U.S. Treasury and the Bank of England, the GCC countries amassed approximately $240 billion during the period 1973-84. This total had reportedly decreased to $205 billion by year-end 1985, with Saudi Arabia holding $90 billion, Kuwait $80 billion, the United Arab Emirates $20 billion and Bahrain, Oman and Qatar collectively holding $15 billion.

With the recent depression in the price of petroleum products continuing throughout 1986 and the extended recession in the Gulf, the disinvestment policy of the GCC members is no doubt ongoing. Additionally, following the U.S. decision to freeze Libyan assets early in 1986, the Arab world—including GCC members—may well diversify their investment strategy by shifting additional funds out of the banking sector into German, Japanese and Swiss government securities and equities. The U.S. equity market may also be more heavily utilized as an investment vehicle with the thought being that it is more difficult to isolate and freeze movement in equities than sovereign bank deposits.

Should there be a continued disinvestment of dollar-based holdings, additional pressure on the U.S. dollar may occur, making it necessary for the GCC countries to consider pegging their currencies to a basket of currencies (as does Kuwait) rather than to the U.S. dollar. With the bulk of GCC foreign-reserve holdings denominated in U.S. dollars, a continuing reassessment of investment strategy will be necessary to preserve purchasing power. The ongoing strategy review will obviate a further evolution in the Gulf financial industry, which represents the second most important revenue producer in the GCC after petroleum and related products.

A GENERAL HISTORY OF ARAB BANKING IN THE GULF

A brief history of Arab banking will help the reader to understand the development of banking in the Arabian Gulf. The first records of commercial banking in the Arab world appear to date from the establishment of an institution in 1856 known as the Egyptian Bank in Cairo, which was privately owned by British interests. The Anglo-French-owned Imperial Ottoman Bank, established in 1863, began to open branches in the principal trading centers in the Near East before the turn of the century, while the French Crédit Foncier also established branches in major commercial and trading centers. This nucleus of banks, controlled by colonial interests, seems to have dominated the Arab world until the establishment of certain indigenous banks in the period following World War I.

Under Turkish rule, banking in Syria and Lebanon was established to assist the colonial power in its administrative responsibilities. The former Banque du Syrie for Syria and Lebanon actually functioned as a subsidiary of the Ottoman Bank and performed the role of central banker to both Syria and Lebanon until 1955 and 1964, respectively, when the Central Bank of Syria and Banque du Liban (Central Bank of Lebanon) were established. The National Bank of Egypt was also established as a private-sector bank in 1898 and performed certain limited functions of a central bank until the formation of the Central Bank of Egypt in 1960. It was only after World War I when the first Arab private commercial bank was established, acknowledged to have occurred in 1920 with the formation of the Banque Misr in Cairo, to provide a vehicle to finance the prospering Egyptian cotton trade. Similarly, the Banque Sabbagh and Banque Tohme were established in Beirut to formalize the business of two leading Lebanese moneylenders, a move that prompted the eventual formation of dozens of small, family-owned Lebanese commercial banks, many of which have continued to prosper throughout the lamentable deterioration of the Lebanese economic and political systems since 1975.

The movement spread southeastward to Jerusalem in 1930 with the formation of Arab Bank Ltd. by Abdulhameed Shoman and continued into Saudi Arabia in 1938, when the merchant families of Kaki and Mafouz established the National Commercial Bank in Jeddah. Both Arab Bank Ltd. and Banque Misr established branches in the major neighboring trading centers of Beirut and Damascus, and Arab Bank Ltd. extended its branch network to Amman and Cairo.

The National Bank of Iraq, founded in 1949, was the precursor of a widespread nationalistic movement throughout the area following World War II, when certain quasi-government as well as private financial institutions, established to protect colonial interests, were nationalized.

The National Bank of Iraq commenced operations in 1949 to absorb the functions of the British-controlled Iraqi Currency Board. Hereafter, issuance and control of Iraqi currency would be centralized in Baghdad instead of London, and the National Bank of Iraq would be reconstituted in 1956 as the Central Bank of Iraq. Similarly, in Egypt the decade of the fifties witnessed the nationalization of all foreign private banking interests, including those of Arab Bank Ltd., and the transformation of the National Bank of Egypt to a commercial bank when the aforementioned Central Bank of Egypt was established in 1960.

For 150 years— up to the formation of the United Arab Emirates in December 1971—banking in the Arabian Gulf outside of Saudi Arabia had, with some exceptions, been predominantly controlled by British interests. The British Bank of the Middle East obtained a 30-year concession in Kuwait in 1941, which included an exclusion of all other foreign banks from the country. It was also granted a 20-year exclusive concession in Oman in 1948. The Eastern Bank, a British financial institution later to become Chartered Bank, established a branch in Bahrain in 1920 and would eventually serve as the official banker to the Bahraini government until 1975. The Eastern Bank also established the first banking presence in Qatar in 1949.

With the history of Arab banking dominated by colonial interests, and specifically by British interests in the Gulf states, the formation and development of national banking institutions was generally delayed until the fifties. The National Bank of Kuwait, the first indigenous bank to be established in that country, was founded in 1952, and the National Bank of Bahrain (established as Bahrain Bank) was formed in 1957. Somewhat later, the Qatar National Bank was established in 1965 and the National Bank of Oman in 1973. The Saudi Arabian Monetary Authority (SAMA) was established in 1952 and has always operated as the central banking authority in Saudi Arabia, leaving the commercial banking sector in such private hands as the National Commercial Bank (1938), Riyad Bank (1957), and a select group of foreign branches which have since been Saudiized for the purpose of permitting greater national control over the kingdom's banking system. SAMA, however, maintains a 38 percent interest in Riyad Bank and thus participates indirectly in the business of Saudi commercial banking. It is interesting to note that the first organized banking presence in Saudi Arabia was in the form of a branch of the Dutch Algemene Bank in Jeddah, a presence that helped to finance the Moslem pilgrimages from the Dutch East Indies to Mecca as well as the commercial and trading interests of the East India Company.

ing the 1960s this basic banking structure was broadened to modate several venturesome Western banks which established es, representative offices or assumed management contracts with indigenous banks. In 1961 in Kuwait the foresightedness of Abdlatif Al-Hamad—a young, well-educated Kuwaiti from a prominent merchant family—was instrumental in establishing the first indigenous investment bank in the Arab world, and the Kuwait Investment Company (KIC) quickly became a model financial institution staffed by young Kuwaitis trained in Europe and the United States. Within this framework, trade and commercial activity was conducted between Western and Arab worlds on the usual documentary basis without any specific need to effect systemic changes.

In the late 1960s Arab banking stepped out of the confines of the Middle East to establish joint-venture consortium banks with traditional European financial institutions, and the first such venture, Banque Franco-Arabe d'Investissements Internationaux (FRAB) was established in Paris in 1969. Until that time Arab banking was largely domestic in nature but anxious to acquire expertise in international capital markets. Several leading Arab banks took the giant step to the European continent. The action by FRAB was the harbinger of a massive Arab presence in the major European capital cities that would eventually serve to broaden the importance of Arab banking internationally. The FRAB experiment was rapidly followed by the formation of the Union des Banques Arabes et Françaises (UBAF) in 1970 in Paris under the direction of Dr. Mohamed Abushadi, a leading Egyptian financier; the European Arab Bank in 1972 in Luxembourg and the Banque Arabe et Internationale d'Investissement (BAII) in Paris in 1973.

Recognizing the success of these consortium banks, the Gulf International Bank was established in 1975 which, instead of being a consortium of financial institutions domiciled in Europe, was a joint venture of the governments of the Gulf states of Bahrain, Oman, Kuwait, Qatar, Saudi Arabia and Iraq. Uniting their financial forces they established this major wholesale commercial bank, based in Bahrain that was capable of participating effectively in the principal international capital markets.

This movement coincided with the oil price revolution in late 1973 and early 1974, the demise of Beirut as the principal Arab commercial center in 1975, the subsequent birth of the Bahrain offshore banking concept in 1975 and the development of the Eurocurrency markets. Furthermore, with the prevailing instability of the major international currencies, the Gulf Arabs quickly recognized that an active presence in the international financial community would protect and enhance their expanding economic interests. The list would continue with the formation of Saudi International Bank in London in 1975 with strong shareholder support from SAMA (50 percent) and Morgan Guaranty Trust (20 percent), and with smaller equity participations of Banque Nationale de Paris (5 percent), Deutsche Bank (5 percent), National

Westminster Bank (5 percent), Union Bank of Switzerland (5 percent) and the two leading Saudi Banks, National Commercial Bank (2.5 percent) and Riyad Bank (2.5 percent).

Morgan Guaranty has a long history of close cooperation and assistance with the Gulf state governments and their financial institutions, and a SAMA-Morgan association in Saudi International Bank was a logical development. Even when the Bahraini offshore banking movement was initiated in 1975, precipitating a flood of American banks to the area, Morgan Guaranty abstained from establishing a banking unit in the Arabian Gulf since the concept was not compatible with its overall objectives. Their strategic relationships with certain Gulf-state finance ministries, central banks and a selective list of wealthy merchants did not necessitate a physical presence in the area. They viewed the offshore banking movement as being too dependent upon the vagaries of the Gulf-state finance ministries, and they reasoned that their London branch could accommodate the foreign exchange and other operational requirements of the Arabian Gulf area. Besides, Morgan Guaranty took on the role of managing the Bank of Kuwait and the Middle East in Kuwait under contract during the period 1976-82, after which the bank was controlled by the Kuwaiti Ministry of Finance.

The culmination of Arab consortium bank formations occurred in January 1980 with the establishment in Bahrain of the Arab Banking Corporation, a joint venture between the governments of Kuwait (Ministry of Finance), Libya (Secretariat of the Treasury) and Abu Dhabi (Abu Dhabi Investment Authority) that was created with an authorized capital of $1 billion, of which $750 million was quickly paid in. Soon after being established, this bank came to be known by its acronym, ABC, and during the next five years would become a major force not only in Gulf banking but in international merchant banking. ABC's foresight to expand globally merits commendation, and internal sources point out that this was done "to eliminate any advantage an Arab bank might have enjoyed from the external financial surpluses and large development expenditures of Arab oil-producing states."

Furthermore, the creation of ABC Investment & Services Company as a tax exempt company in Bahrain confirms ABC's commitment to the GCC region and to assisting in the development of regional capital markets. In short, the stage was set for Gulf Arabs to accept the challenge of productively utilizing the massive wealth being generated by the export of petroleum and petroleum products.

During the formation and development of the Arab consortium banks, Western financial technology was an integral part of the early successes enjoyed by these banks, and the American banking and financial community played an important role in the training of young Arab bankers.

The major U.S. money center banks, investment banking houses and brokerage firms extended invitations to their counterparts in the Arabian Gulf to offer in-house training facilities which were eagerly sought and utilized. The interdependence of global financial institutions is vital to the success of its participants, and the Americans quickly sought to strengthen their rather weak banking relationships in the Gulf in order to affirm their own credibility as a viable link in the chain of international finance.

In a speech to the Arab Bankers Association in London in June 1982, Abdulla Saudi, President and CEO of Arab Banking Corporation, stated that the Arab shareholder had four objectives in collaborating with Europeans in forming the consortium banks as follows: (1) to initiate Arab penetration of the international capital markets, (2) to provide training for young Arab bankers, (3) to help to cater to the financial needs of Arab countries and (4) to share in the management of their own funds. Saudi concluded that although the consortium banks had achieved some of these objectives in the early years, there were certain conflicts in meeting the criteria of surplus and deficit countries, i.e., should the consortium bank facilitate the international lending process by offering attractive terms to the deficit countries or should the banks be seeking higher margins in order to improve their own profitability?

He further indicated that certain activities undertaken by the consortium banks such as portfolio management and correspondent banking encroached on similar established activities of the foreign shareholder, thereby diminishing the effectiveness of the consortium. Only when the second wave of consortium banks was established in the mid-seventies, with Arab shareholders primarily from surplus countries and with specific geographic lending criteria, were the Arabs able to more fully accomplish their objectives. By the early eighties there had emerged an elite group of well-trained Arab commercial and investment bankers who had worked alongside seasoned professionals in the London, New York and Paris capital markets, so the need to depend on the expertise of a foreign shareholder had considerably diminished.

Consider, for example, the abundance of indigenous financial institutions that were established in GCC countries capable of providing feasibility studies, initiating investments in industrial and development projects and sourcing both equity as well as medium- and long-term credit, including export credit from the major international agencies. While foreign expertise was initially essential to enable the indigenous and consortium banks to compete effectively with the major international banks, it was the knowledge of the area and the traditional practices of the marketplace that provided the Arab banks with the ability to effectively penetrate the financial and business community.

OFFSHORE BANKING AND GCC REGIONAL BANKING DEVELOPMENT—AMERICAN BANKS ESTABLISH A PHYSICAL PRESENCE IN THE ARABIAN GULF

No discussion of Gulf Arab banking would be complete without an analysis of the Bahrain offshore banking market which originated in 1975 through the initiative of the Bahrain Monetary Agency, the predecessor of the Central Bank of Bahrain. The original concept of developing an offshore banking center in Bahrain stemmed from the fact that with oil reserves depleting over a period of 25 years, Bahrain would eventually lose its primary source of revenue and become more reliant upon three major revenue generators: the ALBA aluminum smelting operation, the BALEXCO aluminum extrusion works and the Arab Shipbuilding and Repair Yards (ASRY), a $340 million shipyard complex owned jointly by the seven OAPEC countries (Saudi Arabia, Bahrain, Kuwait, Qatar, UAE, Libya and Iraq) that was established in November 1974 to service the Gulf tanker business.

Although Beirut had served as the commercial center for the Middle East for decades, its location was far from the income-generating Gulf states, and its viability was becoming more questionable due to the Lebanese political and social disorder. There was definitely a need to establish a new financial center away from this turbulence, but there were few alternatives since most Arab Gulf states did not permit a foreign banking presence. It was felt that a vibrant offshore banking business could transform Bahrain into a service community, attracting substantial investment in infrastructure that would have a positive impact on the social and economic needs of the community.

Initially, there was some competition from the United Arab Emirates to establish a parallel offshore banking system in both Abu Dhabi and Dubai with "Restricted Banking Licenses" to be issued by the Emirates Currency Board. Citibank and First National Bank of Chicago had already established full commercial branches in Abu Dhabi and Dubai, and while other American banks examined the possible alternative of a presence in the UAE, 15 American banks eventually opened offshore banking units (OBUs) in Bahrain. Altogether, 185 foreign banks and financial institutions from 34 different countries established either an OBU, or representative office in Bahrain during the period 1975-85, including Merrill Lynch and E.F. Hutton, with Investment Banking Licenses. The asset growth of the Bahraini offshore banking units reached a peak of $63.5 billion in March 1984, but has since declined to a still very significant level of $56 billion.

Similar to the Singapore offshore banking system which had been established several years prior, the Bahrainis structured their system to attract banks desirous of maintaining a physical presence without competing for the limited onshore dinar business with the Bahraini banks. The American banks were delighted to find a country in the heart of the Arabian Gulf area that was willing to permit the establishment of a physical presence. It was not the dinar-based business that American banks coveted but access to the dollar-denominated transactions that would put them in closer contact with the rapidly developing Gulf market. The annual OBU license fee was $25,000 and the Bahraini Monetary Agency demanded strict compliance with the island's banking regulations. American bankers were familiar with the success of the earlier Singapore system, but there were other factors that favorably supported the feasibility of an offshore banking market in Bahrain.

Communications between other global financial centers were excellent, and the island served as a strategic link between the Far East and Europe. With a four-hour time difference between Bahrain and Hong Kong, a position in foreign exchange at Hong Kong's close of business could be passed on to Bahrain and worked in that market before the opening in Paris one hour later, or in London two hours later, enabling the major U.S. and other international banks to maintain a 24-hour working linkage in the foreign exchange markets for the first time ever.

Furthermore, the infrastructure of the Bahraini market provided an excellent base for those foreign banks that wanted to develop stronger relationships with the Gulf state governments, their associated financial institutions and private corporate entities.

Initially the OBU bankers targeted only prime corporate names in Saudi Arabia, Kuwait, the UAE and Oman, but as competition for business increased and margins for prime borrowers were squeezed, the approach for new customers changed. The aggressive young marketing officers from Bahrain soon identified a middle-market range of corporate borrowers and a new lending emphasis was centered upon these lesser capitalized but creditworthy and well-managed names. Most of the early financing was arranged at attractive yields and was liquidated promptly at maturity, without rescheduling or workout problems, factors which encouraged the Bahraini banking community to continue lending despite continuously deteriorating conditions.

The rapidly expanding Saudi corporate market, however, lured OBU bankers to Jeddah, Riyadh and Dhahran, and although foreign banks are prohibited from branching in Saudi Arabia, the Eastern Province of the kingdom is only a 20-minute flight across Gulf waters from Bahrain. With the indigenous Saudi banking community in a developing stage with regard to multinational corporate lending techniques, the foreign banks from Bahrain undertook a strong solicitation effort of prospective borrowers of Saudi riyals and dollar funds that the OBUs were attracting.

OBUs, American Banks and the Saudi Market

Citibank was the only American bank with a full-service branch operation in Saudi Arabia prior to the Saudiization process in 1979 which required all foreign banks with branches in the kingdom to incorporate as local Saudi banks with 60 percent Saudi national ownership. Although reduced to a 40 percent ownership, most of the foreign banks managed to retain their original operating identity by arranging management agreements, but over time these banks are becoming increasingly Saudi-styled and managed. Chase Manhattan Bank helped to establish the Saudi Investment Banking Corporation in September 1974, a joint-venture investment bank based in Saudi Arabia in which a group of foreign banks held one-third of the capital, a group of Saudi institutional investors held one-third, and the remaining third was held by approximately 3,600 Saudi individual investors. The bank was established with an authorized capital of $10 million denominated in Saudi riyals and was structured to extend medium-term loans for Saudi corporate development projects. Chase's participation continues to be 20 percent of the equity and responsibility for management.

Other foreign banks participating in the joint venture were Commerzbank in Germany, the Industrial Development Bank of Japan and Schroeder Wagg, while Riyadh Bank, National Commercial Bank, and Al Jazira Bank were among the Saudi institutional shareholders. The joint venture never developed its full potential in the Saudi marketplace, due probably to the fact that Saudi project development peaked soon after the bank became fully operational. In addition, Chase Manhattan Bank signed a ten-year technical-service agreement with the Saudi Industrial Development Fund in 1974 which was established to finance the fixed assets of projects falling within the National Development Plan. For security, SIDF requested a mortgage over the land and fixed assets, and the maximum term of the loan could not exceed 15 years. The Fund was successful in providing development capital for much-needed industrial projects.

As the offshore riyal market developed, the Saudi Arabian Monetary Agency (SAMA) recognized the dangers in permitting such a market to proliferate without proper controls. Unlike the Central Bank of Kuwait, which prohibited Kuwaiti banks from depositing Kuwaiti dinars in the Bahrain offshore market from the inception of the OBUs, SAMA permitted offshore riyal deposits by Saudi banks, probably to encourage the participation of the OBUs in large Saudi construction projects, allowing the foreign banks to fund themselves by obtaining riyals from Saudi sources. But SAMA grew wary that the continuation of this would serve to internationalize the riyal and issued an edict in ibiting foreign banks from participating in public-project riyal without SAMA approval. A second circular by SAMA, moving to enforce a withholding tax of 15 percent on all interest payments by Saudi corporations, dealt the Bahrain offshore market a further blow, but both measures had a positive effect on Arab banking by enhancing their competitive status in the region. It also forced the foreign banks to offer new, more sophisticated products which had a beneficial effect on the regional financial market.

The American financial presence in the United Arab Emirates was limited to branches of Citibank and First National Bank of Chicago in Abu Dhabi and Dubai and representative offices of Chemical Bank in Dubai and of Bank of America in Abu Dhabi. In addition, Bank of America maintained a 30 percent ownership of Bank of Credit and Commerce International, a Luxembourg domiciled bank established in September 1972 with its principal regional office in Abu Dhabi (the remaining 70 percent ownership was in the hands of individual Middle Eastern shareholders of which the most significant was Sheikh Zaid, the ruler of Abu Dhabi). Bank of America liquidated its ownership in BCCI in June 1980 but during their eight-year involvement in the joint venture the active participation of the Bank of America provided a solid organizational and credit structure on which BCCI would later prosper.

The Kuwaiti Ministry of Finance still prohibits foreign banks from branching as well as establishing representative offices, and American banking has penetrated Oman and Qatar only to the extent of Citibank branches in the capital cities.

The crash of the Kuwaiti stock market, the Souq al Manakh, in 1982 with losses on paper of $92 billion, and the subsequent plummeting oil prices in 1983 caused a substantial slowdown in Arabian Gulf construction, infrastructural development, trade and payment delays. Additionally, this coincided with a global business recession and the debt-servicing problems of the LDCs in the early to mid-eighties, forcing banks to scrutinize operating costs. Staggering debt problems of such well-known names as Arab Gulf businessmen Shobokshi, Galadari and Pharoan began to surface in 1983, and over the next three years repayment problems in the region were exacerbated as positive cash flows from once viable business operations slowed to a trickle or turned negative. The boom and near bust of the widespread Shobokshi empire alone epitomizes the excess in business expansion in the golden years of the Gulf boom.

These elements combined have caused many banks to reassess the viability of maintaining a Bahraini OBU presence, and some of the financial institutions in the Arabian Gulf have already begun to wind down their commercial banking activities in order to prepare for the new demands of the marketplace. There will probably be further consolidation of the banking industry as both Arab and foreign banks reassess their structures, personnel composite and product lines. The

American OBUs have already experienced some staff reductions and realignments as they shift their current emphasis from corporate lending to foreign exchange and transaction processing, and they will certainly enhance their merchant banking capability. During the past two years, several American OBUs and representative offices have closed due to the Gulf recession, and more closings may follow despite the warning of the Bahrain Monetary Agency that those banks that close will not be permitted to return.

GULF ARAB BANKING AND INVESTMENT IN THE UNITED STATES: COMPLETING THE INTERDEPENDENCE CHAIN

As Arab financial institutions established operating entities in European capitals in the 1970s in an effort to emulate the early success of the Arab consortium banks in Paris and London, it was a natural extension of Arab finance to establish a presence in the United States. The government of Kuwait had already targeted the United States as a principal investment base for its excess oil revenues and in February 1974 the Kuwait Investment Company (KIC) purchased Kiawah Island near Charleston, South Carolina. The same year, KIC invested further in the Atlanta Hilton in a 50-50 partnership which they later bought out, and in 1981 the Kuwait Petroleum Company purchased 100 percent of the Santa Fe Drilling Company in California for $2.5 billion, primarily for its C.F. Braun engineering and construction subsidiary. While Kuwait diversified its foreign investment portfolio by purchasing 15 percent of Daimler Benz, 25 percent of Korf Stahl Steel, 24 percent of Hoechst and 10 percent of Metalgesellschaft, all of West Germany, reliable sources have reported that Kuwaiti reserves were invested in approximately 480 of the top "Fortune 500" American companies, yielding substantially more for Kuwait in dividends and interest than its petroleum export revenue.

In order to facilitate the stock equity purchases in the United States by Gulf Arab investors, Arab banking took to American shores to further broaden their limited offshore banking operations that had already been established in London and Paris. The American market provided a variety of investment opportunities as well as the stability and security essential to any successful investment environment.

This new wave in international banking, let us call it the Arab wave, was dissimilar from the previous three American, European and Japanese waves which resulted either directly or indirectly from the appearance of the multinational corporation. Aptly christened "Le Défi Amér- Servan Schreiber, this "American challenge" was responded pean and later Japanese firms which for competitive reasons to expand internationally. Thus, the primary motive behind the internationalization process of the first three banking waves from the industrial countries of the OECD was to follow their multinational customers abroad, and the process occurred at an opportune time because many of the banks had reached maturity in often overbanked domestic markets. While the Arab banks did not have multinational customers to lead them abroad, the tug of international markets proved to be irresistible.

In 1976 UBAF Arab American Bank became the first majority Arab-owned bank to be established in the United States. The consortium bank was an Arab joint venture with four major U.S. banks—Bankers Trust New York Corporation, First Chicago Corporation, Texas Commerce Bankshares and Security Pacific Corporation—selected to afford a strategic geographic coverage of the United States. These four banks each initially owned 5 percent of the UBAF's equity, with the remaining 80 percent owned by 16 Arab financial institutions representing each country in the Arab world. The bank was founded as a New York state-chartered wholesale commercial bank with its fundamental objective to promote and expand U.S.-Arab trade relations as well as to serve both American and Arab investment interests. While these objectives were successfully met during the first decade of operations, UBAF Arab American Bank has recently reassessed its market strategy and has established an active merchant banking group in order to take advantage of present market dynamics.

Because of federal and state reciprocity laws, the boom in Arab banking in the United States was delayed until the enactment of the U.S. International Banking Act of 1978 and the subsequent abolition of reciprocity laws in New York State in 1980. The "Rule of Reciprocity" in banking terminology basically stipulates that a Saudi bank, for example, cannot establish a branch in New York State if a New York State chartered bank is prevented by Saudi legislation from establishing a branch in Saudi Arabia. Once such reciprocity legislation was abolished, the Arab banking wave into the United States was underway, and it was the Gulf-based banks that spearheaded the drive.

Today there are approximately 24 Arab banks represented in the United States either with a branch, agency or representative office. While most banks entered the American market with a representative office or a branch of the head office, Banque Arabe et Internationale d'Investissement (BAII) chose to establish a unique, New York State Banking Law Article 12 investment bank in May 1984 as a joint venture between BAII Holdings (47 percent), Banque Exterieure d'Algerie (24 percent), Kuwait Real Estate Consortium (24 percent) and Chemical First State Corporation (5 percent). The Article 12 structure restricts the bank only insofar as it cannot accept deposits from within the state of New York but the thrust of the bank is to "initiate and direct investment flows into and out of the United States, and to develop corporate and merchant banking relationships with American companies," as described in their annual report.

Several Arab individuals have purchased equity interests in American banks dating from the early 1970s. Most of these investments have been motivated by a desire to participate in the ownership of an American domiciled financial institution through which the Arab owner can channel personal investment funds. While many of these investments have been short-lived, they have served the dual useful purposes of acquainting the Arab investor with the fundamentals of the American financial system, as well as providing needed capital to an often struggling institution. Should there be a shortage of investment opportunities in the Arabian Gulf, some of the wealthy merchants may well seek to invest in a small to medium-sized American bank. Such investments have been well received by the American public, and by and large the Arab has not taken an active role in the management of the bank but has either retained the existing management or added a few selected personnel. Thus, Arab investment in U.S. financial institutions continues to enhance the development of common interests between Gulf investors and the American business community.

THE FUTURE OF ARAB BANKING IN THE GULF AND U.S.-GULF ARAB BANKING AND INVESTMENT

When the Gulf Investment Corporation (GIC)[1] was conceived in November 1982 by the GCC finance and economy ministers and established in Kuwait in 1984, representing the first joint venture to be established under the aegis of the GCC, no one could have predicted that within a few years the price of oil would have plunged to $10 per barrel and that the entire Gulf economy would be set back by recession. And yet it was a propitious beginning for the GIC, for the corporation gained a valuable head start on a declining economic situation that would necessitate a complete reassessment with respect to its viability. The founders of the GIC could well project the completion of infrastructural development in the area and anticipate the need for a GCC-sponsored investment company to initiate and motivate both public and private investment in the area's corporate sector, but it was indeed fortunate that the GIC had enough lead time to staff and structure prior to the economic downturn.

---

[1]For a complete description of the Gulf Investment Corporation, see pp. 247 in the Documentation section of this book.

With an authorized capital of $2.1 billion of which $540 million had been paid in as of September 30, 1985, the GIC was established for the following reasons as stated in its charter:

—To contribute to the economic development and integration of the shareholding states.

—To promote the development of the shareholders' financial resources.

—To assist the shareholding countries to diversify their sources of income.

—To provide a commercially acceptable return on the shareholders' investment.

Furthermore, the Directorate, consisting of twelve members of whom six are the finance ministers of the member countries, have identified two priority areas for action. First, the GIC will undertake to identify, structure, finance and promote new ventures within the GIC member-state economies. These projects will be undertaken with either public or private sector interests and may well include foreign corporate joint-venture participations. Investments will not be restricted to GCC countries, but will include investments in nonmember states where the project is determined to be in the best interests of the GCC. Second, the GIC will strive to develop and promote a GCC capital market which will play a major role in financing the expansion of the industrial, agricultural, commercial, mining and service sectors.

As a Gulf capital market develops, there will be numerous opportunities for foreign investment bankers to participate in attractive joint ventures with GCC partners, and this prospect should motivate American capital market interests to maintain close contact with ongoing GCC activities.

Dr. Khaled Al-Fayez was an appropriate choice to be named as the first chief executive officer of the GIC for he had gained a depth of experience as the first general manager and chief executive officer of Gulf International Bank's widespread banking activity. Al-Fayez has publicly stated that the GIC's role is to identify and finance feasible projects in the productive sector; namely, industry, agriculture and the services.[2] He feels that much of the imported value added in the processing industries could be eliminated by establishing indigenous plants to provide the specialized features to basic commodities vital to the area's consumer markets.

Furthermore, the GIC has indicated its desire to assist in building and supporting an integrated GCC capital market which would lend

---

[2]See Khaled Al-Fayez, "The Gulf Investment Corporation," *American-Arab Affairs*, No. 11 (Winter 1984–85), pp. 34–37.

enormous support to sustaining economic development in the area. While this is a substantial undertaking, the GIC appears to be the logical vehicle through which to proceed with the creation of a strong financial industry which is so vital in accomplishing all of the desired objectives of the GCC. By functioning as an economic and financial catalyst as well as an investment adviser, the GIC can direct the development of the Gulf-states' economies in such a constructive way as to serve the best interests of all concerned. During these formative years of the GCC, it is essential to have an experienced investment council representing all of the constituents.

Despite the current rationalization of the Gulf banking industry, the process is normal for any industry caught in the throes of recession, and the result is generally a healthier, more efficient sector. While conventional commercial banking will continue to be the lifeblood of the Gulf banking industry, the Gulf banks will have to adapt to a changing world and provide their clientele with more sophisticated products. We have already seen certain banks restructure to provide investment banking services, and with the acceptance of the Society for Worldwide Interbank Financial Telecommunication (SWIFT) by the Arab League, electronic banking will assume a more important role in the future of Gulf banking.

SWIFT is a worldwide highspeed, low-cost communications network interconnecting commercial banks for the purpose of providing member-users with more efficient telecommunications. Utilization of SWIFT services will further help to integrate the Arab banks into the international financial community.

The Arabization of the GCC financial sector will continue to proceed at a pace that is contingent upon the rational absorption of qualified human resources, and the issue will not be forced as an inappropriate accommodation which would be equivocal to misrepresentation. The intention of the Gulf banking and financial sector is to build a strong base that will enable it to compete with the best names in the industry. As the Gulf banking center in Bahrain consolidates and diversifies into financial service activities, the linkage between Arab and American financial institutions will continue to strengthen. The mature U.S. capital market and broad array of investment opportunities provide an attractive product mix for Gulf investment funds, and in order to assure a source of new product and financial technology, strong ties will have to be maintained which will prove to be mutually rewarding.

The following statement of purpose appeared in the preface of the Gulf International Bank 1985 Annual Report and underscores the commitment that most Gulf banks have toward financial technology and state of the art product knowledge:

Our objective is to remain one of the most professional international merchant and wholesale commercial banks, headquartered in Bahrain but with physical presence elsewhere when justified. The specialty role of our Bank is to be emphasized through its ability to service the full range of needs of the Gulf and Middle East by development of expertise in merchant and investment banking, in portfolio management, and in industries most closely associated with the area. We intend to maintain our commitment to technological advancement. The need to train an increasing pool of Gulf nationals in banking skills is recognized as the key to our success.

Only by strengthening the linkage with the major money centers in the world can the aforementioned commitment be accomplished, and this will result in a further mutual dependency within the global financial system.

The recent collapse of oil prices has caused substantial conjecture among economists about the future of the oil industry and the effects of possible price scenarios on the Gulf producers. Some feel that an irreversible set of factors has been triggered that will cause U.S. demand for oil to outstrip its projected production capacity within a five-year time frame, thereby renewing U.S. dependence on Arabian Gulf oil. Should this happen, oil prices would certainly climb back to the $20 per barrel level where most agree there would be price stabilization in order to avoid disruptions on OPEC economies. Others argue that there are three factors that augur for a continuation of present price levels. First, there is considerable excess capacity in today's world oil production that is likely to continue for years to come. Second, over a prolonged period the price of oil has a significant impact on demand, and the major producers may be reluctant to force prices to excessive levels in the future with the same alacrity as in the past. Finally, the U.S. Strategic Petroleum Reserve currently total 500 million barrels, which is sufficient to accommodate demand for three months under current import requirements.

The capping of marginal U.S. wells which became unprofitable when oil declined below $15 per barrel has already reduced U.S. production by 100,000 barrels per day over the past year and by the end of 1986 it was estimated that daily production had been reduced by up to one million barrels per day. Should oil prices escalate back to $15 by 1990, an additional three million barrels in daily production will be cut, creating a further demand for imported oil. With oil imports projected to increase 11 percent this year to 5.5 billion barrels a day, some experts estimate that imports could reach eight million barrels per day by 1990 even without further demand for oil.

The present uncertainty in the petroleum sector indicates that the recession in the Gulf is cyclical and that imbalances in oil production and consumer demand will eventually cause petroleum prices to escalate. Since the health of the banking and financial service industry is directly related to the price of oil, the current financial rationalization process will determine whether the Arab banks have the resiliency to adjust to the downturn in the area.

The GCC is also positioning itself for any eventuality. While its acknowledged strength lies in the quantity of petroleum reserves of its member countries, a further unrecognized dimension of the GCC's potential impact on global affairs in years to come is the flexibility and maturation of its financial institutions.

Above all, the determination of its founding fathers and the spirit of the membership they represent will help the GCC to occupy its rightful place in the world's leading economic communities.

Chapter 4

ECONOMIC INTEGRATION OF THE COOPERATION COUNCIL OF THE ARAB STATES OF THE GULF: CHALLENGES, ACHIEVEMENTS AND FUTURE OUTLOOK

Abdullah Ibrahim El-Kuwaiz

His Excellency Dr. El-Kuwaiz is the Associate Secretary-General for Economic Affairs, the Cooperation Council of the Arab States of the Gulf (the Gulf Cooperation Council).

The following chapter deals with the economic integration of the Gulf Cooperation Council (GCC) member states from several perspectives. At first it lists the objectives set up by the GCC as shown in its formal documents; then it examines whether these objectives are reasonable in the light of the GCC's present economic environment. Finally, the chapter presents what has been accomplished in GCC economic integration to date.

OBJECTIVES

The GCC's economic objectives were set out in five official documents, all of which have been adopted by the GCC Supreme Council. These are the GCC Charter, the Unified Economic Agreement, Common Objectives and Policies for Development Plans, the Unified Industrial Development Strategy and Common Agricultural Policy.[1] For the sake of brevity only the first two documents will be looked at initially.

---

[1] See p. 246 for GCC memorandums on food security.

Article 4 of the GCC Charter outlines the basic objectives of the organization as follows:

1. To implement coordination, integration and interconnection among member states in all fields in order to achieve unity among them.
2. To deepen and strengthen relations, links and scopes of cooperation in various fields now prevailing among their peoples.
3. To formulate similar procedures, rules and regulations in various fields including the following:
   a. Economic and financial affairs
   b. Commerce, customs and communications
   c. Education and culture
   d. Social and health affairs
   e. Information and tourism
   f. Legislative and administrative affairs
4. To stimulate scientific and technological progress in the fields of industry, mineralogy, agriculture, water and animal resources; to establish scientific research centers; to implement joint projects and encourage cooperation by the private sector for the good of their peoples.[2]

These are broad and comprehensive objectives which require more substantially defined methods to be implemented and achieved. The Unified Economic Agreement, signed by the GCC heads of state in November 1981, almost immediately after the creation of the GCC as an organization, was created to do just that. The Agreement catalogues the details and specifics of the Charter's objectives and sets terms to coordinate and unify economic, fiscal, monetary, industrial and trade policies of GCC member states in an organized and specific fashion. The ultimate aim of the Agreement is to provide a vehicle for the integration of the economies of the individual six member states into one large, regional economy.

The Agreement's emphasis on streamlining and harmonizing development efforts are spelled out in a number of articles and provisions, of which the following are the most important:

—Coordinating industrial activities and formulating policies and mechanisms aimed at creating an integrated and well-diversified manufacturing base (Article 12, item 1).

—Standardizing industrial legislation and regulations and encouraging local production to meet domestic needs (Article 12, item 2).

—Allocating industries among member states according to relative advantages and economic feasibility, and encouraging the establishment of basic as well as ancillary industries (Article 12, item 3).

---

[2]See page 217 for the complete text of the GCC Charter.

—Establishing joint ventures among member states in the fields of industry, agriculture and services, and supporting these ventures with public, private and mixed capital (Article 13).

—Giving citizens of member states the right to establish commercial, industrial and agribusiness ventures on an equal footing with citizens of a host member state (Article 8).

—Setting up a common investment strategy and free movement of both labor and capital (Articles 8 and 21).

—Coordinating training and labor policies and efforts to acquire technology (Articles 14 and 16).

—Liberalizing trade among GCC member states, including waiving customs duties on interstate trade in agricultural products, animal husbandry, natural resources and manufactured goods made from materials obtained in a member state, and manufactured goods made from imported raw materials if domestic value added constitutes at least 40 percent of the cost of the finished product and GCC nationals own at least 51 percent of the equity of the firm producing them (Articles 1, 2 and 3).

—Exempting from fees and taxes member states' products passing in transit, and granting national treatment for all means of transportation, including ships, and exempting passengers and goods aboard them from taxes and fees (Article 18).

—Establishing a common minimum external tariff as a step to unify it with or without the purpose of protecting national products from unfair external competition (Article 4).

—Coordinating export and import policies, strengthening bargaining power vis-à-vis foreign supplies, and building up common strategic food stocks (Article 7).

—Coordinating oil policy throughout all stages of the industry (Article 11).

The question to be asked now is how responsive are the present economies of the GCC member states to these broad and comprehensive objectives? To answer this question we have to look more closely at the economies of the GCC.

ECONOMIC STRUCTURE AND LIMITATIONS[3]

The sectoral composition of the gross domestic product (GDP) indicates a number of features which make the economies of the GCC member states look markedly different from any other major regional economy. The mining sector (of which oil extractions is the most impor-

---

[3]This section is drawn from material prepared by the author and delivered at a conference sponsored by *Middle East Economic Digest* in Bahrain, February 27, 1985.

tant) accounted for more than 47 percent of total GDP of the GCC states collectively in 1983. Although this high percentage reflects the excessive dominance of the oil sector, it should be noted that the contribution of this sector was even higher in the past. It accounted for more than 65 percent of the total GCC collective GDP in 1976. The role of agriculture in the GDP of the GCC states is still relatively insignificant, yet some major strides are hoped for in the future as a result of GCC-sponsored initiatives.

The services sector, both public and private, contributed over 32 percent to the GDP in 1983, while the contribution of the construction sector accounted for about 12 percent. Manufacturing, including refining oil into petrochemical by-products, however, accounted for more than six percent of the GCC total GDP in the same year, up from four percent in 1976.

About two-thirds of the GCC total GDP is currently generated in Saudi Arabia (64 percent) and 16 percent in the UAE, while Oman and Qatar contributed an almost equal share of four percent each in 1983. Only three percent of the total GDP was generated by the Bahraini economy in the same year (up from two percent in 1976). The contribution of the Saudi economy in 1976 was only 59 percent of the GCC total GDP, the increase reflecting their significant expenditure on industrial development, while that of Kuwait declined during the period from 17 percent in 1976 to nine percent in 1983. The remaining GCC member states have managed to maintain their share in the total GDP during the period 1976-1983 as summarized in Table I.

The economies of the member states of the GCC have grown rapidly in the past decade. In current prices the gross domestic product of these states more than doubled in size during the eight-year period 1976-1983, rising from a level of $79.4 billion to $186 billion, with an annual com-

TABLE I
Member States' Contribution in GCC Total GDP
(percent)

Year/Country	Bahrain	Kuwait	Oman	Qatar	Saudi	UAE	Total
1976	2	17	3	3	59	16	100
1983	3	9	4	4	64	16	100

pound growth rate of about 12.9 percent. The most important source of this remarkable growth was the services sector, which accounted for 40 percent of the total GDP growth. More than one-third (34 percent) of the growth in the GCC economy during the same period was attributable to the mining sector, of which oil is the main component. Nevertheless, the other non-oil sectors were growing at sharply higher rates during the period, but due to their relatively small initial base their contribution to the growth of the total GDP is still less significant than the oil sector. Table II illustrates GDP growth rates by sector in each of the GCC states.

As can be seen from Table II, the manufacturing sector was the fastest-growing sector in the GCC economy during the period 1976-1983, achieving a compound growth rate of 25.8 percent annually. Electricity generation (including water desalination) ranked second in rate of growth during the same period, while the agricultural sector ranked third. The mining sector, on the other hand, was the slowest-growing sector during the same period, attaining a rate of only 7.8 percent per annum.

The overall GCC economy was, as stated before, growing at a healthy compound growth rate of 12.9 percent per annum. Among the GCC member states, the Bahraini economy was the fastest-growing during the period (21.6 percent), followed by Oman (18.4 percent) and Saudi

TABLE II
Recent Sectorial and Total GDP Growth Rates of the GCC Economy 1976–1983
(percent)

Sector/State	Bahrain	Kuwait	Oman	Qatar	Saudi	UAE	Total
Agriculture	10.1	18.1	14.6	13.3	28.0	18.4	24.5
Mining	12.5	3.0	15.4	8.0	8.8	6.2	7.8
Manufacturing	21.3	8.3	39.9	43.2	17.2	51.2	25.8
Electricity	27.6	9.0	29.8	8.5	28.3	33.0	25.6
Construction	15.6	13.1	12.3	5.4	19.8	12.8	17.3
Other Sectors	29.1	2.7	26.2	25.1	24.0	19.7	20.6
Total GDP	21.6	3.8	18.4	12.9	14.3	12.7	12.9

Arabia (14.3 percent). Due mainly to the low growth in the mining sector (3.0 percent), Kuwait's economy was growing at a relatively modest rate of only 3.8 percent per annum during the period, reflecting a growth pattern in which the oil sector is indeed the prime generator of growth and development in the GCC member states. The states that maintained high overall economic growth rates were those with the highest growth rate for their oil sectors (e.g., Bahrain, 12.5 percent, and Oman, 15.4 percent).

The manufacturing sector was growing at a remarkably high rate in both the United Arab Emirates (51.2 percent) and Qatar (43.2 percent) during the eight years ending in 1983, while industrial growth in Bahrain and Oman took place at an annual compound rate of 39.9 and 21.3 percent, respectively, during the same period. The growth rates of manufacturing in the remaining GCC member states were also high, far beyond the eight percent target growth rate set by the International Development Strategy for the second U.N. development decade.

GCC member states as a group and individually have a number of very real limitations to prolonged economic growth, however, among which are the following:

—The six member nations are overly dependent on the export of crude oil.

—Although the private sector has increased its share in the gross domestic product of the GCC states, from around 30 percent ten years ago to almost 55 percent currently, its role in the industrialization process is still below what it should be.

—Given GCC geographic and economic constraints the group still faces a somewhat chronic scarcity of human resources, both skilled and unskilled.

—The GCC's domestic markets are rather limited and highly scattered.

—If the GCC concentrates on international markets, it has to compete vigorously with the well-established manufacturers of industrial countries and other developing countries. It also has to enter into contractual agreements dealing with the very complicated subject of international trade, an area for which the GCC as an organization and the member states individually do not have any acquired expertise or long-term experience.

—Other than hydrocarbons, the GCC has very limited mineral resources and a scarcity of natural water.

—Although almost all infrastructure facilities are in place in the Arabian Gulf, interconnection among these facilities is almost nonexistent.

—Industrial regulations and legislation, as well as industrial incentives, are different in nature and application in each of the member states.

—The Arabian Gulf states do not have an indigenous technological base with which to encourage industrial growth and development.

While the process of regional integration is proceeding relatively satisfactorily, the main decisions regarding application of national resources are still made on the national level. The issue of national sovereignty is still very dear to the people and leadership in each of the six Gulf states. The GCC, as a regional integrating institution, does not have power over national entities. In other words, there is as yet no GCC supranational government with which regional development priorities can effectively supersede national ones. The GCC, however, is attempting to influence regional development with rational and sound policy perspectives that will encourage individual member growth as well as simultaneously encourage regional development.

A general consensus among economists is that economic integration among nations presupposes a certain degree of complementarity; it is an application of the division of labor and a convenient vehicle for mobilizing factors of production and facilitating movements of goods across borders. The GCC experience is quite different, however. The GCC member states more or less are trading in one line of production, i.e., the export of oil and petroleum products. They all import their consumer, industrial and other required goods from major industrial areas. By implication, interstate trade in the Gulf to any great degree is missing. Thus liberalization of trade by itself would not create economic integration similar to, say, the European Economic Community, as targeted in both the GCC Charter and the Unified Economic Agreement. That calls for a new approach. To that effect the GCC started with building joint institutions, harmonizing laws and regulations and setting up joint-venture projects to create a productive capacity which would promote integration. The question of integration in our case, therefore, was the problem of *development*, which makes economic integration more difficult than in the case of the industrialized countries. We believe that the GCC has successfully passed the test of approaching and overcoming that difficulty.

ACHIEVEMENTS

What follows is not intended to be an exhaustive list of what has been done regarding the economic coordination and integration of the GCC member states. It is, rather, intended to highlight these efforts in an attempt to explain the pattern in which these efforts fall. These can be divided into six categories:

1) Adopting Common Regional Strategies and Policies

In the area of common strategies and policies there are new official documents that give general guidelines such as the Common Objectives and Policies for Development Plans, adopted in 1984. There are also documents dealing with specific sectors such as the GCC Common Agricultural Policy, adopted in 1985, and the GCC Unified Industrial Development Strategy, adopted in 1985.

The GCC Secretariat is now working on two draft policy papers, the first dealing with coordination of monetary and fiscal policies in accordance with Article 22 of the Unified Economic Agreement and the second dealing with GCC transportation policy.

2) Building Institutions and Harmonizing Regulations

In the area of institution building the Gulf Investment Corporation, with a capital of $2.1 billion, was created by the GCC in 1983.[4] Its objectives are to discover, study, promote and participate in economically feasible projects in almost all sectors. The GCC Organization for Measures and Standards was created in 1984. It was given the *sole* responsibility of adopting standards for GCC imported as well as manufactured goods and following up their implementation. The membership of the Gulf Technical Bureau for Communications was increased to include all GCC member states, and it has been annexed to the GCC Secretariat General and given more power and responsibilities to coordinate not only the distribution of air frequencies but also to find additional ways and means to further the coordination among members in the area of communications generally. Additionally, procedures are also being finalized to create in the Secretariat a new office for the registration of industrial property rights.

Several laws, rules, regulations, standards and procedures were commonly adopted by all GCC members. These include:

—regulations related to customs, such as forms, standards and procedures;
—common regulations for port handling;
—common regulations for ship registrations;
—common regulations and forms for banking inspections;
—common laws related to agriculture, including fertilizer handling, pesticides, water conservation, preservation of marine life, quarantines, etc.; and
—common standards such as standards for building highways and expressways in the GCC states and 50 other standards adopted by the GCC's Organization for Measures and Standards.

---

[4]See page 247 for a full description of the Gulf Investment Corporation.

—Finally, the draft of GCC Industrial Regulations is now under discussion and the GCC Unified Commercial Law is under preparation.

3) Creating a GCC Economic Citizenship

Economic citizenship has been dealt with in Articles 1, 2 and 3 of the Unified Economic Agreement for the free movement and equal treatment of goods, including the elimination of customs duties on domestically produced goods. All of these articles have been implemented since March 1983. Articles 18 and 20 give citizens of GCC member states the same rights and treatment accorded to those belonging to their own citizens, specifically both land and sea transportation of cargo and passengers. This was also implemented in 1983.

Article 8 of the Unified Economic Agreement instructs GCC member states to give all GCC citizens the same treatment granted to their own citizens without any discrimination or differentiation regarding freedom of movement, work and residence, right of ownership, freedom of exercising economic activities and free movement of capital. In the years from 1983 to 1985, a number of steps were taken to implement Article 8. These steps include equal treatment of any GCC citizen in investments in industry, agriculture, fisheries, natural resources, animal husbandry, contracting, hotels, restaurants, maintenance, commerce (trade) and real estate for personal use, and discussion is now underway to include other commercial activities and insurance. Equality is also awarded to most professionals, including accountants, physicians, pharmacists, engineers, economists and a number of others. All types of technicians and tradesmen that are GCC citizens were also given equal treatment in other GCC member states as of 1984. In a very few years, we believe, full GCC economic citizenship and complete equality will be achieved.

4) Creating Regional Infrastructures

When discussing the linkage of the infrastructures of the GCC, it should be realized that the member states have built over the last decade the majority of the infrastructural necessities of modern nations. Integrating roads, telecommunications, services such as health care, electricity and water, and other areas still are in a development stage, although we have made a significant effort in studying methods of linking the GCC member states' infrastructures and economic activity.

For example, a study of the present modes of transportation in the Gulf has already been commissioned by the Arab Fund for Social and Economic Development at the request of the GCC. Several other studies have recently been completed dealing with the integration of GCC ports, including the need for any possible expansion; a regional pipeline carrying crude oil from major GCC oil fields to the Gulf of Oman; a GCC railroad network; a major highway connecting all the members of the GCC; a high-voltage regional electric grid; and an integrated communications system.

All these studies are now under consideration by GCC members. It is possible, however, that the present conditions in the oil market will adversely affect GCC ambitions in these fields. Steps toward integrating these vital infrastructural areas will be made on a priority basis as resources will allow.

5) Developing Joint-Venture Projects

Long before the emergence of the GCC, joint projects were entered into by member states at both the Arab regional and Gulf subregional levels. The formation of the Council, however, further stimulated this trend and opened new possibilities for the GCC region. Several manufacturing and agricultural projects are either under advanced study or in the implementation phase. Such projects include a refractory company, a tire plant, a poultry plant and the production and marketing of agricultural seeds. In the areas of transportation and communications, a Gulf coastal transport company and a land transport company are under consideration, as is a communications cable maintenance venture. With active overall promotion and coordination for these projects from the GCC Secretariat General and the Gulf Investment Corporation, the private sectors in GCC-member states have shown keen interest in implementing these projects, frequently with the Gulf Investment Corporation acting as an investment partner.

In the area of finance, a joint-venture company for reinsurance to be created by the existing national insurance companies is also under study.

6) Coordinating External Policies

The last but not least of current GCC preoccupations is developing a common, GCC member-state position vis-à-vis other countries, regional and international groupings and multilateral institutions. At present this is taking four forms:

—Joint GCC purchase of essential, commonly imported items to reduce overall costs to GCC member states by virtue of purchasing larger quantities, e.g., joint purchases of rice and other foodstuffs. In the near future more positive steps will be taken to engage in joint export promotions in the form of joint trade and other exhibitions abroad similar to the one undertaken annually in the Arab Gulf capitals hosting the GCC summit meetings.

—Joint approach to regional development assistance.

—Negotiating as a group with GCC trading partners, namely the European Economic Community, the United States and Japan.

—Joint positions and representation in multilateral institutions such as Arabsat, Anmarsat, international civil-aviation organizations, GATT, SWIFT and other international organizations.

ASSESSMENT AND FUTURE OUTLOOK

In reflecting on what has been accomplished in the past five years, a great deal of ground has been covered in the economic area. In most cases the sailing has been smooth and welcomed by member states. However, as we continue the going will get less smooth, as has been the case in all similar economic groupings. The GCC is not an exception.

A slowing down of integration, therefore, is expected and quite natural. First, agencies and ministries in member states concerned will need additional time to study and review advanced steps toward integration and their local implications. Second, these agencies and ministries will also need increased time and effort to prepare themselves to cope with the structural changes required for integration. The legislative and administrative processes are a third element of the deceleration of integration. It is hoped that shortening the bureaucratic circuit of decision making within the GCC will arrest this process.

Of paramount importance, moreover, are the concerted efforts designed to create a suitable environment for development through common policies. The GCC has adopted the Common Objectives and Policies for Development Plans, the Common Agricultural Policy and the Unified Industrial Development Strategy to help create such an environment. The latter is of particular importance to the region's industrial development. Industrialization can contribute to the important economic objectives of the GCC member states by diversifying the economic structure and increasing self-reliance and stability; creating skills and experience that will, in the future, lead to a more rapid increase in productivity and more flexible and fast-growing economies; and by providing investment opportunities for the region's surplus funds.

The Unified Industrial Development Strategy (UIDS) embodies these objectives and spells out policies and programs to achieve them. Specifically, it is designed to direct efforts to accelerate the industrialization process within the framework of a GCC integrated economy. It involves closer coordination of existing industrialization programs and plans and more cooperation in facing common industrial constraints. The basic objectives of UIDS include raising the participation of citizens in industrial growth among the GCC member states, attaining an acceptable degree of self-reliance in basic manufactured goods, creating an indigenous base for applied sciences, research and technology, and integrating the oil sector with other sectors of the economy, especially the manufacturing sector.

Private-sector mobility is of utmost importance in the future economic development of the GCC. A relatively generous incentives package for industrial investors has already been devised in the UIDS. The positive response of the private sector to these incentives is keenly awaited. It is hoped that the private sector in the Gulf will rearrange its priorities and move away from its traditional concentration on trade and services toward active participation in the economic and industrial development process.

Reflection on these internal factors reveals the need for readjustment of the role assigned to the GCC and its institutions. With far-reaching comprehensive objectives, it is imperative that the GCC and its institutions develop themselves to increasingly assume the role of a supranational government—a crucial step in the implementation of GCC objectives. The GCC has to consolidate a management structure that would effectively supervise and follow up its work. A step forward in this direction would be to strengthen the hand of the Secretariat General beyond the role assigned to it in the GCC Charter. On its own initiative the Secretariat General, through position papers, has pioneered some steps to make integration possible. However, it needs more teeth from the Supreme Council to see that these steps and others approved by the Council are firmly put into action.

As for the GCC's trading partners, they should be more understanding and accommodating than they have been to date. They should respond positively to the call for the reallocation of industrial production shares worldwide, so as to effectively exploit the comparative advantages of each region.

This reallocation is in the interests of the GCC's trading partners. On the one hand, goods will be produced where they are more efficiently manufactured, making them cheaper as inputs to the final products of our trading partners. On the other hand, a true partnership is one that is based on a mutual and permanent relationship. It requires joint investment in productive assets. It also calls for unconditional access to each other's markets.

Seen from the GCC side, negotiations with major trading partners have several objectives. In addition to protecting the GCC's interests, the negotiation process will assist in developing institutions in the GCC to become more receptive to their increasing regional role. Negotiations also have direct impact on bringing members closer to each other in order to unify their positions vis-à-vis the outside world.

In conclusion, and with positive response to these factors, the prospects for the GCC look fairly promising in the long term. In the context of financial resources and infrastructure, the GCC member states are in a good position to trigger and consolidate development opportunities both within the region and with the GCC's trading partners. With over one-third of world oil reserves in GCC territories, a comfortable income is guaranteed well into the next century, thereby increasing the GCC's potential for successful economic development and integration.

Finally, it should be stated that the success of the GCC experience will have a spillover effect on the Arab world at large. The GCC will enhance relationships among other Arab nations through rationalizing spending, which will allocate more resources for development; increasing Arab productive assets; creating a bigger market for goods produced within the region; opening additional opportunities for employment; developing a strong economic entity that is part of the Arab world; and creating a workable model for Arab unity.

Chapter 5
EVOLUTION OF A GCC OIL POLICY

Hossein Askari and Babak Dastmaltschi

Hossein Askari received his Ph.D. in Economics in 1970 from the Massachusetts Institute of Technology. He has been an adviser to Executive Director at the International Monetary Fund and adviser to the Minister of Finance of Saudi Arabia. For the last three years he was the Director of the Economics and Finance Department of the Consulting Center in Riyadh; in this capacity he directed the development of energy planning models (international, domestic and GCC) for the Ministry of Planning of Saudi Arabia. He is currently visiting professor of International Finance at George Washington University. Babak Dastmaltschi has for the last three years been directing efforts to design and develop the Long-term Energy Plan for the Kingdom of Saudi Arabia. He has also done numerous feasibility studies for industrial projects in the GCC. He is currently a consultant on issues of privatization to the Ministry of Finance of Saudi Arabia.

The importance of the Gulf Cooperation Council (GCC) countries in the world oil market is evident and can be gauged by a glance at some simple statistics. The GCC possesses over 40 percent of world crude oil reserves and in excess of 60 percent of OPEC's reserves (see Table I). The GCC has, at times, accounted for up to 30 percent of the non-Communist world oil production, and up to 58 percent of OPEC production (see Table II and Figures 1 and 2). In recent years, both OPEC and GCC oil production, as well as the share of the GCC in OPEC and non-Communist world production, have decreased markedly. Nevertheless, the relative importance of the GCC in the future of the world oil market is, in the long run, largely a function of its extensive share of proven and potential oil reserves.

TABLE I
Proven Crude Oil Reserves
1984

	Billion Barrels	Ratio of GCC (Percent)
GCC	303.2	100.0
OPEC	476.3	63.7
World	707.2	42.9

SOURCE: *BP Statistical Review of World Energy, 1985*

For the economic security of the United States and the rest of the West in the medium- and long-run, the role of the GCC is critical. Oil production in the United States is on the decline, production in the North Sea will start to decline in the early 1990s or before, while consumption in the West will increase. Simultaneously, oil consumption in other developing countries is expanding at a faster pace than in the West. Given such expectations, the importance of oil supplies from the GCC will increase. Projections by the authors show that by the end of this century the GCC could account for over 50 percent of the world's trade in oil. Under such conditions, it is difficult to exaggerate the importance of the stability and security of the GCC to the United States and to the West in general. Some observers have erroneously downgraded the importance of the GCC; their error lies in gauging the importance of GCC oil to Western interests by looking at the limited current oil flows from the GCC to the United States. First, as has been mentioned above, the role of the GCC will increase over time. Second, it matters little where GCC oil is currently consumed. If GCC supplies were to somehow be terminated, then all consumer nations would have to compete for the remaining available supplies. This in turn would likely result in higher prices.

In this chapter, the interest of the GCC within the context of the world oil market is examined, and some policy recommendations, incorporating the nature of GCC economies, are made.

TABLE II
Oil Production
(thousand barrels per day)

	1974	1975	1976	1977	1978	1979	1980	1981	1982	1983	1984	1985
GCC	13,680	11,785	13,725	14,230	13,340	15,020	14,405	13,570	9,625	8,340	8,145	6,965
OPEC	31,055	27,530	31,090	31,690	30,275	31,470	27,450	23,390	19,935	18,475	18,345	17,225
Total World	58,620	55,700	60,085	62,560	63,050	65,775	62,745	59,375	57,020	56,705	57,800	57,340
Share of:						(Percent)						
GCC/OPEC	44.1	42.8	44.1	44.9	44.1	47.7	52.5	58.0	48.3	45.1	44.4	40.4
GCC/World	23.3	21.2	22.8	22.7	21.2	22.8	23.0	22.9	16.9	14.7	14.1	12.1
OPEC/World	53.0	49.4	51.7	50.7	48.0	47.8	43.7	39.4	35.0	32.6	31.7	30.0

SOURCE: *BP Statistical Review of World Energy*

FIGURE 1

World Oil Production
(millions of barrels per day)

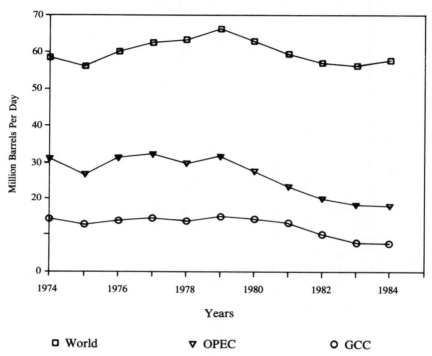

Years

□ World   ▼ OPEC   O GCC

NATURE OF GCC ECONOMIES AND THE ROLE OF OIL

The GCC member countries, with the exception of Bahrain, share one dominant common characteristic, namely oil. Their economies are largely based on the extraction and export of a single commodity which, in turn, is derived from a *depleting* economic base. This factor—the economic dependence of the GCC countries on a single depletable resource—is the overriding common element among these economies.

The depletable nature of oil resources means that each barrel of oil extracted today reduces the number of barrels to be produced in the future by an equivalent amount. This distinguishes oil exporters and, for that matter, exporters of all depletable resources, from exporters of agricultural or manufactured products, since the income or output of the latter is derived from a *sustainable* economic base. Current oil

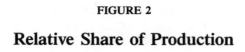

FIGURE 2

Relative Share of Production

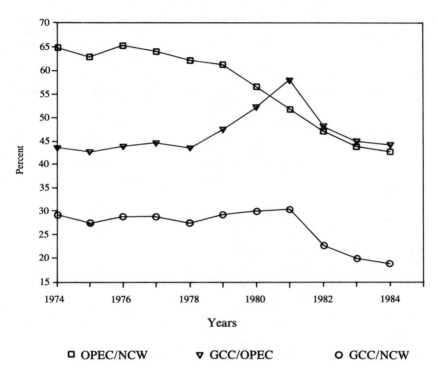

Years

□ OPEC/NCW   ▽ GCC/OPEC   ○ GCC/NCW

production, in a sense, reduces the aggregate national capital stock or wealth of oil-producing countries and, in turn, the future flow of income if the oil had not been extracted today. Future income and consumption levels can only be protected from declining if the revenues derived from oil wealth are transformed into productive domestic or foreign assets.

A simple comparison of a diversified economy to an economy based totally on oil may be useful. In a diversified economy, economic output from agriculture and industry can be expected at a constant level for all future generations as long as the soil does not deteriorate, capital is replaced and natural disasters do not occur. More likely, if the capital base is increased through investment, technological change, and other measures to enhance productivity, output will in fact increase over time.

In an economy totally based on the extraction of exhaustible resources, this constancy or growth of national product is not assured. At the

89

extreme, if a country had x units of oil reserves and it produced them all in the first year, then its national product, given standard national income accounting practices, would be the price of oil multiplied by x. But, in the second year, its national product would be only a fraction of its national product in the first year, because even if it invested all its revenues from the first year, the return on investments would, in all likelihood, be less than 100 percent. From the above example, it can be seen that, in essence, the national product of an extractive economy is not comparable to the national product of a diversified, nonextractive economy. Conventionally, national product in these countries embodies a great proportion of *asset transformation* as opposed to economic production. A direct implication for an economy that is extraction based is that these economies should have high national savings rates. An appropriate national savings rate (higher than that in a comparable economy with no extractive industry) is necessary if the economy is to maintain its level of national output after its extractive resource is depleted.

Similarly, although current-account surpluses are normally viewed as surplus funds, for the GCC countries, given the source of the temporary surplus, that is, the depletion of their oil wealth, the current-account surplus should be interpreted differently. Current-account surpluses are derived from the sale of oil assets and should be used to derive alternative sources of income, through foreign investments and ultimately through a diversified domestic economic base.

In such a setting, the GCC countries should be keenly aware of the current savings and investment needs of their economies if economic output is to be maintained as oil is depleted.

In assessing dependence, there are a number of measures that can be used. One is the ratio of exports of the exhaustible commodity to total exports. Table III shows that in 1980, oil represented over 90 percent of export earnings for five of the six GCC members.

Dependence on oil is also illustrated by the high ratios of oil exports to GDP (gross domestic product). In some respects, this statistic is more significant since it reveals not only the high ratio of oil exports to total exports, but also the high ratio of the value of oil exports to the *total* output of all goods and services. Again, in five of the six countries (Kuwait, Oman, Qatar, Saudi Arabia and the United Arab Emirates) oil exports averaged 69 percent of GDP in 1980. That ratio has clearly declined recently, as oil exports have dropped rapidly (more rapidly than GDP) over the past three years. Yet, current GDP is still substantially financed from past export earnings.

The reliance on oil is also manifested in the contribution of oil revenues to government revenues (see Table III). In the absence of a national

TABLE III
Dependence on Oil

	Ratio of Oil Exports to Total Exports 1980	Ratio of Oil Exports to GDP 1980	Ratio of Oil Revenues to Government Revenues 1979
Bahrain	33.6	85.0[1]	77.0
Kuwait	90.0	74.7	82.0
Oman	92.4	57.7	86.0
Qatar	95.0	77.4	94.0
Saudi Arabia	99.9	87.8	91.2
UAE	94.0	65.7	96.0

[1]Ratio of Petroleum Exports to GDP

SOURCES: International Monetary Fund, International Financial Statistics, Country Sources.

system of taxation, oil provides the lion's share of government revenues.

As can be seen in Table IV and Figure 3, almost all GCC countries counted on their large current-account surpluses during the latter part of the 1970s. Today those surpluses have been eroded considerably. For the GCC countries as a whole, their current-account surplus exceeded $70 billion in 1981, and dropped to a deficit of $20 billion in 1984. Past current-account surpluses have afforded these countries the accumulation of adequate financial reserves to weather recent current-account deficits, but not for a prolonged period.

Given the dependence and thus the importance of oil to the GCC countries, oil policy becomes one of the two critical components in their long-run economic performance; the other element being the soundness of their domestic and foreign investments to compensate for the depletion of oil. It is the author's opinion that GCC oil policy should be designed to maximize discounted long-run revenues from oil. In the remainder of this paper, the execution of GCC oil policy in achieving revenue maximization is assessed.

PAST OIL POLICIES OF THE GCC

The Period Prior to 1981

The period prior to 1981 can be characterized as a period without a concrete GCC oil policy. Although the GCC was not formed until 1981,

TABLE IV
Balance on Current Accounts
(millions of U.S. dollars)

	1973	1974	1975	1976	1977	1978	1979	1980	1981	1982	1983	1984
Bahrain	(66)	117	(203)	(361)	(423)	(339)	(262)	390	550	664	243	(11)
Kuwait	2,067	8,308	6,714	7,151	5,480	6,129	14,032	15,302	13,778	4,873	5,115	5,570
Oman	(67)	228	(44)	(17)	47	(67)	549	942	1,369	547	477	148
Qatar	252	1,593	1,161	1,035	461	707	1,884	3,119	--	--	--	--
Saudi Arabia	2,520	23,025	17,417	17,581	15,806	(2,212)	11,167	41,404	38,353	(1,047)	(16,293)	(24,036)
UAE	676	4,640	3,907	4,625	3,673	3,161	6,548	11,916	--	--	--	--
Total	5,382	37,911	28,952	30,014	25,044	7,379	33,918	73,073	54,050	5,037	(10,458)	(18,329)

SOURCES: International Monetary Fund, International Financial Statistics, Country Sources

-- = Not Available

92

FIGURE 3

GCC Balance on Current Account

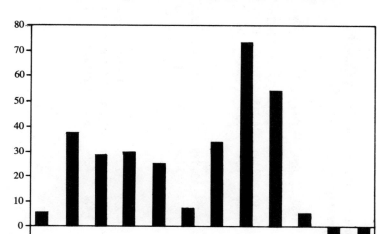

Years

individual countries should have still shared the same goal of revenue maximization. However, as can be seen from the production figures in Table II and from comparative statistics on excess production capacity (Table V), production was essentially demand driven.

The only concrete policy to speak of was that of Kuwait, aimed at putting some limits on production. Saudi Arabia acted as "swing producer," filling any gaps in demand, to the extent possible, by increasing output and thus moderating price increases.

Excess capacity for the OPEC members of the GCC countries was at its lowest in 1979, largely as a result of the decline of production in Iran and Iraq, which in turn was due to the Iranian revolution and the war between the two nations. Saudi Arabia was producing close to 10 million barrels per day (mbd) for the period 1979-81. During the period 1974-1981, the share of GCC production in OPEC output increased from 44 percent to 58 percent.

1982 to 1985

Demand for oil in the non-Communist world declined after 1979 (world consumption decreased from 51.2 mbd in 1979 to 45.7 mbd in

TABLE V
Comparative Statistics on Oil Production: Capacity, Output, and Excess Capacity
(thousand barrels per day)

		1976	1977	1978	1979	1980	1981	1982	1983	1984	1985
OPEC	capacity	39,225	39,300	40,215	35,235	34,435	34,435	32,135	32,220	28,230	27,425
	output	30,461	31,137	29,881	31,470	26,799	22,491	18,445	17,581	17,490	16,063
	excess cap.	8,764	8,163	10,335	3,765	7,636	11,944	13,690	14,639	10,740	11,362
Mideast-OPEC	capacity	28,050	28,225	29,315	25,035	24,235	24,235	22,135	22,170	18,860	18,625
	output	21,226	21,545	20,541	21,375	17,874	15,054	11,706	11,021	10,708	9,546
	excess cap.	6,824	6,680	8,774	3,660	6,361	9,181	10,429	11,149	8,152	9,079
GCC-OPEC	capacity	19,320	18,275	18,325	16,735	17,235	17,235	17,635	17,670	14,060	13,725
	output	13,751	13,617	12,711	14,725	13,761	12,841	8,838	7,590	7,318	5,921
	excess cap.	5,569	4,658	5,614	2,010	3,474	4,394	8,797	10,080	6,742	7,804

SOURCE: *Petroleum Intelligence Weekly, BP Statistical Review of World Energy*

GCC-OPEC: Saudi Arabia, Kuwait, Qatar, UAE.
Mideast-OPEC: GCC-OPEC plus Iran and Iraq.

1985, or by about 11 percent). Concurrently, non-Communist world oil production decreased by 17 percent over the same period, OPEC production decreased by 42 percent and production of GCC countries in OPEC dropped even further (46 percent). Again, the major contributing element in this decline was the role of Saudi Arabia as a swing producer. This time, however, Saudi Arabia curtailed output to maintain higher price levels.

The strategy of acting as a swing producer has had some consequences which will be partially highlighted later. Export levels of the swing producer are much more volatile. Just as an increase in world demand implies a large export increase for the swing producer, a downturn in world demand implies a large export reduction. The policy implication for swing producers, from a long-run perspective, is quite significant. Within OPEC swing producers lose relatively more revenue during a phase of production contraction and gain disproportionately from a production expansion. The question is, will other OPEC members allow the swing producers to take the lion's share of any expansion? If they will not, yet insist on swing producers absorbing most of a contraction, the swing producers will find themselves in a classic "kinked demand curve" situation. In such a situation, any status quo automatically becomes the optimum.

More importantly, what are the effects on the economy and the policies of a swing producer? As can be witnessed in the case of Saudi Arabia, the production differential during the past five years between the highest and lowest level of production was eight mbd. Such fluctuations in production translate in similar swings in export revenues, and in the case of a highly oil-dependent economy such as Saudi Arabia, on its government revenues. Worst of all, this strategy does not allow for the implementation of a consistent policy to maximize long-term discounted revenues, as it only serves to satisfy short-term world oil market needs and to maintain short-run cohesiveness within OPEC.

This strategy has cost Saudi Arabia and the other GCC member states dearly. Their share of production within OPEC decreased from 58 percent in 1981 to 44 percent in 1984. However, the real loss can be seen from the decline of the share of GCC members of OPEC, from 30.4 percent of non-Communist world production to 19 percent in 1984. Indeed, within the OPEC countries the GCC members of OPEC were the only countries in the aggregate where excess production capacity exceeded oil production between 1982 and 1985 (see Figure 4).

The results of this policy for the GCC were the following:

—a significant loss in market share;
—proportionally lower export and government revenues than other OPEC countries due to their high degree of reliance on oil exports;

FIGURE 4

GCC-OPEC Oil Production:
Capacity, Output, Excess Capacity

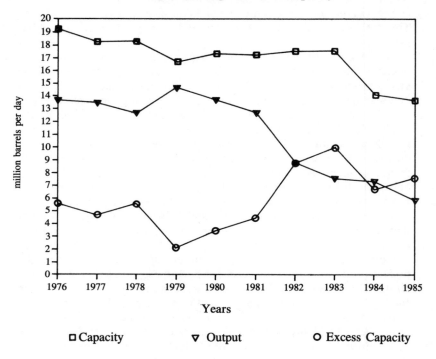

□ Capacity   ▽ Output   O Excess Capacity

—current-account and budget deficits that are being financed from earlier savings; and

—although not a result of GCC policies, the above-mentioned losses were aggravated further due to the recent depreciation of the U.S. dollar. Since oil exports are denominated in dollars, the loss in revenue due to the decline in sales was further aggravated by the reduction in purchasing power.

RECENT POLICY—1985 TO PRESENT

Given the aforementioned changes in the world oil market and the impact on the economies of the GCC, Saudi Arabia decided to abandon its role as a swing producer and increase output up to its OPEC quota. Consequently, world crude oil prices dropped for a while below $10 per barrel. Was such a strategy in Saudi Arabia's best interests or, more generally, in the best interests of GCC countries?

In December of 1985, OPEC's announced objective was to increase market share. This implied that OPEC's aggregate share was the target. However, if OPEC tried to attain this through collusive behavior and allocations, then disputes would have again arisen within OPEC regarding the appropriate level of individual shares or quotas. The December 1985 meeting of OPEC may have had as its target OPEC's aggregate share, but all indications were that each member would try to get some "appropriate" market share for themselves resulting in a larger aggregate share for OPEC. What would have exactly motivated each country's decision regarding its share, and the resulting aggregate share, was in practice unclear.

In August of 1986 OPEC reached what might at best be characterized as a "temporary" agreement. The agreement was to set an aggregate quota of roughly 16.8 mbd. This agreement was made possible by other OPEC members, especially Iran, excluding Iraq from any output limitations. The October 1986 meeting of OPEC excluded this fragile agreement with a slight production increase for the remainder of the year. But an important question still remains—while the agreement may be helpful to the GCC in the short run, is it in their best long-run interest? In our opinion, the agreement will be detrimental to the GCC if it does not result in their long-run revenue maximization.

Realistically, it is unlikely that OPEC can agree for long on individual shares. Additionally, expanding the size of OPEC will again fail because as the membership is expanded, it will be even more difficult to come to any agreement.

Past experience may be useful in determining how OPEC and the GCC might emerge from the present crisis, despite the August and October 1986 agreements. First and foremost, OPEC production policies appear to have been in error. OPEC oil production was too low, resulting in an inappropriately high price. This high price level induced conservation, the development of alternative sources of energy, and increased exploration and production of oil outside of OPEC. Over time, these developments resulted in a continual reduction in OPEC's share of world oil output leading to the crisis of 1985-1986. Second, since OPEC is unable to effectively allocate shares in a shrinking market for a long period of time; an enlargement of OPEC to new members will also—in the long run—fail. Third, pricing in dollars adds an inherent instability to the market as movements in the exchange value of the dollar will substantially change market demand and also impact on the real value of revenues to OPEC members. In short, OPEC must be more market oriented if it is to succeed in the future.

Market orientation for OPEC implies realistic long-term production or pricing policies. How does this translate itself into practice and how will OPEC and the GCC emerge from the present situation?

In our opinion, OPEC should pick a production level that would result in a price that maximizes discounted long-run revenues, as opposed to focusing on short-run and medium-run results and on market shares which should not be an end in themselves. Whether or not this approach will work will depend on the convergence or divergence of the economic interests of individual OPEC members.

Some simple calculations will illustrate OPEC's long-run interests, the interests of individual members and especially the interests of the GCC. In the calculation, two extreme alternatives for OPEC behavior can be examined: 1) OPEC increasing output at a constant pace to satisfy increasing demand and 2) OPEC maintaining a constant output and allowing prices to rise. In reality OPEC would pursue a policy in between the two extremes. The purpose of such an exercise is to determine whether OPEC policy is likely to be closer to the first or the second alternative.

The results will depend on demand for oil, which in turn depends in large part on world economic growth, income elasticity of demand for oil, price elasticity of demand for oil, and supply of oil and other sources of energy in OPEC and in non-OPEC countries.[1] Projected world economic growth from International Monetary Fund (IMF) statistics and other sources would indicate optimistically an annual figure of around 2.8 percent. Estimates for average income and price elasticities of demand for oil are given as follows: The income elasticity for developing countries is 0.5 to 0.6 in the short run, and 1.3 to 1.9 in the long run. For industrial countries a uniform income elasticity of 0.8 will be used. The price elasticity of the developing countries is -0.1 in the short run and -0.25 to -0.35 in the long run; for industrial countries these are -0.16 and -.40 respectively.

The other element is oil production. As a reasonable scenario, we could assume zero increase in production outside of OPEC. OPEC has roughly an additional 18 million barrels maximum sustainable capacity (see Table VI). Of this, it is estimated that an additional 2 to 3 million barrels a day would go to domestic consumption by the year 2000, leaving 15 to 18 million (18 in 1986 and going down to 15 in 2000) barrels per day for exports (see Table VI). The question, therefore, becomes how much should OPEC produce for exports? To answer this, we can examine two simple alternatives for OPEC behavior. Table VII gives the necessary background information to assess OPEC behavior and prices.

---

[1] Income elasticity of demand for oil measures the percentage increase in the demand for oil resulting from a one percent increase in income. The price elasticity of demand for oil measures the percent increase in the demand for oil resulting from a one percent decrease is the price of oil.

TABLE VI
Maximum Sustainable Crude Oil Production Capacity
(millions of barrels per day)

	1985	1990	2000
OPEC	31.6 - 33.0	29.1 - 34.3	27.8 - 33.5
Mideast-OPEC	22.6 - 24.0	22.1 - 25.4	21.4 - 25.2
GCC-OPEC	15.1 - 16.4	14.5 - 16.9	14.4 - 16.7

SOURCE: *Petroleum Intelligence Weekly, BP Statistical Review of World Energy, IEA World Energy Outlook*

GCC-OPEC: Saudi Arabia, Kuwait, Qatar, UAE.
Mideast-OPEC: GCC-OPEC plus Iran and Iraq.

We have made the following simplifying assumptions: 1) average income growth of 2.8 percent in the world economy for the period 1986-1995, 2) constant world oil prices, 3) an average long-term income elasticity of roughly 1.0, and 4) an average price elasticity of -0.3.

Based on these assumptions, we have derived the world demand (Table VII, row 1). In this scenario (with no extra output outside of OPEC), all of the 1986-1995 increase in demand would be satisfied from OPEC sources. In the third row the implied extra revenues to OPEC are calculated, assuming a constant price of $17 per barrel. In row 4 we estimate a price level (using a price elasticity of -0.3) that would develop if OPEC did not increase output. In row 5 the addition to OPEC revenue is calculated. Should OPEC follow the dictates of revenues of row 3 or row 5? In row 6 the difference in the respective increase in revenues due to each policy is calculated.

Before discussing the results, it is noted that the two outcomes, i.e., rows 3 and 5, are intended as extreme cases. Clearly, through 1988, OPEC revenues would be slightly higher if output was increased as opposed to letting prices rise (see row 6). Beginning in 1988, OPEC behavior would depend on whether individual members would benefit more by increasing output or increasing prices. Given the high levels of excess capacity in some OPEC countries, the future of oil prices depends on the relative benefits of the two scenarios for individual member countries. Taking rough production figures available for the end of 1985, one can see that roughly 11.5 million bpd, or around 70

TABLE VII
OPEC Oil Output and Revenues–Two Simple Scenarios to the Year 1995

	1985	1986	1987	1988	1989	1990	1991	1992	1993	1994	1995
1) World Oil Demand (million barrels per day)	57.6	59.2	60.9	62.6	64.3	66.1	68.0	69.9	71.8	73.9	75.9
2) OPEC Production (million barrels per day)	16.0	17.6	19.3	21.0	22.7	24.5	26.4	28.3	30.2	32.3	34.3
3) Increase in OPEC Oil–Revenues relative to 1986 at constant price of $17.00 per barrel (millon $/day)	--	27.4	55.6	84.6	114.4	145.0	176.5	208.8	242.1	276.3	311.4
4) Oil Prices if OPEC does not increase output but allows prices to rise ($/barrel)	--	18.6	20.3	22.2	24.3	26.6	29.0	31.7	34.7	38.0	41.5
5) Increase in OPEC Oil Revenues relative to 1985 at constant level of production but with rising prices (million $/day)	--	25.4	53.1	83.5	116.7	152.9	192.6	236.0	283.4	335.2	391.9
6) Difference in Revenue Increase; Scenario Row 5 Less Scenario Row 3 (million $/day)	--	-2.0	-2.5	-1.1	2.3	8.0	16.1	27.2	41.3	58.9	80.5

percent of the extra capacity, was in three OPEC countries—Kuwait, Saudi Arabia and the United Arab Emirates—while about 35 percent of OPEC exports at that time (a low of two mbd for Saudi Arabia) was in these same countries.

The issue then becomes, is it to the advantage of these countries to get 70 percent of the scenario presented in row 3 or 35 percent of the scenario presented in row 5? Clearly, prior to 1988, revenues in row 3 are higher than in row 5, so that the GCC countries in OPEC are better off with exporting more oil, as opposed to letting prices go up, even if the percentages were 50-50. However, given their low level of exports (resulting in a total share of only 35 percent of OPEC exports), they would be better off in every year by getting 70 percent of row 3, as opposed to 35 percent of row 5. Additionally, it should be noted that the scenario represented in row 5 is a much larger overestimate than that of row 3 because in the scenario for row 5 substantial extra energy output should be forthcoming from non-OPEC sources, thus moderating price increases and OPEC revenues. This further supports the likelihood of the scenario represented in row 3. In reality, if the first scenario is pursued prices will also rise somewhat as excess capacity is reduced. All of this would indicate less volatility in oil prices, with prices increasing gradually but at an increasing rate as excess capacity is reduced.

In the 1979 to 1981 period the reverse of this situation existed. The financial incentive was to let prices increase. These calculations are illustrative and simplistic, but the basic point is evident—assuming any reasonable price elasticity, a few members which have the lion's share of excess capacity (the GCC member states of OPEC), but have a minority of current output, are better off by increasing output.

These results lead us to one inescapable fact—OPEC can be divided into at least two groups with divergent interests. One group—with little or no excess capacity or with policy reasons not to increase output—would like to maintain the OPEC shares prevailing in 1985 and let prices rise. The other group—with substantial excess capacity—would like to increase its output, and thus its share, even if it means a lower price. For the long run, these differences are even more important as the members with more capacity and reserves would like today to pursue policies which preserve a future market for their oil; while the countries with low capacity and reserves would like to sell their limited oil at a high price in the short run and have less interest in long-run market outlook. As was pointed out earlier, OPEC's production policies prior to 1981 (some of which were beyond OPEC's control) have resulted in the difficulties of OPEC members today. These policies resulted in a price that was too high in relation to the long-run equilibrium price. This price level choked off demand and induced high levels of oil exploration and the development of alternative sources of energy. These developments may have eventually occurred, but they were artificially accelerated by restrictive oil production policies.

For the GCC the recent (December 1985 to October 1986) strategy of expanding output makes sense also for the following reasons:

—it will increase GCC revenues, despite the drop in price,

—the long-run benefits of this strategy to the GCC is that lower oil prices will not only make production less feasible for some new entrants into the world oil market but will also dissuade further exploration and development of alternative sources of energy in the future,

—when the Iran-Iraq war ends, due to the high absorptive capacity of both of their economies, both countries are likely to argue for higher production shares in OPEC. With a higher relative share of production to begin with, the GCC would be in a better bargaining position than if negotiations began from a lower production level,

—although temporary agreements were reached in August and October 1986, they were made possible because of the hardships that increased GCC oil production had caused for other OPEC countries and non-OPEC producers such as Mexico, Norway and the Soviet Union, and finally

—one cannot ignore the devastating impact that lower oil prices have had on the limited exports of Iran and therefore on Iran's ability to finance its war effort.

Where does this leave us? In retrospect, it becomes obvious that Saudi Arabia and the other GCC members of OPEC did forego their long-run shares by following a production policy that sustained high prices and were subsequently forced to continually reduce production in order to maintain prices. The recent abandoning of the swing-producer strategy appears to have been to the benefit of the GCC members, both economically and politically—at least within the Gulf region. If anything, the GCC can afford to produce even more in order to regain a larger share of the market, also resulting in higher short- and long-run revenues.

EMERGENCE OF A GCC OIL POLICY

The importance of a sound, international oil policy for the GCC nations cannot be overemphasized. The overwhelming importance of oil to their economies has been established; an importance which will continue for years to come. In short, the nature of their economies indicates one common denominator now and in the future—oil. A sound, coordinated oil policy, therefore, is of paramount importance.

Simultaneously a stable GCC oil policy is also helpful to all importers, such as the United States and the rest of the Western industrialized world, as well as all oil producers.

In the past, the GCC states have not given due emphasis to their special interests within OPEC. Several OPEC countries have relatively little or no excess capacity and would like to maintain the OPEC shares prevailing in 1985 and let prices rise. The GCC on the other hand—with large reserves and substantial excess capacity—should increase its output and thus its share, even if it results in a lower price; as this would still increase revenues. OPEC policies prior to 1981 have in large part created the difficulties of OPEC members today, especially for the GCC states. These policies resulted in a price that was too high in relation to the long-run equilibrium price; reducing demand and inducing high levels of oil exploration and the development of alternative sources of energy.

Instead of pursuing policies which would have tended to maximize discounted long-run revenues, GCC countries basically went along with OPEC decisions and acted largely as swing producers, especially Saudi Arabia. This policy, while benefiting the GCC in the period from 1979 to 1981, has had several negative medium- and long-term manifestations:

—a dramatic and disproportionate decline in oil output after 1981,
—a dramatic and disproportionate decline in market shares,
—a dramatic and disproportionate decline in oil revenues, and
—a dramatic and disproportionate increase in GCC excess capacity.

Given this historical perspective on GCC oil policies, what should be the fundamentals of a GCC oil policy? A coherent oil policy should include the basic principles and action outlined below.

Long-run Revenue Maximization
The GCC should pursue policies within OPEC which maximize discounted long-run reserves for the GCC. If this means increased output, so be it. Revenues, not prices or output, should be the target.

GCC Oil Quota
Once the GCC pursues discounted revenue maximization as its objective in OPEC, the GCC should establish a combined GCC quota as opposed to maintaining individual country quotas within OPEC. This would allow representation of a group of countries with similar objectives while affording the GCC the opportunity to internally determine each of its members' quotas. This would be beneficial to the GCC because it would afford member countries internal flexibility regarding production levels while keeping overall production high enough to preserve market share. For example, if one of the members wishes to produce less than its share, another country can produce more, so as to prevent a loss in the overall GCC market share. The existence of

such an overall GCC quota would have been beneficial during the October meeting of OPEC.

Capacity Development

The current situation of excess production capacity is expected only to last into the early 1990s. The prognosis is for the oil market to tighten thereafter. In order to continue to have an important impact on the international oil market into the 1990s, the GCC should continue to invest in capacity expansion so that it can prevent the mistakes of the late 1970s from recurring; namely, letting prices increase too rapidly thereby reducing demand and encouraging exploration in other parts of the world. By always maintaining some level of excess capacity, and by satisfying demand while letting prices increase slowly, the GCC can prevent another price shock and thus discourage new oil exploration and investment in alternate energy sources.

Denomination of Oil Prices

In order to reduce significant price fluctuations and to stabilize the real purchasing power of revenues, the GCC should persuade the rest of OPEC to denominate oil in terms of a basket of currencies with appropriate weights reflecting OPEC's import denominations.

OPEC Membership

The GCC should not argue for enlarged OPEC membership as it would further polarize OPEC. However, if Oman and Bahrain could qualify, it would be in the interest of the GCC for these two countries to join OPEC, resulting in added bargaining power for the GCC.

If the implementation of these policies is not workable within an OPEC context, then the GCC should seriously consider withdrawing from OPEC. Non-GCC OPEC countries have more to lose than the GCC from such an eventuality since any reduction in GCC output is beneficial to non-GCC OPEC members.

If the GCC pursues the indicated oil policies, what will be the likely course of oil prices? Oil prices should increase slightly between now and 1990; at about the rate of the general price level. After 1990, in the absence of unforeseen external shocks, prices should increase at a rate somewhat above the general price index, and at an increasing rate towards the end of the decade. The expectation would be that prices would also be much less volatile than over the period 1978 to 1986.

Finally, success for the GCC in the economic field will be measured by success in their joint oil policy. Agreements on uniform tariffs, uniform subsidies, coordinated exchange rate policies and a uniform commercial code, while helpful, are dwarfed in their importance by the need for a sound and coordinated GCC oil policy. Given the overriding importance of oil in their economies, the future economic success of the GCC will depend on its achievements in oil and oil-related policies. The actions of late 1985 constitute a step in the right direction. However, the agreements of August and October 1986 might be a step backward because it is questionable whether the production levels agreed to are in the long-run interests of the GCC and would result in revenue maximization. Kuwait's position of demanding a higher production quota in the October meeting of OPEC was in our opinion motivated by considerations outlined in this chapter. It thus appears that at least some GCC states have started on the road to forming an oil policy. But there is much more to be achieved in developing a sound and coordinated GCC international oil policy.

Chapter 6

IMPACT OF THE GCC ON THE DEVELOPING LEGAL SYSTEMS OF THE GULF COUNTRIES

Nicholas B. Angell

Mr. Angell is a partner in the law firm of Chadbourne & Parke with offices in New York City and Washington, D.C., and in Dubai, Abu Dhabi and Sharjah, United Arab Emirates, under the name of Chadbourne, Parke & Afridi. Mr. Angell was resident in Dubai 1979 to 1986 and has now returned to the firm's New York office.[1]

T he legal systems of the nations that comprise the Gulf Cooperation Council—Bahrain, Kuwait, Oman, Qatar, Saudi Arabia and the United Arab Emirates—have recently undergone dramatic change and development, which is continuing. The major trend has been greatly increased codification of law and administered regulation, which entail increasing substitution of institutionalized procedures for the traditional informal, discretionary exercise of authority.

The GCC, formed in 1981, has already served as a vehicle for increased associations and concerted policies and actions among the member states, and it is also having an influence on their legal systems. Although it is very likely that the GCC will have an increasing influence on the further development of the legal systems of the member states, the shape of this influence cannot be predicted right now.

It is the purpose of this article to examine the elements that will condition the various forms this influence may take. These elements

---

[1]The author wishes to acknowledge the assistance in the preparation of this article of his colleagues Gary R. Fuelner and Charles S. Laubach of Chadbourne, Parke & Afridi, United Arab Emirates. The author is also grateful to W. M. Ballantyne for making available his private collection in London of the Official Gazettes of the Gulf countries.

include the current stage of development of the legal systems of the GCC countries, the legal structure of the GCC, its current authority and objectives and the actions taken by the GCC since its formation in 1981 that affect the policies, laws and regulatory structures of the member states.

CURRENT STATE OF DEVELOPMENT OF THE LEGAL SYSTEMS OF THE GCC COUNTRIES

Brief Historical Background

The legal systems of the Gulf area, like the societies in which these systems function, have always reflected a significant number of shared features, including, most importantly, their shared Islamic religious heritage and with it the rich and scholarly heritage of Islamic law. The shared features also reflect in part the relatively uniform geographic and economic characteristics of the area. Throughout the Gulf area a distinction developed between the economies of the inland areas, which because of severe aridity could support only nomadic animal husbandry, and the coastal villages, where trade, commerce and seafaring activities developed. This rural/coastal economic dichotomy was accompanied by a dichotomy of legal systems. In the rural areas, adjudicative functions were performed, when necessary, by tribal elders, and the law was composed largely of tribal custom. In the coastal communities law was administered in a system of courts, and after the spread of Islam the law was largely Islamic law.[2]

With the intrusion of British political influence into the coastal Gulf countries beginning in the late 18th century came an introduction of British legal institutions. Under the British foreign jurisdiction acts, British legislation was given extraterritorial effect in the principalities of Bahrain, Qatar and the Trucial Coast. British jurisdiction did not supplant local jurisdiction but instead was introduced parallel to it, governing non-Muslim foreigners resident in the Gulf countries, while Muslim residents remained subject to the jurisdiction of the local authorities. Under British influence much of the legislation adopted by local authorities was borrowed from the common law codes of India. Judges trained in British law were introduced to administer justice in a parallel court system. Final appeal from a decision of extraterritorial British courts lay to the Privy Council in England.[3]

---

[2]See, e.g., W. M. Ballantyne, *Legal Development in Arabia* (London: Graham & Trotman, 1980), p. 25 (hereinafter cited as *Legal Development*).

[3]Sayed Hassan Amin, *International and Legal Problems of the Gulf* (London: Middle East and North African Studies Press; Boulder, CO: Westview Press, 1981), p. 11, n. 2; *Legal Development*, pp. 7-10, 13-15, 23-25.

The British retroceded extraterritorial jurisdiction in Kuwait in 1961, Oman in 1967 and the UAE, Qatar and Bahrain in 1971.[4] Kuwait, immediately following the withdrawal of British extraterritorial jurisdiction, set a very important precedent which was widely followed among the other Gulf countries by turning not to British common law but to an emerging body of Arab civil law as a source for new legislation (based largely on Egyptian statutory models, influenced primarily by the French civil law tradition). The government of Kuwait first indicated this new departure by commissioning the famed Egyptian jurist, Abdul Razzaq Sanhouri, to draft a commercial code and other items of major legislation.[5]

The heartland of the Kingdom of Saudi Arabia, unlike the other members of the GCC, never fell under the extraterritorial jurisdiction or became a sphere of influence of Britain or any other European power. Abd Al Aziz ibn Saud, the founder of modern Saudi Arabia, was declared king in 1932, culminating his family's long rise to power, and until recently legislation in Saudi Arabia has been framed by its rulers largely without reference to common or civil law based codes. However, in response to economic and development issues similar to those facing the other Gulf states, Saudi Arabia has also been required to formulate new policies and has done so, in some cases in advance of the other states. Much recent Saudi legislation has been influenced by the same body of Arab civil law that has influenced legislation in the other GCC states, and consequently a number of Saudi laws resemble laws in force in the other GCC states. In general, though, the Saudi government has been less willing than the other GCC member governments, especially Kuwait's, to adopt legislation from her more westernized and secularized Arab brethren, and the influence of the Islamic *sharia* legal system remains especially strong. Indeed, overall the Islamic *sharia* continues to exercise a major practical influence and to provide the cultural milieu for the development of the legal systems of all the Gulf nations, and in most of their constitutions it is stipulated to be a principal source of legislation.

Recent economic development in the Gulf and the sudden emergence of the countries of the area as major participants in worldwide finance and commerce has depended, of course, on the exploitation of their enormous petroleum resources. Bahrain was the first Gulf country in which oil was discovered (1932), soon followed by Saudi Arabia. Oil was discovered in Kuwait and Qatar in the 1940s and in the UAE and

---

[4]*Legal Development*, pp. 11-12, 15, 23; W. M. Ballantyne, "The Constitutions of the Gulf States: A Comparative Study," 1 *Arab Law Quarterly* , Feb. 1980, p. 58 (hereinafter cited as "Constitutions").

[5]Generally, *Legal Development*.

Oman in the 1960s.[6] In the 1970s the Gulf countries, led by Saudi Arabia, assumed control of production (and thereby world supply and price); oil prices rose dramatically and substantially enhanced revenues began to flow to the Gulf area. There followed a decade of very rapid economic growth accompanied by a greatly increased influx of foreign services and labor and other major changes the eventual consequences of which have still not been fully realized.

Legal Institutions

Constitutional Powers

Despite their common cultural and historical heritage, the GCC countries do not have governments of uniform structure. Four of the member countries, Kuwait, Bahrain, the UAE and Qatar, have written constitutions, while Saudi Arabia and Oman do not. In five of the member countries supreme executive, legislative and judicial authority is vested in the central government, while in the UAE authority is divided between the federal government and the constituent emirates. Finally, the philosophy of separation of powers is embodied to varying extents in the governmental systems of the member countries. While all six countries have separate judicial systems, only in Kuwait and Bahrain is there a clear distinction between the legislative and executive branches of the government. The distinction is observed in the UAE and Qatar, but the legislatures there are accorded primarily a consultative role. In Oman and Saudi Arabia the executive exercises substantially unfettered legislative power.

Kuwait

The constitution of Kuwait was adopted on November 11, 1962. It declares Kuwait to be a sovereign, Islamic and democratic state. Kuwait is ruled by an amir whose office is hereditary but who shares power with his cabinet, the National Assembly and the courts.

Executive power is exercised by the amir and the cabinet. The cabinet is composed of individuals appointed by the amir, who need not be members of the National Assembly. In addition to executive powers, the amir is accorded limited authority to rule by decree. Legislation may be proposed by the amir or by a member of the National Assembly, but the National Assembly is accorded prime responsibility for framing new laws. After drafting a law, the National Assembly submits it to the amir. The amir may then either enact it or return it to the National Assembly for reconsideration. The amir is required by the constitution

---

[6]Fuad Hamdi Basisu, *Al-Taawun Al-Inmai Bayn Aqtar Majlis Al-Taawun Al-Arabi Al-Khaliji* [Developmental Cooperation Among the Countries of the Arab Gulf Cooperation Council] (Beirut: Arab Unity Studies Center, 1984), p. 38.

to enact any draft law which he has returned to the National Assembly and which the National Assembly has thereafter approved by a vote of two-thirds. The National Assembly is an elected body of 50 members who must be native Kuwaiti citizens literate in Arabic. The Kuwaiti constitution guarantees an independent judiciary.

The National Assembly was disbanded from 1976 to 1980 and again in July 1986.

Bahrain

The constitution of Bahrain was adopted by a constituent assembly on December 6, 1973, and is patterned after and substantially similar to the Kuwaiti constitution. Bahrain is ruled by an amir whose office is hereditary but, as in Kuwait, power is divided among the amir and his cabinet, the National Assembly and the courts.

In late 1975 the National Assembly of Bahrain was disbanded, and the ruler and his Council of Ministers have since exercised all legislative powers.

United Arab Emirates

The UAE provisional constitution of 1971 declares the UAE to be a sovereign Islamic union of the seven constituent emirates and provides for the division of power between the federal government and the emirate governments.

The highest authority of the federal government is the Supreme Council, composed of the rulers of the seven emirates or their deputies. The Supreme Council elects a president and vice president of the union from among its members; the president, with the consent of the Supreme Council, appoints a prime minister and cabinet. The cabinet is declared to be the executive authority of the federation, under the control of the president and the Supreme Council.

In addition to executive power, the cabinet is accorded responsibility for originating and drafting legislation, which it must ordinarily submit to the Federal National Council, a consultative deliberative body of 40 members chosen by the individual emirates, for nonbinding approval, rejection or amendment. Following consideration by the Federal National Council, legislation is submitted to the Supreme Council. The bill as approved by the Supreme Council is then promulgated by the president. The law as promulgated is not constitutionally required to embody any amendments which the National Council may have made to the law, and indeed a law may be enacted notwithstanding any objection by the National Council.

The UAE provisional constitution also provides for an independent judiciary.

Qatar

In Qatar, the Amended Provisional Basic Regulation of 1972 functions as the provisional constitution. The regulation declares Qatar to be an independent, Islamic and democratic state. The head of state is the amir, whose office is hereditary. Executive power rests with the amir and with a cabinet which the amir appoints. Legislative power is accorded primarily to the cabinet, which drafts laws prior to promulgation by the amir. A 20-member Consultative Council is provided for in the regulation to debate proposed legislation, but its opinions are not binding upon the cabinet. The Consultative Council is intended by the regulation to be elected, but elections have been postponed by amiri resolutions amending the regulations. Judicial powers are exercised by an independent system of courts governed by rules framed by the justices themselves.

Oman

Oman has no written constitution. The government of Sultan Qaboos rests upon the legitimacy of the Al Said dynasty, which has ruled Oman since 1741. In accordance with the traditional nature of the regime, full executive and legislative power rests with the Sultan. There is no elected legislative or consultative body, and all legislation is drafted by the sultan and his appointed Advisory Council, whose deliberations are not public, and promulgated by decree of the sultan.

Saudi Arabia

The Kingdom of Saudi Arabia has no constitution. The Saudi government draws its constitutional legitimacy from its adherence to the Islamic *sharia*, whose principles serve it in much the same way as the common law serves the government of England. Saudi political theory regards the *sharia* as the only true "law" to such an extent that the various legislative enactments, no matter how fundamental, are referred to formally as "regulations" rather than laws. These may be promulgated variously by royal decree, cabinet decree, or ministerial order or circular.

The kingdom is a benevolent monarchy with its political roots and instincts in traditional tribal patterns. The process by which new rules and regulations are initiated, drafted, considered and promulgated does not involve a public procedure. The Saudi royal family is large but is known for its collegial approach to decision making, and it is believed that most significant policy initiatives are adopted by a process of substantial consensus involving the senior levels of the family.

Judicial Institutions

All of the Gulf states have formally established, substantially independent and actively functioning judicial systems, four of them under their written constitutions. Arbitration procedures are available and generally are respected and encouraged as a means of resolving disputes, although local procedures are normally preferred to foreign facilities.

Bahrain

The Bahrain judicial system includes civil, criminal and *sharia* courts, with the *sharia* courts in turn divided into Jafari and Sunni branches. Apart from a separate petty claims court, the only significant administrative body which decides disputes in Bahrain is the Labor Court, which has jurisdiction to decide employment disputes.[7]

As under the judicial systems of all the Gulf states, there is no doctrine of precedent in Bahrain, and the courts are therefore not governed by previous court decisions. Also, as in the other Gulf states, there is limited publication of court decisions.

The most important institution for administering arbitration in Bahrain is the Chamber of Commerce and Industry, which has a specialized committee that administers arbitrations and also provides a conciliation facility. Arbitration procedures are governed by the Bahrain Civil and Commercial Procedure Law and by the bylaws of the Bahrain Chamber of Commerce.

An arbitration award rendered in Bahrain is enforced by lodging it in court and then petitioning the court for an enforcement order. Under Bahraini law a foreign arbitral award may be enforced by court order. Bahraini courts will grant enforcement orders for awards that are rendered in jurisdictions that accord reciprocal treatment to Bahraini awards, if the original panel of arbitrators had jurisdiction, if due process was observed, if the arbiter's award represented a final disposition of the dispute and if enforcement would not result in conflict with Bahraini law or public policy. Arbitral awards may also be enforced in Bahrain under the Geneva Protocol of 1923, the Geneva Convention of September 26, 1927, and the New York Convention of June 10, 1958.[8]

Kuwait

The court system of Kuwait is divided into six different branches: personal, criminal, commercial, administrative, leases and civil. Appeal lies to a Court of Appeal and a Circuit of Cassation within the Court of Appeal.

The six courts are assigned different subject matter jurisdiction (i.e., criminal, commercial and administrative matters). The personal courts

---

[7]Based in part on oral communication with David Renton, Esq., Bahrain, by telephone, July 13, 1986.

[8]Based in part on Samir Saleh, *Commercial Arbitration in the Arab Middle East* (London: Graham & Trotman, 1984), pp. 275-289.

have jurisdiction over matters of the personal status of Muslims, in particular family and inheritance law. The civil court has jurisdiction over all noncriminal cases not dealt with by the other branches. Both the personal and civil courts formerly applied *sharia* law directly but are now subject in the first instance to a personal status law and a civil code, respectively.[9]

For parties who have agreed to arbitration, a number of arbitration facilities exist in Kuwait, governed in general terms by the Kuwaiti Code of Civil and Commercial Procedure. As in Bahrain, the Kuwaiti Chamber of Commerce administers arbitration and conciliation procedures according to internal regulations of the Chamber of Commerce. The Kuwait Society of Engineers administers arbitration proceedings concerning disputes in the construction industry. Finally, if a lawsuit has been filed in court the parties can request arbitration to be administered by the Minister of Justice and the trial court. Arbitration clauses and arbitration agreements are generally given effect by the Kuwaiti courts, and foreign arbitration awards are normally enforceable in accordance with the same principles applicable in Bahrain. Foreign arbitral awards may also be enforced in Kuwait under the New York Convention of June 10, 1958, or the Arab League Convention of September 14, 1952.[10]

Oman

Oman has three principal judicial tribunals: *sharia* and criminal courts and the Authority for the Settlement of Commercial Disputes. The *sharia* courts hear cases dealing with the personal status of Muslims, the criminal courts hear criminal prosecutions and the Authority for Settlement of Commercial Disputes has exclusive jurisdiction to hear all commercial disputes. The authority is staffed by three full-time judges and by representatives of the Ministry of Commerce and the Chamber of Commerce.

In addition, there are two administrative bodies for settlement of disputes in Oman: the Labor Court administered by the Ministry of Labor and Social Affairs, which settles employment disputes, and the Lease Disputes Committee administered by the Ministry of Housing, which decides disputes related to residential leases.[11]

Arbitration may be held under the administration of the Authority for Settlement of Commercial Disputes or the Oman Chamber of Com-

---

[9]Based in part on oral communication with Ali Al-Baghli of Al-Baghli, Al Molah and Associates, Kuwait, by telephone, July 13, 1986.

[10]Based in part on Saleh, pp. 252-274.

[11]Based in part on oral communication with Stephen Cake, Esq., Muscat, Oman, by telephone, July 14, 1986.

merce. Domestic arbitral awards are enforceable in Oman if they are rendered in consistency with *sharia* principles. However, foreign arbitral awards are not enforceable in Oman and must be submitted to the Authority for Settlement of Commercial Disputes for reconsideration of the merits.[12]

Qatar

The court system of Qatar is divided into the civil courts and the *sharia* courts. The civil courts deal with civil and criminal matters in separate sections. These courts have jurisdiction over essentially all cases except those relating to the personal status of Muslims and some criminal matters in which Muslims are involved. In practice, however, the *sharia* courts have routinely accepted all types of civil and criminal cases which normally fall within the jurisdiction of the civil courts. There are no administrative courts, but the civil courts adjudicate in certain administrative matters.[13]

There is no clear doctrine in Qatar with respect to the effect which courts give to arbitration clauses and agreements. Parties who wish to conduct arbitration in Qatar may arbitrate under the administration of the Chamber of Commerce, which administers arbitration only between Qatari nationals, or may conduct *ad hoc* arbitration.

The enforcement of arbitral awards rendered in Qatar is largely at the discretion of the civil court as no statute applies to court enforcement of such awards. A draft Qatar civil code (not promulgated but widely followed by judges) provides that arbitral awards are enforceable if no objection to the award has been lodged within seven days of its being rendered and if no independent ground for nonenforcement of the award exists.

The enforcement of foreign awards in Qatar requires that the case be tried anew by a Qatari trial court. Qatar is not a party to any treaty or bilateral accord that provides for enforcement of foreign arbitral awards.[14]

Saudi Arabia

In Saudi Arabia, just as the only "law" is the *sharia*, the only "courts" are the *sharia* courts. These exist in each city and town and are administered by one or more *qadis* trained in Islamic law. Decisions of the local courts may be appealed to a central appellate body which has relatively broad authority.

Nevertheless, there has been created alongside the *sharia* court system a number of specialized but important administrative tribunals

---

[12]Based in part on Saleh, pp. 370-392.

[13]Based in part on oral communication from Dr. Majdalany, Majdalany & Partners, Doha, Qatar, by telephone, July 14, 1986.

[14]Based in part on Saleh, pp. 322-341.

which, from the point of view of most modern commercial disputes, are of much greater significance. Jurisdiction is assigned to these specialized tribunals by decree, regulation or order.

For example, most private commercial disputes, including commercial agency disputes, are referred to the Committee for Settlement of Commercial Disputes (sometimes called the "commercial courts") which is established within the Ministry of Commerce. This body consists of a panel of three "judges" in each Saudi province. Disputes based on promissory notes or other commercial paper are referred to a further special committee, the Negotiable Instruments Committee of the ministry. Disputes involving insurance matters were also referred to a separate panel within the Ministry of Commerce until recently, when arbitration of insurance disputes was made mandatory.[15]

The Saudi Grievance Board has jurisdiction over essentially all disputes between the government and private parties. Its jurisdiction and authority to adjudicate claims have been defined by regulation.[16] Among other things, the Grievance Board handles all disputes concerning the many government contractors in the kingdom. Finally, the Ministry of Labor has its own three-tier system of labor "courts" with jurisdiction over all labor disputes within the kingdom.

By promulgation of arbitration regulations, the kingdom has attempted to encourage arbitration as a means of dispute settlement.[17] The arbitration regulations provide that all arbitrations will be conducted under the supervision of the body otherwise having jurisdiction of the dispute, and arbitration awards are subject to approval by such authority (most frequently, in business matters involving foreign companies, this would be the Committee for the Settlement of Commercial Disputes or the Grievance Board). Additionally, arbitration does not eliminate certain of the perceived problems of the application of *sharia* law. For example, under the arbitration regulations all arbitrators must be Muslims and awards must not be contrary to the *sharia*.

Recently, in December 1985, a special committee at the Ministry of Commerce was appointed prospectively to adjudicate the banking cases (particularly loan collection cases) of the sort now pending in the king-

[15]Andreas Haberbeck, "Insurance under Saudi Arabian Law," 2 *Lloyd's Maritime and Commercial Law Quarterly*, May 1986, p. 246; David Renton, "The Settlement of Banking Disputes: Major Developments," *Middle East Executive Reports*, Vol. 9, No. 2 (Feb. 1986), p. 25.

[16]Royal Decree No. M/51 of 1402 A.H. See J. Robert Steelman, "The Grievance Board in Saudi Arabia—An Overview of Royal Decree M/51," *Middle East Executive Reports*, Vol. 6, No. 5 (May 1983), p. 8.

[17]Arbitration Regulation of 1983, Royal Decree No. M/46 of 1403 A.H. as supplemented by the 1985 Implementation Rules, Council of Ministers Resolution No. 7/2021/M of 1405 A.H.

dom in large numbers. However, it is considered unlikely that the committee will be able to overcome the most significant problem in the resolution of these banking disputes, which is the question of the legality of interest.

Arbitration awards rendered outside the kingdom can be enforced as such under Saudi domestic law only if rendered in conformity with the *sharia*, or under the International Center for the Settlement of Investment Disputes Convention or the Arab League Convention of 1952, to which the kingdom is a signatory.

United Arab Emirates

When the United Arab Emirates was established in 1971, a new federal judicial authority was also established, and the constitution was drafted to divide jurisdiction between the emirates' courts and the federal courts. However, all of the emirates except for Dubai (which retains its own judicial system) have transferred the jurisdiction of all civil disputes to the federal courts. All the emirates also have separate *sharia* courts.

The *sharia* courts are courts of general jurisdiction, and unless their jurisdiction is specifically prohibited by law, a plaintiff may institute any type of lawsuit in them. However, in practice jurisdiction in commercial cases is usually assigned or transferred to the civil courts pursuant to existing amiri decrees or court rules.

The federal civil courts have jurisdiction over all civil matters and all criminal matters referred to them by the federal public prosecutor. The federal civil courts, the *sharia* courts and the Dubai courts all have appellate procedures.

The most important administrative institutions for resolving disputes in the UAE are the Labor Ministry, which provides a venue for conciliation between parties to a labor dispute, and ministerial committees set up by the governments of the UAE and of Abu Dhabi to hear disputes with government contractors.

Arbitration in the UAE is enforceable and may be supervised by the federal and Dubai judicial systems. In addition, the chambers of commerce of the various emirates offer conciliation or arbitration facilities. In either case, to enforce an award a party must seek judicial confirmation of the award and issuance of a court enforcement order. Foreign arbitration awards are usually enforceable in accordance with the same principles as in Bahrain and Kuwait. The UAE is a party to the Arab League Convention on the Enforcement of Foreign Judgments and Awards of September 14, 1952.

Regulation of the Legal Profession

Each of the GCC member states provides for the licensing of advocates (who may appear before the courts) and legal consultants. Saudi

Arabia licenses only nationals to practice advocacy and legal consultancy. Foreigners wishing to practice legal consultancy must be employed by a local licensed practitioner, but foreigners may not practice advocacy.[18] The UAE is more permissive, allowing legal consultants of any nationality to open offices (subject to strict licensing requirements) and allowing persons with a degree from an Arab faculty of *sharia* or law to obtain a license to practice advocacy.[19] Oman's requirements are generally quite similar to those of the UAE, Kuwait's are similar to those of Saudi Arabia, and those of Bahrain are more restrictive than the UAE but less so than Saudi Arabia and Kuwait.[20]

Legal Education

At present, only three of the six GCC member states (Kuwait, Saudi Arabia and the UAE) have universities where law is taught. Oman is expected to join this list soon with the opening of the new Qaboos University.

The Faculty of Law at the University of Kuwait, founded in 1967, has about 1,000 students. There is a recently established faculty of *sharia* and law at the University of the United Arab Emirates in Al Ain, Emirate of Abu Dhabi, and there are three institutions in Saudi Arabia where *sharia* and law are taught: the Islamic University of Imam Mohammad bin Saud, founded in 1974, with branches in Riyadh, Qasim and Abha; King Saud University; and the Islamic University in Medinah.

Legislation

Though not comprehensive, there has been developed in most of the GCC states a considerable structure of written laws and regulations governing many of the principal aspects of commercial, political and social life. A good many of these laws are recent, dating only from the current decade. Others are much older. The development of written law has proceeded at different rates in the various GCC states. Kuwait has generally been the earliest to enact laws in many areas, and as a result its body of legislation is probably the most complete and the most sophisticated. At the other extreme, Qatar has been notably relaxed in promulgating formal legislation. In all of the GCC states, of course, new

---

[18]Ministerial Resolution No. 116 of 12.7.1400 A.H.; Ministerial Order No. 1190 of 16.2.1402 A.H.

[19]Amjad Ali Khan, "The Courts and the Legal System in the U.A.E.," *Middle East Executive Reports*, Vol. 6, No. 8 (Aug. 1983), p. 24.

[20]See, e.g., "New Law Cuts Back Expatriate Lawyers," *Middle East Executive Reports*, Vol. 4, No. 5, May 1981, p. 6 (Bahrain); Decree Law No. 26 of 1980 (Bahrain), reprinted in *Middle East Executive Reports*, Vol. 4, No. 5 (May 1981), pp. 20-24.

policies and regulations are sometimes introduced administratively by means of circulars and interpretations which may be announced within the relevant government bureaucracy, but are not generally advised to the public at large. Increasingly, however, changes in government rules, regulations and policies are reported officially and in the local press.[21]

Major Trends and General Considerations

The legal systems of all of the Gulf states are evolving in the direction of increasing government regulation of economic activity and the corresponding growth of administrative bureaucracies. This development is perhaps most pronounced in Kuwait, Saudi Arabia and, within the UAE, in the Emirate of Abu Dhabi. Other states, such as Qatar, the Emirate of Dubai, and to a lesser extent Oman, seem to have resisted this trend and have retained more informal, less institutional procedures.

All of the GCC states are concerned with their heavy dependence on petroleum resources and their susceptibility to world economic factors beyond their control. All are also concerned with the need to develop and protect an economic base beyond the simple production of crude oil or natural gas. In response to this, Saudi Arabia, the UAE and Oman have made a serious attempt at the development of viable local industries serving regional markets. The effort to develop local industry has inevitably been accompanied by pressures for protection. Kuwait and Bahrain appear to have concentrated more on the investment of their existing wealth and the development of sophisticated banking, financial and other service sectors. The Emirate of Dubai has attempted to follow both courses.[22] All of the Gulf states have enacted a variety of legislation which is intended to protect the interests of local merchants.

Responsible authorities in the GCC states seem well aware that they are actively involved in fashioning essentially new societies, however much grounded in older values. But the rapid social and economic changes that these states have undergone in the last two decades and a deep traditional conservatism, along with the extreme vicissitudes of the oil market over the past decade, plus very real political fears arising from the current Iran-Iraq war, have combined for the present to pro-

---

[21]Many of the references to statutes cited in this article were obtained from W. M. Ballantyne, *Register of Laws of the Arabian Gulf* (London: Lloyd's, 1985).

[22]For purposes of considering either domestic legislation or the reception of GCC initiatives, the UAE cannot always be treated as a single entity. The individual emirates retain considerable authority over the regulation of commerce within their borders, and the Emirate of Dubai in particular has taken a relatively energetic position in favor of the encouragement of international trade and foreign investment in the local economy.

duce a prevailing philosophy of caution rather than active social and political engineering.

Notable Absence of Certain Regulations

From a Western point of view, the GCC states are remarkable for the absence of legislation and enforcement in certain areas. For example, there are no exchange controls on foreign currency in any of the GCC states. Additionally, none of the GCC states imposes an individual income tax on either foreigners or national citizens, although several states do impose a social security tax. Corporate taxation exists and is discussed below.

A less favorable omission is the absence of formal bankruptcy laws or regulations in several of the Gulf states. Coupled with the absence or uncertainty of procedures for the perfection and enforcement of security interests, this has worked to the significant detriment of both foreign and local creditors during the recent economic downturn in the Gulf.

Kuwait has an official stock exchange, and Saudi Arabia regulates trading in shares of Saudi companies, which is limited to banks, but Bahrain, Oman, Qatar and the UAE have no such provisions.

Formal protection for intellectual property is also the exception rather than the rule. Bahrain and Kuwait have patent and trademark laws and Saudi Arabia and Qatar have trademark laws alone.[23] In the UAE a patent and trademark law has been drafted but not enacted, although some trademark protection has been available under theories of unfair competition or consumer protection. None of the GCC states has copyright laws, and the area is generally recognized as a major market for pirated musical tapes, publications and other products.

An example was set in Kuwait for the codification of law in civil law fashion. Kuwait first enacted a commercial code, drafted by the author of the Egyptian civil code, in 1961, and now has both a revised commercial code[24] and a new civil code.[25] Saudi Arabia and the other Gulf states, with the exception of the UAE, show little sign of moving in the direction of such detailed codification, although Saudi Arabia already has an elaborate negotiable instruments regulation[26] and an equally elaborate commercial code regulating land and maritime commerce[27] left over from an earlier era. In the UAE, on the other hand, a civil

---

[23]The Bahrain Patents, Designs and Trade Marks (Procedure) rules, 1955; Law No. 4 of 1962 (Kuwait); Law No. 3 of 1978 (Qatar); Royal Decree No. M/5 of 1404 A.H. (Saudi Arabia).

[24]Decree Law No. 68 of 1980, *Al-Kuwait Al-Yaum*, No. 1338 of 1981.

[25]Decree Law No. 67 of 1980, *Al-Kuwait Al-Yaum*, No. 1335 of 1981.

[26]Royal Decree No. 37 of 1383 A.H.

[27]Order No. 32 of 1350 A.H.

code[28] on the Egyptian-Kuwaiti model has recently been put into effect, and there is considerable official encouragement for the development of a commercial law as well.

Forms of Doing Business

In each of the GCC states, businesses may be organized locally as sole proprietorships or as one of a number of types of commercial companies. Each of the GCC states has now enacted a companies law,[29] although implementation of the commercial companies law in the UAE has been suspended until 1987.

The types of commercial companies recognized by law follow the European civil law classification and include general and limited partnerships, joint stock companies, limited liability companies, partnerships limited by shares and contractual joint ventures. The individual GCC states incorporate minor variations on this general theme. For example, Kuwait omits the category of partnership limited by shares, Qatar provides only for joint stock companies and cooperative companies and the UAE distinguishes between public and private joint stock companies. Bahrain provides for an entirely separate category of offshore exempt companies,[30] which are the basis of its reputation as a regional banking center.

Investment by foreign companies and individuals in companies organized within the GCC states is subject to restrictions. Except in Oman, foreigners are not permitted to hold more than a 49 percent interest in a local company. In most GCC states foreign parties are prohibited from being general partners in a partnership company or from being shareholders in a joint stock company.

Foreign companies may establish permanent branch offices in Bahrain and the UAE under the sponsorship of local citizens. The branch-office option is available in other GCC states only on a temporary basis in connection with government projects, or by special exemption.

All business enterprises are centrally registered, and registration in the Commercial Register is the principal formality required for operation. The commercial registration number of a company is frequently required to be shown at its premises and on its stationery. A separate license or approval prior to registration, usually from the Ministry of Commerce, is normally required prior to commercial registration for all companies, and companies having foreign participation may require the

---

[28]Federal Law No. 5 of 1985.
[29]Decree Law No. 28 of 1975 (Bahrain); Law No. 15 of 1960 (Kuwait); Law No. 4 of 1974 (Oman); Law No. 3 of 1961 (Qatar); Royal Decree No. M/6 of 1385 A.H. (Saudi Arabia); Federal Law No. 8 of 1984 (UAE).
[30]Ministerial Resolution No. 25 of 1977.

approval of additional bodies established for that purpose. The fore-going pattern is varied somewhat in the UAE where businesses, both foreign and domestic, are licensed at the level of the individual emirates, whose policies may differ considerably. Under any circumstances, licensing and registration of a business having foreign ownership nor-mally requires documentation at a minimum of the company's articles of incorporation and financial history.

In addition to being limited to a minority interest, foreign investment in the GCC states may also be limited to certain kinds of enterprises. For example, the Foreign Business and Investment Law of Oman[31] and the Foreign Commercial Investment Law of Saudi Arabia[32] restrict foreign investment to projects important to economic development or which promise a transfer of technology. At present, in most, if not all, of the GCC states, certain activities such as trading, local transportation and ordinary construction are limited to wholly locally owned firms.

A major exception to the foregoing generalizations is the recent estab-lishment by the Emirate of Dubai of the Jebel Ali Free Zone (JAFZA) at the Port of Jebel Ali, Dubai. JAFZA offers foreign companies the opportunity to establish an industrial, assembly, warehouse or other site in the Arabian Gulf region without the normal requirement for a local sponsor or partner. JAFZA also handles all administrative require-ments relating to personnel visas and labor permits. Free zone com-panies are exempt from income tax and are guaranteed the right to repatriate profits for at least 15 years. The imports and exports of free zone companies, other than their sales within the UAE, are duty free. The development of the Jebel Ali Free Zone may make it an increasingly active center for internal as well as external trade.

Labor and Immigration Regulations

Immigration

Owing to their attraction for workers from other Arab countries, the Indian-Pakistani subcontinent and parts of Asia, and in defense of their own small native populations, all of the GCC states pursue restrictive immigration policies. Visas are required to enter any of the GCC states for either visit or employment purposes. Forty-eight-hour transit visas are available in Bahrain, but otherwise every visitor must have a local sponsor for visa purposes. Admission for employment requires the separate approval of labor authorities and the issuance of a separate labor permit. However, there is no visa or other entry requirement for other GCC nationals.

---

[31]Sultani Decree No. 4 of 1974.
[32]Royal Decree No. M/4 of 1399 A.H.

Because of the sponsorship requirement and the cost of recruitment of expatriate labor, foreign employees are generally not free to change employment at will, but must have the permission of their original employer/sponsor. Apparently there has been some recent dissatisfaction with the existing severe restrictions on transfer of employment, perhaps because of the growing number of experienced expatriates now available locally owing to employment cutbacks during the current recession. In any case both Saudi Arabia and the UAE have recently relaxed their procedures for transfer of employment visas and have reversed the earlier presumption against the consent of the original sponsor. In Saudi Arabia, however, each request for the grant or renewal of an employment visa is scrutinized to determine whether the position can be filled from the growing Saudi labor force.

Labor

Employees throughout the GCC countries have the benefit of relatively favorable and paternalistic labor laws, which are surprisingly regular throughout the GCC states.[33] These laws follow broadly the provisions of the Kuwait Labor Law, passed in 1964. They customarily distinguish between employment for a specified or unspecified term, require that employers must give priority in hiring to nationals, provide for a probationary period upon commencement of employment and prescribe special conditions of employment of women and juveniles. They further determine when wages are to be paid, applicable working hours and holidays, minimal working conditions, and compensation for work-related accidents and illnesses. They also provide for express statutory benefits upon termination of employment. The provisions of these laws and their administration are generally favorable to employees.

Commercial Agencies

Each of the GCC states provides for the establishment of commercial agencies, which are a prominent feature of the Gulf commercial landscape. In general, the commercial agency provides a means for a foreign company to conduct organized marketing efforts without establishing a registered local presence of its own.

Commercial agencies are defined broadly by the statutes,[34] and include most types of distributors, dealers, sales representatives, general sales

---

[33]Decree Law No. 23 of 1976 (Bahrain); Law No. 38 of 1964 (Kuwait); Sultani Decree No. 34 of 1973 (Oman); Law No. 3 of 1962 (Qatar); Decree No. M/21 of 1389 A.H. (Saudi Arabia); Federal Law No. 8 of 1980 (UAE).

[34]Amiri Decree No. 23 of 1975 (Bahrain); Law No. 36 of 1964 (Kuwait); Sultani Decrees No. 26 of 1977 and No. 82 of 1984 (Oman); Law No. 12 of 1964 (Qatar); Royal Decrees No. 11 of 1382 A.H., No. 5 of 1389 A.H., No. 32 of 1400 A.H., and Ministerial Order No. 1897 of 1401 A.H. (Saudi Arabia); Federal Law No. 18 of 1981 and Ministerial Decree No. 22 of 1981 (UAE).

agents, forwarding agents, etc., whether or not these buy and sell for their own account and whether or not they have the power to bind the principal. All commercial agencies must be registered with a central authority, usually the Ministry of Commerce, and unregistered agencies may not take advantage of favorable provisions of the relevant commercial agency law and in some cases may not rely on local adjudication of any claims in connection with an unregistered agency agreement.

In each of the GCC states, commercial agencies are limited to national citizens, and only in Oman may local companies which are not 100 percent locally owned be commercial agents. In all except Kuwait, an agency is automatically deemed to be exclusive for the specified territory. In the UAE, individual emirates may be specified as the territory, and in Saudi Arabia agencies are sometimes limited by province.

Perhaps the most significant feature of the various GCC commercial agency laws is their express provision for compensation to the agent in the event of termination without justification. In practice, justification is seldom found in the absence of gross neglect of the agency or substantial breach of the agency contract. Indeed, the UAE Commercial Agencies Law expressly provides that a commercial agency may not be terminated, even upon the expiration of the specified term of the agency contract, without appropriate compensation. In this respect the GCC states follow the civil law example in treating commercial agencies as a property right rather than a contractual right.

Compensation for termination is intended, according to the statutes, to reimburse the agent for his efforts and expenditures leading to the success of the agency, but it has largely become a weapon for commercial leverage to prevent the free transfer of agencies. The compensation requirement was originally designed in large part to prevent major commercial agents from acquiring successful agencies away from smaller competitors. However, the result in practice has been that powerful agents are still able to secure agencies of their choice, but foreign companies have been left with less flexibility in dealing with smaller local agents in their efforts to establish the success of new agencies.

Regulation of Industry

Industrialization was initially seen by many as the most promising way to mitigate the extreme dependence of the GCC states on the production of crude oil. Local industrial advantages included a wealth of available capital and a cheap supply of petroleum both for energy and as a feedstock for downstream industries. The cement industry was another in which it was felt that local advantages existed and for which there existed a ready regional market in connection with construction during the boom years of the late 1970s and early 1980s.

Now, however, owing to a decline in the petroleum market, duplication of industries, high labor costs, a disinclination on the part of the local private sector to invest in industrial rather than trading enterprises, and the Gulf recession generally, some of the enthusiasm for industrialization is wavering.

Generally, industrial ventures require at least majority local ownership.[35] Bahrain and Kuwait require 100 percent local ownership of industrial enterprises. Each of the Gulf states except Saudi Arabia requires the approval of the Ministry of Industry for the establishment of an industrial enterprise, and Saudi Arabia requires such approval in order for an industrial facility to qualify for various benefits, such as favorable rental and utility rates, subsidized raw materials and interest-free loans. Official approval entails certain benefits in the other GCC states as well, although these are generally limited to tax holidays, customs incentives and government purchasing preferences.

In the UAE, the existing industrial law has not been enforced at the federal level except in order to certify national industries as such for the purpose of customs exemptions in other GCC states. Industrial enterprises in the UAE continue to be licensed by the individual emirates, although there has recently been some emphasis on review and coordination of industrial policy in order to prevent duplication of industry and to insure that markets for industrial products will exist.

Government Tenders and Contracts

Government contracting, too, follows a standard pattern in the GCC states. Most significant contracts are awarded on the basis of either public or limited tenders. In some states there exist formal prequalification and/or contractor classification requirements for bidders.

The standard tender procedure requires a bid bond in an amount of one to five percent of the contract value, and award of a tender requires a performance bond, usually in the amount of 10 to 15 percent of the contract value. Contract terms are essentially nonnegotiable, a habit that was formed during the boom years.

Formerly, an advance payment of 10 to 20 percent of the contract value was customary in connection with construction contracts. This practice has been curtailed as a budgetary measure. Contract payments are customarily released according to the progress of the works, and a final payment of five to ten percent is retained, in addition to the performance bond, pending final acceptance by the project owner.

Tender supervising authorities vary. In some states approval of tenders by a single central authority is required, while in others authority

---

[35]See Decree Law No. 6 of 1984 (Bahrain); Law No. 6 of 1965 (Kuwait); Sultani Decree No. 1 of 1979 (Oman); Law No. 11 of 1980 (Qatar); Royal Decree No. 50 of 1381 A.H. (Saudi Arabia); Federal Law No. 1 of 1979 (UAE).

is dispersed according to the subject matter and value of the tender. As government budgets are tightened, there appears to be a tendency for increasingly centralized control and coordination of government contracting.

In several states, including Kuwait and the UAE federal government, government contracting is restricted by statute to national citizens and companies. At least in the UAE, this requirement is not rigidly enforced where specialized foreign expertise is required. At a minimum, arrangements can be made for the establishment of a limited purpose joint venture which will satisfy local authorities. The GCC states are also relatively uniform in giving national companies a ten percent or more price advantage in competitive tender situations. Recently, however, cost conscious governments have effectively converted this preference into an option for national companies to reduce their bid to match the price of a foreign bid within the preference range.

In Saudi Arabia, which does not limit government tenders to national companies, there is nevertheless a hierarchy of preference favoring wholly Saudi-owned companies, then majority Saudi-owned companies and lastly foreign-owned entities. In addition, Saudi Arabia has imposed the so-called 30 percent rule, which requires that non-Saudi government contractors must subcontract at least 30 percent of the value of their contract to Saudi companies. Initially, Saudi companies were defined for purposes of both the burden and the benefit of this rule to mean only wholly Saudi-owned companies. Thus, joint venture companies were required to subcontract 30 percent of their contracts and were not eligible to serve as subcontractors under the rule. This interpretation was formally revised in early 1986 in conformity with Saudi government initiatives to promote joint ventures in the kingdom, and now majority Saudi-owned joint ventures need not subcontract their own work under the rule.

Banking Regulation

In contrast to many other areas of commerce, regulation of banking varies widely among the GCC states. Bahrain has had a large and renowned offshore banking sector which was particularly active in financing in the Gulf area during the boom years. Foreign banks may also obtain licenses for representative offices or investment banks in Bahrain. In Kuwait and Saudi Arabia, by contrast, all banks must be organized locally and must be at least majority owned by local citizens. In Kuwait, minority ownership is further limited to other Arab nationals only. Joint venture banks have often been managed under contract by the foreign partners.

In the UAE and Oman, foreign banks may operate branch offices and may compete on a relatively equal basis with locally organized commercial banks. The UAE in particular is considered to be over-banked, and the licensing of new banks, whether local or foreign, is not foreseen except in connection with the merger of existing banks. In Oman, as a practical matter, few foreign bank branches have been licensed and only one or two are regarded as successful.

In each of the GCC states, establishment of a bank or branch office requires the approval of the national central bank or monetary authority, as the case may be. All banks are normally required to submit and publish their balance sheets annually. Regulation by government authorities typically requires minimum capital, specified capital/loan ratios and, recently, provision for bad loans.

A system of exchange houses exists in parallel with the commercial banking system in most of the GCC states. These have played a significant role in facilitating the remittances of foreign workers in the Gulf region and have also engaged at least to some extent (but without official authorization) in the taking of deposits.

Despite considerable rhetoric, to date only the UAE has enacted an Islamic Banking Law,[36] and there exists only a small number of Islamic banks operating in the GCC states.

Corporate Taxation

Most of the GCC states impose an income tax on the profits of foreign companies operating locally.[37] However, most of the income tax statutes of the GCC states are relatively old and are frequently not enforced in strict accordance with their terms, oil revenue having superseded income taxation as a principal source of revenue.

In Kuwait and Saudi Arabia corporate income tax includes a tax on the profit share of foreign companies holding an interest in Kuwaiti or Saudi joint-venture companies. A Saudi partner in such companies is liable only for payment of the *zakat* on its share in the company. The *zakat* is a religious tax perhaps best defined as a 2.5 percent tax on income-producing assets. Ownership by other GCC nationals is treated as Saudi ownership for tax purposes.

In Qatar the statutory corporate income tax is levied in practice only on foreign companies, and in Bahrain income tax is effectively imposed only on oil-producing companies. There is no federal income tax in the UAE, but most emirates have income tax statutes or decrees which by their terms apply to corporate entities in general. However, in practice

---

[36]Federal Law No. 6 of 1985.

[37]See, e.g., Decree No. 8 of 1955 (Bahrain); Decree No. 3 of 1955 (Kuwait); Sultani Decree No. 47 of 1981 (Oman); Decree No. 1 of 1954 (Qatar); Royal Decree 17/2/28/3321 of 1370 A.H. (Saudi Arabia); Abu Dhabi Income Tax Decree of 1965; Dubai Income Tax Decree of 1969; Ras Al Khaimah Income Tax of 1969; Sharjah Income Tax Decrees of 1968 and of 1973.

income tax in the UAE is payable only by oil-producing companies and by a limited number of foreign banks which have not been able to secure exemption. In Oman, the law provides for taxation of all companies (including partnerships) and "permanent establishments," both foreign and domestic alike, but 100 percent Omani companies have received a temporary exemption from the income tax which has been repeatedly extended, most recently until 1987.

LEGAL STRUCTURE OF THE GCC

Formation of the Structure

The GCC was formally established when the heads of state of the six countries met in Abu Dhabi and on May 25, 1981, signed its Charter.[38] The Charter was signed pursuant to an agreement to form the GCC reached on February 4, 1981, by the six foreign ministers meeting in Riyadh.[39]

It may be that the outbreak of the war in the Gulf between Iran and Iraq in 1980 and the common interest of the six countries in working toward a solution to the war may have been the final catalyst for the formation of the GCC,[40] but the historical, cultural and other ties among these countries are extensive and deep, dating back centuries. The countries have a common language, religion and geography with similar natural resources and political systems and have essentially free enterprise economies linked with the industrialized democracies. The six countries pursue a foreign policy in cooperation with the League of Arab States and the Islamic Conference Organization and are not aligned with either the NATO or Warsaw Pact countries.

---

[38]The Charter of the GCC, Art. 1 (hereinafter cited as Charter), states that the official name is the Cooperation Council for the Arab States of the Gulf. The date and place of signature are set forth at the end of the Charter. The Charter is reprinted, among other places, in No. 7 of *American-Arab Affairs,* Winter 1983-1984, as well as p. 217 of this book. The Charter has been ratified through implementing legislation in the member countries, e.g.: Decree Law No. 6 of 1981, *Bahrain Official Gazette* No. 1461 of 1981; Law No. 44 of 1981, *Al-Kuwait Al-Yaum* No. 1367 of 1981; Decree No. 6 of 1983, *Qatar Official Gazette* No. 2 of 1983; Decree 76 of 1981; *UAE Official Gazette* No. 97 of 1981.

[39]*The Secretariat General "in Brief"* (Riyadh: GCC Secretariat General, n.d.) ; *The Way Forward, Co-operation and Unity in the Gulf* (Sultanate of Oman: Ministry of Information, 1985) (hereinafter cited as *The Way Forward*), p. 15, reprints the final statement of that meeting. *The Way Forward*, published on the occasion of the sixth meeting of the GCC Supreme Council in Muscat in November 1985, outlines at pp. 13-16 the preparatory steps taken between the Febraury 4, 1981 meeting and the first summit on May 25, 1981.

[40]The final communiques of each of the first six meetings of the GCC Supreme Council have dealt in part with the Iran-Iraq war. The final communiques of the first five meetings are reprinted in *The Way Forward*, pp. 79-88.

With so much in common, the six Gulf countries cooperated to a considerable extent even before the formation of the GCC. By 1981, the six apparently had concluded that they could more effectively pursue their common interests through a more formal, visible and permanent vehicle for cooperation.

Authority and Goals

The GCC is not a supranational institution with independent legislative and judicial authority. The member states have not ceded sovereignty to the GCC.[41] Policies, resolutions and other actions taken in implementation of the Charter have the effect of law under the legal systems of the member states in accordance with their individual constitutional or other requirements.

It is notable, however, that under Article 27 of the Unified Economic Agreement signed by the ministers of economy and finance in Riyadh in implementation of the Charter on June 8, 1981, only two weeks after the Charter itself was signed, it was provided that "in case of conflict with local laws and regulations of member states, execution of the provisions of this Agreement shall prevail." The Unified Economic Agreement was ratified by the Supreme Council at the November 1981 summit and was further ratified through implementing legislation of the member states.[42] Although Article 27 was intended to confer the status of law to the provisions of the Unified Economic Agreement and adds strength and legitimacy to such provisions and their implementation, it probably carries no greater authority than treaty law and clearly falls short of relinquishing sovereignty.

Nevertheless, the goals of the leaders in establishing the GCC appear to be ambitious and potentially far-reaching. Article 4 of the GCC Charter establishes the principal goals and directs the GCC to promote the "coordination and integration between the member states in all fields with the ultimate aim of achieving their unity"; to deepen and strengthen ties and existing cooperation; to establish "similar systems in various fields" including legislation and administration as well as economic and financial affairs, commerce, customs, communications,

---

[41]Indeed, such a surrender of sovereignty would conceivably create a problem under the constitutions of Bahrain, Art. 1(A); Kuwait, Art. 1; Qatar, Art. 2; and the UAE, Art. 4. E.g., however, Abdullah El-Kuwaiz, "The Gulf Cooperation Council and the Concept of Economic Integration," *American-Arab Affairs*, No. 7 (Winter 1983-1984), p. 47.

[42]E.g.: Decree Law No. 26 of 1981, *Bahrain Official Gazette* No. 1468 of 1981; Law No. 58 of 1982, *Al-Kuwait Al-Yaum* No. 1443 of 1981; Decree No. 51 of 1982, *Qatar Official Gazette* No. 8 of 1982; Law No. 6 of 1983, *Qatar Official Gazette* No. 3 of 1983; Law No. 1 of 1984, *Qatar Official Gazette* No. 3 of 1984; Decree No. 47 of 1982, *UAE Official Gazette* No. 105 of 1982.

educational and cultural affairs, social and health affairs, information and tourism; to further "scientific and technological progress" in various fields; and to set up joint ventures and encourage private-sector participation in development projects.

The United Economic Agreement referred to above reinforces the venturousness of the Charter by referring to the goals of the GCC as "economic integration" and to the intention of the parties to "coordinate and unify their economic, financial and monetary policies, as well as their commercial and industrial legislation, and customs regulations."

Governing and Working Bodies

Under the Charter, the Supreme Council is the highest governing authority of the GCC. The principal bodies which implement the work of the Council are the Ministerial Council, the Secretariat General and various specialized committees.

The Supreme Council is composed of the heads of state of the six member countries and is chaired by its members on a rotating basis. Each member has one vote. The Supreme Council may pass resolutions at validly convened meetings at which a quorum of two-thirds of its members attend. Resolutions dealing with substantive matters require the unanimous vote of members attending, while a majority vote will pass a resolution dealing with a procedural matter. The Charter provides that the Supreme Council may examine any question of interest to the member states; draw up major GCC policy; examine recommendations, reports, studies and joint ventures referred to it by the Ministerial Council; discuss reports and studies prepared by the secretary-general; adopt policies for dealing with other nations and international organizations; and amend the Charter. Its sessions are governed by rules of procedure that were approved concurrently with the Charter.[43] The first session of the Supreme Council was held in Abu Dhabi in May 1981, and it has held sessions (commonly called summits) each November since then in the capital cities of the member countries on a rotating basis.

Much of the more detailed work of the GCC is performed by the Ministerial Council, a body composed of the foreign ministers of the member states that meets every three months. Like the Supreme Council, its chairmanship rotates among its members, and its meetings are governed by the same quorum and voting requirements as are Supreme Council meetings. The Ministerial Council is empowered to initiate

---

[43]The Rules of Procedure of the Supreme Council of the GCC are reprinted in *The Way Forward*, pp. 27-32, and p. 223 of this book.

policies and studies related to cooperation and coordination between the member states in various fields, to make recommendations to the Supreme Council on the coordination of existing activity, to submit its recommendations to the relevant ministers for implementation, to encourage private sector cooperation among the member states, to submit proposals to specialized committees for study, to recommend amendments to the Charter, to prepare for Supreme Council summits, and to examine matters referred to it by the Supreme Council. Its sessions are also governed by rules of procedure that were signed concurrently with the Charter.[44]

The Secretariat General is entrusted with the day-to-day operations of the GCC. It is headed by a secretary-general appointed by the Supreme Council. The secretary-general since the establishment of the GCC has been H.E. Dr. Abdulla Y. Bishara, a respected Kuwaiti diplomat.[45] The Secretariat General is provided authority under the Charter to prepare studies relating to cooperation and coordination of programs of the member states, prepare reports on GCC activities, supervise implementation of resolutions of the Ministerial Council and Supreme Council, prepare reports and conduct other activity at the request of the Ministerial Council or Supreme Council, draft administrative and financial regulations governing the GCC, prepare GCC budgets and final accounts and prepare the agenda and final resolutions for sessions of the Ministerial Council. The Secretariat General has 275 employees in its offices in Riyadh.[46] It has a number of departments that prepare reports and conduct research on specific types of issues: the Office of the Secretary-General, the Legal Affairs Department, the Economic Department, the Political Department, the Man and Environment Department, the Information Department, the Military Department, the Finance and Administration Department, and the Information Center.[47] The member states contribute equally to the budget of the GCC Secretariat General.

---

[44]The Rules of Procedure of the Ministerial Council of the GCC are reprinted in *The Way Forward*, pp. 35-41, and on p. 229 of this book.

[45]For a statement of the views of the Secretary General see Abdulla Yacoub Bishara, "The Gulf Cooperation Council: Achievements and Challenges," *American-Arab Affairs*, No. 7 (Winter 1983-84), p. 40; see also *Emirates News*, Nov. 29, 1984, announcing his reappointment until November 1987.

[46]Statistics for June 1986, obtained from the GCC Secretariat General, Riyadh.

[47]*The Secretariat General "In Brief."* In June 1986, based on statistics obtained from the GCC Secretariat General in Riyadh, the employees were distributed as follows: 20 in the Office of the Secretariat General; 11 in the Legal Affairs Department; 63 in the Economic Department; 18 in the Political Affairs Department; 22 in the Man and Environment Department; 11 in the Information Department; 13 in the Ministry Department; 107 in the Finance and Administration Department; and 30 in the Information Center.

Specialized Committees

Aside from the Supreme Council, the Council of Ministers and the Secretariat General, a number of specialized committees have been established to deal with particular problems or subject matters.

The Charter establishes a Commission for the Settlement of Disputes which operates under rules of procedure signed concurrently with the Charter[48] and which is designed to settle disputes relating to the interpretation of the Charter. The members of the Commission are to be named by the Supreme Council for each dispute that may arise. Each particular Commission will hear and decide only one particular dispute. Fortunately, it has not yet been necessary to refer any such disputes to the Commission. When such disputes have arisen, they have been settled by discussions among the member states' representatives.[49]

In addition, several committees have been established parallel to the Ministerial Council. Such committees have been formed by the ministers of the member states and deal with problems falling within their areas of expertise. While there is no express authority in the Charter for the establishment of such committees, their existence is clearly implied.[50] The ministers of oil, health, power and electricity, and finance and economy have all formed separate committees within the GCC. Many of these ministerial committees have formed subcommittees. For example, the Finance and Economy Committee has established a Permanent Subcommittee on Monetary Policy, and an Environmental Subcommittee. The Power and Electricity Committee has formed a subcommittee to monitor the performance and quality of government contractors. The Health Committee has established a Subcommittee on Pharmaceuticals.[51]

The GCC finance and economy ministers established the Gulf Investment Corporation in November of 1982 to encourage the industrialization and economic development of the Gulf.[52] It has an authorized

---

[48]The Rules of Procedure for the Commission for Settlement of Disputes of the GCC are reprinted in *The Way Forward*, pp. 43-46, and on p. 236 of this book.

[49]Based in part on oral communication from Mohamed As-Sayari, Director General of the Legal Department, GCC Secretariat General, on June 18, 1986.

[50]Charter, Art. 12 reads in part as follows:

"The Ministerial Council shall exercise such powers which include:

To submit its recommendations to the relevant ministers in order to draw up the policies required for putting decisions adopted by the GCC into effect."

[51]Ian Meadows, "The GCC 'Oil Wing,' " *Middle East Executive Reports*, Vol. 5, No. 11 (Nov. 1982), p. 9; Eugene R. Sullivan, Jr., "Gulf Integration: A Status Report," *Middle East Executive Reports*, Vol. 6, No. 6 (June 1983), p. 7.

[52]Agreement of Incorporation of the GIC and Articles of Association of the GIC, reprinted in *The Way Forward*, pp. 53-63. Also see p. 247 for a full description of the GIC.

capital of $2.1 billion and is jointly owned by the GCC member states.[53] A number of other organizations, many of which were established with GIC financing, exist for the purpose of promoting various types of industrial and economic activity in the Gulf.[54]

ACTIONS TAKEN BY THE GCC

Most of the actions taken by the GCC that relate to the economies and legal systems of the member states have been within the framework of the Unified Economic Agreement.[55] These actions may be grouped into four categories:

1. Steps taken to achieve equal legal treatment for nationals of the GCC states in each of the member states with respect to their economic activity;
2. Establishment of common economic policies;
3. Establishment and promotion of joint ventures in the public and private sectors; and
4. Development of common institutions and laws.

Equal Legal Treatment

The Unified Economic Agreement provides for the unhindered import and export among the member states of "agricultural, animal, industrial and natural resource products that are of national origin," for member states to accord such products of national origin from another member state "the same treatment as national products" and for all such products of national origin to be "exempted from customs duties and other charges having equivalent effect." The term "national origin" is defined as applying to all products produced in a facility within a member state at least 51 percent owned by nationals of member states, having at least 40 percent of their final value added in a member state, and accompanied by a certificate of origin authenticated by an agency of the government of the country of origin.[56] The ministers of finance and economy of the member states meeting in Riyadh in August 1982 reached an agreement to implement these provisions of the Unified Economic Agreement.

Implementation was originally planned to occur on December 1, 1982. In the interim the ministers of finance and economy were to determine how the exempt goods would be identified and certificates of origin issued. It was decided at the November 1982 summit in Bahrain to delay

---

[53]Ibid.; Sullivan, p. 14.

[54]"Focus on the Gulf Cooperation Council" (proceedings of a GCC-sponsored seminar held in the United Kingdom on December 1, 1983), p. 42.

[55]The UEA is reprinted in *The Way Forward*, pp. 49-51; in *American-Arab Affairs*, No. 7, Winter 1983-1984, pp. 177-182; and on p. 239 of this book.

[56]UEA, Arts. 1, 2 and 3.

implementation until March 1, 1983, as some issues, including Oman's desire to be exempted from certain provisions, had yet to be resolved.

Implementation of the agreement opened up larger markets for manufacturers in the member states, especially for manufacturers located in the smaller states, and has the overall effect of protecting and encouraging local manufacturing facilities. However, with respect to a number of products which involve competition among the member states themselves, practical implementation at the borders has been dilatory and uncertain.

The Unified Economic Agreement also directs each of the signatories to grant unhindered transit across its territory to the goods of another member state, with the exception of goods barred from entry into the transit state.[57] Regulations implementing the transit of goods provisions of the Unified Economic Agreement were adopted by the member states to become effective on March 1, 1983, as part of the program that included abrogating intra-GCC tariffs.[58] The agreement also provides that means of transportation for cargo and passengers owned by nationals of a member state shall be accorded the same treatment in each member state that means of transportation owned by nationals of that state receive, and that each member state shall make available port facilities to vessels owned by nationals of other member states on the same terms available to its own nationals.[59].

Under the Unified Economic Agreement not only goods but citizens of member states are to be accorded equal treatment with nationals by all member states (Article 8):

> The member states shall agree on the executive rules which would ensure that each member state shall grant the citizens of all other member states the same treatment granted to its own citizens without any discrimination or differentiation in the following fields:
>
> 1. Freedom of movement, work and residence.
> 2. Right of ownership, inheritance and bequest.
> 3. Freedom to exercise economic activity.
> 4. Free movement of capital.

These provisions were partially implemented effective as of March 1, 1983, by an agreement to provide for a lowering of barriers to the

---

[57]UEA, Arts. 5 and 6.

[58]The Regulations are reprinted in *American-Arab Affairs*, No. 7 (Winter 1983-1984), pp. 183-184, and on page 244 of this book. For an example of legislative implementation by a member state, see Ministerial Decree No. 16 of 1983, *Al-Kuwait Al-Yaum* No. 1461 of 1983.

[59]UEA, Art. 18.

conduct of business and professional activity by nationals of one member state in another member state.[60] It allowed GCC nationals to invest in up to 75 percent of the equity in an industrial, agricultural, animal husbandry, fisheries or contracting enterprise in another member state. After a five-year transition period, a 100 percent equity interest could be owned. It also provided that professionals in the medical, accounting, engineering and legal professions could practice in any GCC state without a residence visa, provided that such persons be citizens of a GCC country and permanently resident in the state in which they set up their practice. Implementation of the accords governing businesses and professions in the UAE was delayed for a year by debates in the Federal National Council over the amount of equity participation that a GCC national should be allowed in a UAE business. However, the law as issued in the UAE conformed to the guidelines set by the GCC.[61] So far it does not appear that any significant advantage has been taken of these liberalizations.

In late 1983, the GCC ministers of economy and finance began to consider seriously whether the foregoing accords should be expanded. Further measures were indeed approved at the Doha summit in November 1983. They provided that GCC nationals could acquire up to 75 percent of the capital in three additional types of businesses—hotels, restaurants or businesses engaged in maintenance activities related to the other permitted activities. They also provided that GCC nationals could practice a number of skilled trades in addition to the professions opened up in the March 1, 1983, accords.[62] At the Doha summit, it was also decided to waive residence visa requirements for GCC businessmen and professionals engaged in the activities covered by these accords.

A further step in allowing the free movement of persons and goods provided for in the Unified Economic Agreement was the lowering of barriers to the ownership of real estate across national boundaries. A committee of GCC legal experts established in 1983 to draft real estate ownership regulations submitted a draft law allowing ownership by

---

[60]Decree Law 3 of 1983, *Bahrain Official Gazette* No. 1525 of 1983; Ministerial Decisions 51 and 52 of 1982, *Al-Kuwait Al-Yaum* No. 1450 of 1982; Ministerial Resolution 6 of 1983, *Oman Official Gazette* No. 265 of 1983; Law No. 6 of 1983, Qatar Official Gazette No. 3 of 1983; Federal Law No. 2 of 1984, *UAE Official Gazette* No. 136 of 1984; Ministerial Resolution No. 24 of 1985, *UAE Official Gazette* No. 149 of 1985.

[61]Federal Law No. 2 of 1984, *Official Gazette* No. 136 of 1984; Ministerial Resolution No. 24 of 1985, *Official Gazette* No. 149 of 1985.

[62]Decree Law No. 4 of 1984, *Bahrain Official Gazette* No. 1581 of 1984; Ministerial Decisions Nos. 43 and 44 of 1983, *Al-Kuwait Al-Yaum* No. 1516 of 1984; Ministerial Resolutions 25 and 33 of 1984, *Oman Official Gazette* No. 288 of 1984; Law No. 1 of 1984, *Qatar Official Gazette* No. 3 of 1984. The implementation in the UAE again took more time than in the other member states.

citizens of member states of up to 1,000 square meters of residential property, with the additional requirement that unimproved land have a residence constructed upon it within two years of its purchase. These proposals were modified in subsequent discussions by the GCC ministers of finance and economy. A final draft, more liberal in terms, was given preliminary approval by the November 1984 summit and, following study by the member states, was given final approval at the November 1985 summit. It provided for maximum ownership of 3,000 square meters of residential property, with construction of a residential dwelling on unimproved land to be completed within five years.

Most recently, in 1986, following implementation of a GCC initiative, companies organized in a GCC state and wholly owned by GCC nationals are no longer required to appoint local agents in order to conduct sales in other GCC states.

Common Economic Policies

Article 4 of the Unified Economic Agreement provides for the adoption of a uniform minimum customs tariff for the protection of national products from foreign competition to be phased in over a five-year period.

Preparatory work for implementing the uniform customs tariff was carried on by the directors of the customs departments of the member states, supervised by the finance and economy ministers, in late 1982 and early 1983. A final accord was presented to and approved by the ministers of finance and economy during a meeting in Riyadh on May 10 and 11, 1983. The guidelines provided for three categories of imports: 1) tax-exempt, applying to food and necessary medical, industrial and agricultural supplies; 2) taxed, subject to a minimum tariff of four percent; and 3) protected, subjected to a maximum tariff of 20 percent. These tariffs were scheduled to become effective on September 1, 1983. The new tariffs required the UAE, Oman, Qatar and Saudi Arabia to raise their minimum tariffs.[63] The member states did not all raise their tariffs before the September 1 deadline, but they were in conformity by the November 1983 summit.[64]

Ancillary to the regulation of imports under the Unified Economic Agreement was the establishment of uniform standards, necessary for

---

[63]Bahrain's tariffs, which were higher, ranged from five percent to 20 percent except on cigarettes and liquor; Kuwait's minimum tariff was four percent; the UAE, Oman, Qatar and Saudi Arabia all had lower minimum tariffs.

[64]Ken Whittingham, "GCC Summit to Focus on Defense," *Middle East Executive Reports*, Vol. 7, No. 11 (Nov. 1984), p. 20; Ken Whittingham, "GCC Summit Conference," *Middle East Executive Reports*, Vol. 6, No. 11 (Nov. 1983), p. 18; John A. Sandwick, "The GCC: An Update," *Middle East Executive Reports*, Vol. 7, No. 4 (April 1984), pp. 14 and 19.

the uniform classification of imports and the protection of the health and safety of citizens of the member states. A standards committee was established following the November 1982 summit, where it was resolved to convert the Saudi Arabian Organization for Specifications and Measurements into the Center for Unified Measures and Specification. The center has gradually been promulgating uniform standards applicable throughout the GCC countries for various categories of consumer, food and technical items.[65] For example, uniform motor vehicle standards are scheduled to come into effect on January 1, 1987.

The common tariffs agreement signed in 1983 established three categories of imported goods, but did not specify what goods would fall under which category. Continuing efforts are being made in this regard. In May 1985 the Ministerial Council considered recommendations submitted to it by a special technical committee that cement, iron ore, aluminum and asbestos from one member country be exempt from all members' tariffs. During the same month the finance ministers met to consider proposals for protective tariffs to be levied on iron pellets, aluminum and cement.

Apart from the subject of trade and tariffs, which has received concentrated attention and action, the Unified Economic Agreement provides for coordination and cooperation in a number of the most important areas of economic and business activity, including economic development planning, strategic food stocks, all aspects of the oil industry, industrial activities, research and applied science and technology, land and sea transportation, and financial, monetary and banking policies. Indeed, the newspapers of the Gulf confirm that since its formation the GCC has provided frequent opportunities for the discussion of problems, issues and objectives relating to all these matters.

Joint Ventures

The GCC has encouraged joint-venture development projects in two different ways. First, the recommendations passed by the GCC concerning the lowering of investment barriers by member states should broaden the pool of financing from which projects in individual states can draw. Second, the GCC has directly encouraged a number of projects, both privately and publicly owned, designed to promote the industrialization and the economic development of the Gulf region as a whole.

The promotion of joint economic development projects, utilizing private sector and public sector funds, is encouraged by the Unified Economic Agreement. Article 13, for example, provides:

---

[65]See, e.g., Ministerial Resolution No. 12 of 1985 (Ministry of Trade and Agriculture) Adopting Gulf Standards and Specifications as National Standards, *Bahrain Official Gazette* No. 1643 of 1985 (labelling of pre-packaged foodstuffs).

Within the framework of their coordinating activities, the member states shall pay special attention to the establishment of joint ventures in the fields of industry, agriculture and services, and shall support them with public, private or mixed capital in order to achieve economic integration, production interface and common development on sound economic bases.

Article 9 provides that the member states shall encourage their respective private sectors to establish joint ventures "to link their citizens' economic interest in the various spheres."

One of the most important GCC entities used to encourage regional projects is the Gulf Investment Corporation.[66] The GIC was approved by the Manama summit in November 1982, following preparatory work by the Financial and Economic Cooperation Committee and the Ministerial Council. Following approval of its formation by the member states, the General Assembly of the GIC was convened on October 12, 1983. The GIC is a joint stock company organized under the laws of Kuwait and headquartered in Kuwait. It has an authorized capital of $2.1 billion, held in equal portions of $350 million by the member states, of which 20 percent has been paid in. It is managed by a board of directors composed of two nominees of each shareholding government.[67] The GIC is not an organization that provides soft loans to development projects,[68] but is intended to operate as a profit-making diversified-investment bank, investing its resources both within and outside the member states in development projects and also securities, commodities, real estate and currencies and also to act as an underwriter and portfolio manager.

The other major regional finance institution in the Gulf countries is the Gulf Organization for Industrial Consulting which, established in 1976, predates the GCC. It is based in Doha with a budget of seven million dollars and is jointly owned by Iraq, Kuwait, Saudi Arabia, Qatar and the UAE (each owning 17 percent of the equity) and Oman and Bahrain (each owning 7.5 percent). The principal functions of the GOIC are to collect information, prepare proposals and evaluate proposed projects, partially with a view to avoiding economically undesirable duplication of projects.[69]

---

[66]See, Decree Law No. 25 of 1982, *Bahrain Official Gazette* No. 1518 of 1982, Approving the Agreement Establishing the G.I.C. (Reprinting the Agreement Establishing the G.I.C. and the G.I.C. Charter); *Al-Kuwait Al-Yaum* No. 1604 of 1985 (same); Sultani Decree No. 2 of 1983, *Oman Official Gazette* No. 256 of 1983, Approving the Agreement Establishing the G.I.C.

[67]GIC Articles of Association.

[68]Remarks by Abdulla Bishara, cited in "Focus on the Gulf Cooperation Council," p. 13; *MidEast Report*, Vol. 17, No. 19 (Oct. 1, 1984), p. 8.

[69]Ken Whittingham, "Where Is the GOIC Going?" *Middle East Executive Reports*, Vol. 5, No. 11 (Nov. 1982), p. 5.

The first jointly owned industrial project to be established in the Gulf is the Gulf Tire Company, based in Bahrain. Feasibility studies were performed in 1984, and the establishment of the plan has been authorized, though it has not yet begun operations. The Gulf Tire Company has an authorized capital of $500 million and is owned 35 percent by Saudi Arabia, 25 percent by Kuwait and 10 percent each by the UAE, Oman, Qatar and Bahrain.[70]

The Gulf United Fiberglass Company, capitalized at $50 million, was approved in 1982 by the GOIC and has been licensed to operate a plant at Jubail, Saudi Arabia. In 1984 the Saudi government granted 70,000 square meters of land for the establishment of its facilities. GUFC is reported to be the first joint stock company established by private-sector GCC investors.

The Gulf Aluminium Rolling Mill Company has been established in Bahrain, also with the active participation of the GOIC. The facility for the mill was put under construction in 1983, and it began producing rolled aluminum in the beginning of 1986.

Other projects that have been studied by GOIC include establishment of a petrochemical refinery, a float glass project in Iraq, an acetic acid plant in Qatar and a petroleum coke project in the UAE at Ruwais.

A number of infrastructural projects have been studied which are intended to contribute to regional economic development. As a first step toward the creation of a regional communications and transportation network, the unification of telecommunications rates was discussed in 1984 and implemented on May 1, 1985. As a further step, the Secretariat has commissioned a feasibility study of a possible railway link between the cities of the GCC and the Iraqi railway network,[71] and the GCC finance ministers have discussed establishing a joint air-freight company. An oil pipeline to transport crude oil to a refinery and port on the Gulf of Oman has also been under study, but representatives of the member states have recently decided not to go forward with the project at this time. It has also been proposed that the submarine communications cable connecting Bahrain, Qatar and the UAE be extended to Kuwait and Saudi Arabia.

Even though the trend in the GCC has been to encourage joint projects and to emphasize coordination rather than competition among the member states, these policies do not foreclose all competition between the member states. One example of such competition is the establishment by the Emirate of Dubai of its own airline, Emirates Airlines (which

---

[70]Ken Whittingham, "GCC: Focus on Joint Projects," *Middle East Executive Reports*, Vol. 8, No. 7 (July 1985), p. 12.

[71]Abdul Kader Bin Ameri, "Interview on the GCC," *American-Arab Affairs*, No. 15 (Winter 1985-1986), p. 71.

commenced service in October 1985), in spite of ongoing discussions on the coordination of rates and schedules of the other three Gulf carriers: Saudia, Kuwait Airlines and Gulf Air.

Uniform Laws

As previously noted, the Charter of the GCC espouses the objective of establishing similar systems of legislation and administration. The Unified Economic Agreement further reflects the intention of the parties to unify their commercial legislation and directs member states to standardize their industrial legislation and regulations, as part of an overall aim to coordinate and integrate economic development.

Currently, the only uniform laws that have been approved by the GCC and adopted by its member states are the uniform laws relating to common tariffs, as discussed above. However, the GCC is encouraging the study of uniform legislation in a number of areas, and several GCC committees, as well as non-GCC organizations that cooperate with the GCC, are involved in the preparation of various uniform laws.

A uniform labor law has been the subject of discussion in the GCC for several years. The first proposal to promulgate a uniform labor law for the Gulf states was made by the labor ministers of the GCC member states and of Iraq. The GCC labor ministers meeting in Riyadh in April 1984 endorsed a plan to prepare a study on the unification of the labor laws of the member states. Discussions of this project have continued at subsequent meetings of the labor ministers, but a draft uniform labor law suitable for submission to the member states for comment has not yet been produced.[72] The GCC has specifically rejected certain aspects of the International Labor Organization's model as unsuitable to conditions within the GCC states.

A draft uniform industrial law is at a more advanced stage of preparation. The GCC Secretariat General originally requested the Gulf Organization for Industrial Consulting to draw up the first draft of a uniform industrial law. The proposal prepared by GOIC was thereafter reviewed by the GCC Secretariat General and the ministers of commerce and industry of the member states. The draft reportedly provides for tax holidays, easy conditions for loans and governmental purchasing priority for nationally owned industries. The draft was studied by the Ministerial Council and by the Supreme Council at its November 1985 summit and has been submitted to the member states for comments.

A proposal generally to make the legal systems of the member states more uniform has been discussed by the justice ministers and is being

---

[72]Based in part on oral communication from Mohamed As-Sayari, Director General of the Legal Department, GCC Secretariat General, Riyadh, June 18, 1986.

studied by the Secretariat General's Legal Department. The justice ministers are in agreement that the legal systems should embody principles of the *sharia* and have accorded particular attention to the provisions of a *sharia*-based model legal system that reportedly has been prepared by the Arab League. The discussions have included a wide range of issues, including an evaluation of the judicial systems of the member states and consideration of the regulation of the legal profession.

Proposals have also been made to unify school curricula, civil service laws, environmental protection laws, building standards and penal codes.

The government of Bahrain has made proposals to the GCC that an arbitration center be established in one of the member countries. The proposal has been considered by the justice ministers of the member states, the Trade Cooperation Committee of the GCC and most recently was discussed by the Supreme Council at the November 1985 summit. However, consideration for such a center is not at an advanced stage. For example, no rules of procedure have been agreed upon (although it is understood that there is serious consideration being given to the use of UNCITRAL rules), and no rules for the administration of the arbitration center have yet been drafted.

CONCLUSION

The GCC member countries have historically exhibited very similar features in their social systems in general and in their legal systems in particular, for they share a common heritage of the Islamic religion and *sharia* principles of law, the Arabic language and geographic and economic conditions. For much of this century the similarity of the legal systems of five of the six states was temporarily augmented as a result of British extraterritorial jurisdiction. In the post-World War II era and following the withdrawal of foreign influence from the area, all six countries have re-installed their own independent legal systems and have generally also attempted to introduce a modern framework of written legislation influenced by each other's efforts and by the previous accomplishments of other Arab nations. Thus, prior to the formation of the GCC, the similarity of the legal systems among the Gulf states had both modern and deep historical roots.

The establishment of the GCC has clearly stimulated the further development of the legal systems of the six member states along increasingly similar lines, particularly due to the adoption by the GCC of the stated goals of the integration of the economies and the unity of the legal systems of the member states combined with the significant implementing actions taken during 1981-86. Developments so far, therefore, have aimed the process in a particular direction. But what further impact, then, is the GCC likely to have on the individual legal systems of its member states?

To consider this question perhaps it may be useful to try to identify different possible models for the future development of the legal systems of the six countries under the continuing influence of the GCC. At least five such possible models suggest themselves:

1. Evolution of the GCC to a full or partial political and legal unity (which is expressly indicated as a goal in the Charter) with some substantial sovereign legislative authority, perhaps reflecting a federal-state division of authority such as currently exists in the UAE;

2. Development of a pattern of promulgation of laws by the Supreme Council or the GCC based on committee work and draftsmanship organized by the Secretariat General and at the ministerial and special-committee level intended in general to be routinely adopted by the legislative authorities of the member states;

3. Development by or through the Secretariat General of an organized, professional capability to prepare in consultation with representatives of the member states model legislation for the consideration and possible enactment by the legislative authorities of the member states (perhaps in various modified versions);

4. Use of the constituent elements of the GCC (the Supreme Council, the Ministerial Council, the various ministerial committees and specialized subcommittees and the Secretariat General) at the various respective levels as forums for discussion, comparative analysis and recommendations with respect to the various aspects of the legal systems of the member states, whether educational, professional, legislative, administrative, judicial or constitutional;

5. Without active involvement of the GCC in the legal affairs of the member states along any of the foregoing lines, encouraging (or perhaps merely permitting) the policies and actions agreed upon by the member states within the framework of the GCC to have their necessary direct and indirect effects on the legal systems and laws of the member states.

These models, of course, are not mutually exclusive and the likelihood is that at least some elements of all five will be involved in the future developmental process.

If the GCC had been established five to ten years earlier, it might well have had a more direct and substantial impact on the future development of the laws and legal systems of the member states. It was during that period that so much of the restructuring of the legal systems and enactment of modern legislation took place. It seems unlikely that, with so much so recently accomplished by all the member states, there will be compelling support in the foreseeable future for the GCC to initiate a program that would replace or significantly revise these accomplishments. Hence, it is probable that the constitutions, the basic judicial, legislative and administrative mechanisms and the existing body of recently enacted commercial legislation will remain substantially unaffected by the GCC. Nevertheless, certainly the developmental and modernization processes will continue in the legal systems of all six countries, so the question remains as to the form of the impact that the GCC will have.

It is suggested that there are three fairly distinct legal spheres in which the GCC realistically could have a substantial and useful influence involving some aspects of all but the first of the five models described above.

First of all, based on the actions taken by the GCC during its first five years as described above, it appears that for the time being the basic influence of the GCC in spheres that most affect the legal systems of the states will continue to involve measures related to 1) creating a free-trade zone within the GCC; 2) providing equal protection from foreign competition for goods manufactured by nationals of the member states; 3) providing equal access to investment, commercial and professional opportunities for nationals of member states in all such states; 4) encouraging and organizing various joint enterprises and projects; and 5) discussion and coordination of policies. To the extent that legal factors are necessary to implement these measures, the legal systems of the member states will be affected. This interplay will undoubtedly continue as various additional measures are adopted.

Second, although much legislation required by modern, business-oriented societies has been enacted by the member states, some of the legislation requires fine-tuning based on experience, and in varying degrees in all of the six states there are still important omissions. Areas requiring attention may include commercial and banking law (especially the problems of collectibility of principal and interest); bankruptcy laws; laws and legal institutions relating to the purchase and sale of investment securities, commodities and currencies; patent, copyright and trademark name protection; arbitration law and facilities; and criminal and civil procedures. In dealing with these matters, rather than involving the GCC directly or indirectly in the promulgation and enactment of uniform laws, it is suggested that a combination of the third and fourth models described above be employed: establishment of an autonomous agency or institute associated with the GCC designed to research and draft model legislation and working in consultation with the committee structure and Secretariat of the GCC. There are a number of successful precedents for this kind of institution, including the American Law Institute in the United States, which has developed both model laws and restatements of case law that are professionally highly regarded and which have been used as a basis for, or have significantly influenced, much legislation in the United States, primarily at the state level. Taking into account the very conservative, practical and traditional instincts of the people and their leaders in the Gulf states and their strong tendency to protect authority and sovereignty at the local levels, the advantage of the suggested approach is that it provides the basis for intelligent solutions to legal problems without requiring a particular result or foreclosing local adaptation.

Third, based on the interest and importance evidenced at the various levels of the GCC relating to joint-venture public- and private-sector projects involving all six member states, it is suggested that the GCC is well-suited to consider the possible establishment, directly or indirectly, of various kinds of institutions or facilities that could be useful in the more effective development of legal systems of the member states. One important possibility, a GCC arbitration center, is already under consideration and should be encouraged because it is needed to provide a middle-ground alternative to the elaborate Western arbitration facilities largely mistrusted by the Arab governmental and business communities and the informal Chamber of Commerce or judicially supervised local arbitrations favored by the legal systems of the member states. A second possibility, a GCC-sponsored institute devoted to the research and preparation of model laws, has already been mentioned and could also include among its functions legal research, developing and making available a first-class legal library, the publication of laws and court decisions in the member states, and organizing conferences, seminars and other programs for legislators, judges and lawyers.

Two other possibly useful initiatives may be appropriate for the GCC to consider. The first would be forming a special committee of the GCC that would concern itself with assistance to the bar associations and lawyers of the member states in establishing guidelines for the organization and activities of bar associations together with the establishment of an umbrella GCC association of the leaders of the local bars. And finally, it may be useful to consider establishing in the GCC region one institution for post-graduate legal education for the most gifted graduates of the law schools of the member states with the objective of providing highest quality legal education and facilities within the Gulf region.

In any event, whatever patterns and structures evolve and are used for the interaction of the developing legal systems of the six member states with the GCC and its policies and programs, it is clear that the stage has been set for a very promising collective enterprise.

Chapter 7

THE SOVIET UNION AND THE GCC STATES: A SEARCH FOR OPENINGS

Stephen Page

Dr. Stephen Page is a visiting associate professor at Queen's University, Kingston, Canada. He is the author of The Soviet Union and the Yemen: Influence in Asymmetrical Relationships.

In the past 15 years, the six Gulf Arab countries that comprise the Gulf Cooperation Council (Saudi Arabia, Kuwait, Bahrain, Qatar, the United Arab Emirates and Oman) have been catapulted into the strategic limelight by an insatiable demand for their oil from Western Europe and Japan and, to a lesser but inevitably growing extent, the United States. Considered by most in the early 1970s to be unstable because of their traditional political systems, dynastic rivalries, and above all the pressures of rapid modernization and accretion of wealth, they appeared to be inviting targets for both domestic revolutionaries and external forces of change.

This situation has presented the leaders of the Soviet Union with difficult choices in tactics: whether to promote revolution, either directly or through proxies, to attempt to weaken the existing governments through other means, and to cooperate with forces of regional instability (in the process risking driving the conservative regimes deeper into the embrace of the United States), or to woo these "reactionaries," to persuade them to put distance between themselves and the "imperialists."

Moscow's choice between these two policy lines (or its decision to use both at once) has been determined largely by local conditions, but whatever tactics have been used, they have been intended to promote a constant set of Soviet interests in the Gulf and its surrounding region. Predominant among these was the Kremlin's perceived need to reduce

Western influence and presence in the Gulf, in particular the U.S. military presence. This need may be said to stem from both "offensive" and "defensive" considerations (although as the debate over Soviet reasons for invading Afghanistan has shown, these are so inextricably intertwined as to make distinguishing between them often an impossible task).

Foremost in the "defensive" category is the desire to prevent this contiguous region from being used as a launching platform for an attack on the USSR. This concern has applied mainly to the Northern Tier countries; however, the Gulf Arab countries' airfields and territorial waters could conceivably be used by an attacker. In addition, the Soviets consider American naval forces in the Indian Ocean (and the Diego Garcia base) to be dangerous and would like to change Gulf Arab rulers' tacit acceptance of this presence. Foremost among Moscow's "offensive" considerations is its recognition of the vital role Gulf oil plays and will continue to play in the economies of the industrialized non-communist world. The Soviets recognize that uncertainty of supply, particularly when it is linked to political questions, creates divisions and weaknesses in the Western alliance, even if that uncertainty falls far short of actual Soviet leverage over supplies. Moreover, should the Soviet Union be able to obtain some leverage or to gain concessionary rates for Arab Gulf oil, its future difficulties in supplying oil to Eastern Europe might be alleviated.

Finally, the Soviets' desire to see Western influence and presence reduced is matched by their desire to increase Soviet influence and presence. They see Southwest Asia as their "backyard," noting at the same time that it is half the world away from the United States; for them, one of the litmus tests of superpower equality (an issue on which they are extremely sensitive) is their ability to affect events in this region. In the Arab Gulf this would mean military equality with the West and a wide range of Soviet personnel on the ground dealing freely with the governments; as a first step Moscow wants to establish economic and diplomatic relations with them. Equality of influence here would necessarily entail a significant reduction in American and Western impact, with substantial results for superpower relations in other parts of the Third World.

SOVIET RELATIONS WITH THE GULF STATES PRIOR TO 1979

Gains have not come easily to the Soviets in the states now making up the Gulf Cooperation Council (GCC), and those that have occurred have mostly been the result of events beyond their control or outside the GCC sub-region. On the whole they have been negative gains; that is, they have reduced Western influence without increasing Soviet influence appreciably. One such gain was the withdrawal of Britain from the Gulf in 1971. This left the principalities, including a barely-formed federation, in an apparent security vacuum, and Moscow with options. It had established relations with Kuwait in 1962 and could use its "good-neighborly ties" to encourage the new Gulf states to develop relations. Or it could encourage radical forces (Iraq, the Arab Nationalist Movement, the People's Democratic Republic of Yemen) which opposed the traditional Arabian Gulf governments. In fact it tried to do both. It recognized the new states, but Saudi pressure apparently convinced them not to proceed with diplomatic relations. At the same time, Moscow was improving its ties to Iraq and the PDRY, two radical states which supported the activities of revolutionary groups in the Gulf, including the Popular Front for the Liberation of the Occupied Arab Gulf, which was waging a guerrilla war in the Dhofar province of Oman in the early 1970s.

Although Moscow's support for this war was limited and never official,[1] it aroused the fear and hostility of the Gulf Arab countries (especially Saudi Arabia), which saw the Dhofar war and Soviet friendship with Iraq, the PDRY and the Yemen Arab Republic as an encircling movement. Soviet involvement also entangled it in the web of broader regional politics, as Iraq made increasing claims on territory belonging to Kuwait and the shah of Iran (whom Moscow did not want to antagonize) moved to compete with Iraq for predominance in the Gulf. Nor was there any sign in the Gulf Arab states that revolution would be successful in the foreseeable future.

However, by 1974 the Soviets perceived a new opportunity for state-to-state relations as the Arab-Israeli conflict spread to the Gulf. When the Organization of Arab Petroleum Exporting Countries (OAPEC) initiated an oil embargo against the West as a result of the U.S. airlift of military aid to Israel during the October war in 1973, Moscow took advantage of the anti-Western mood in the Arab world by applauding the embargo vigorously and reminding the Gulf Arabs of its support of Arab causes; if they truly wished to defeat Israel, the propaganda campaign went, they should reject the United States (Israel's main military and financial supplier) and turn to the USSR.

Once again, however, local conditions negated Soviet efforts. The phenomenal rise in oil revenues in the middle and late 1970s enabled the Gulf Arab states to use economic aid to moderate and deflect local and Arab criticism of their continued conservatism and ties with the West. Moreover, even the widespread distrust and anger at U.S. poli-

---

[1]Stephen Page, *The Soviet Union and the Yemens: Influence in Asymmetrical Relationships* (New York: Praeger, 1985), pp. 125-35.

147

cies in the Middle East could not make the Soviet Union more attractive. To the longstanding ties between Gulf elites and the West, to ideological and religious distaste for communism, and to distrust of the Soviets for their support of revolutionaries, was added the inability of the USSR to provide the high technology and consumer goods wanted by these newly wealthy and rapidly developing societies and the fact that the Soviets did not have a commercial need for Gulf oil.

Thus in the 1970s no other Gulf Arab state followed Kuwait's urgings to establish relations with Moscow, recognizing that although Kuwait had special needs for these ties, the others did not. Kuwait's striving for true nonalignment was (and continues to be) based not only on its distrust of Washington's Middle East policies due to the close ties between the United States and Israel; it also feared the consequences of anger within its substantial Palestinian minority. More important, its precarious situation in the region, with stronger and ambitious countries on all its borders, forces Kuwait to seek its security from a variety of sources, including the Soviet Union and the West. In both the early 1960s and early 1970s the main threat came from Iraq, and Kuwait tried (with some success in 1973) to use its relations with the USSR to moderate Iraq's behavior. In late 1975 Kuwait further emphasized its nonaligned posture by endorsing nonintervention in the Gulf and buying Soviet weapons.

Saudi Arabia and Iran used their increased oil revenues to oppose actively Soviet objectives in the region, turning to the United States for help in building up their security and defense forces. The shah came to the aid of the sultan of Oman, and Iranian forces helped to end the Dhofari rebellion by 1976. Saudi Arabia also provided monetary aid to the sultan to allow him to enact economic and social policies which promised to preserve and improve his leadership of the sultanate. Elsewhere on the Arabian peninsula, Riyadh used its oil money to exert influence on North Yemen and to begin to tie it into an arms-supply relationship with the United States. More ominously for the Soviets, in 1976 the Saudis exchanged diplomatic recognition with South Yemen and appeared to be making a bid to wean it from its Soviet patron.[2] In addition, Riyadh was promoting the idea of a Red Sea security pact aimed at containing Ethiopia and excluding the USSR.

However, Saudi interest in these ventures declined abruptly in the late 1970s. The Soviet intervention in Ethiopia in November 1977 (including an impressive lift of materiel and Cuban troops) and American inactivity (especially when combined with earlier statements in the United States about intervening in the Gulf in the event of a "strangling"

---

[2]Ibid., pp. 57, 60, 171, 173-74.

oil embargo, mutterings which Soviet propaganda used to good effect) made the Saudi leadership reluctant to try actively to counter Soviet moves. Moreover, Riyadh's difficulties in obtaining advanced U.S. weapons (the F-15s, and later bomb racks and auxiliary fuel tanks for them, and the AWACS), due to congressional opposition fortified by the pro-Israel lobby, left the Saudis suspicious of Washington's reliability and unwillingness to take risks to protect American interests. Finally, the July 1978 coup in Aden removed any vestiges of Saudi influence in South Yemen and seemed to solidify Soviet positions at the south end of the Red Sea, while Riyadh's inability to affect the outcome of the brief border conflict between the Yemens in March 1979 served to make the Saudis even more cautious about challenging Soviet interests.[3]

IRAN, AFGHANISTAN AND THE "CARTER DOCTRINE"; 1979 INITIATES SIGNIFICANT CHANGE

The events of 1979 seemed to mark a watershed in Soviet fortunes in the Gulf. It began with the collapse of the "pillar" of American policy in the region and ended with Soviet troops imposing themselves potentially within striking distance of the Strait of Hormuz, a choke-point in the West's oil lifeline. In between, Moscow seemed to make gains in the Yemens and on the Arab-Israeli front which would improve its prospects in the Gulf.

The fall of the shah was a disaster for U.S. regional interests for it removed an ally whose protection was on the whole acceptable to the smaller Gulf states. The only other realistic alternative at the time was a security arrangement openly connected to the United States, and Gulf rulers (with the exception of the sultan of Oman) saw this cure as more dangerous than the disease. Gulf rulers were disturbed by the tendency of American politicians to think in terms of military solutions but also, paradoxically, by the failure of the United States to intervene to save the shah. The Islamic fundamentalism unleashed by the revolution seemed likely to cause considerable difficulties for the modernizing, pro-Western rulers, if indeed it did not overwhelm them. For the United States, the spread of Islamic fundamentalism would entail disruptions in oil supplies and an increased determination among Gulf Arabs to challenge U.S. support for Israel.

The United States and Soviet Union have a zero-sum approach to Third World situations. Moscow, knowing that Washington's positions in the Gulf had been badly shaken by the overthrow of the shah and the

---

[3]Ibid., pp. 184-85.

victory of the Ayatollah Khomeini, moved to enhance its own positions. The Soviets had coexisted quite comfortably with the shah. Now they scrambled to excoriate him while praising the "progressive nature" of the Ayatollah Khomeini. Taking credit for the reluctance of the United States to intervene, they offered their friendship to the Islamic Republic. At the same time, the Tudeh party (Iran's pro-Moscow Communist party) quickly expressed its support of both the revolution and the Ayatollah.

On the other hand the Soviet leaders were aware that a too-enthusiastic embrace would endanger other Soviet interests in the Gulf region. In particular, Iraq was very sensitive to real or imagined shifts in Soviet relations with Iran. Baghdad's longstanding hostility toward Iran was reawakened by the danger of Iranian-sponsored Shiite opposition in Iraq; at the same time Iraqi aspirations to greater regional influence were whetted by the apparent collapse of the Iranian armed forces and by the leading role which Saddam Hussein took in the anti-Camp David movement. This involved a rapprochement with Saudi Arabia and the probability that this would accentuate Baghdad's edging away from Moscow, noticeable since 1978.

The Soviets also recognized the Gulf Arab rulers' fear that events in Iran could spill over into the rest of the Gulf and were concerned lest closer Soviet-Iranian ties encourage increased anti-Soviet sentiment and closer U.S.-Arab Gulf relations despite the growing reluctance of the Gulf states to rely on the United States as an ally. Thus, in January 1979, a Soviet foreign ministry official was sent to Kuwait to reassure that government and the others in the Gulf about Soviet friendship and nonculpability for events in Iran.[4] Earlier, Leonid Brezhnev reportedly sent two messages to Riyadh expressing a desire to reestablish diplomatic ties. For several months the Soviet media published articles flattering to Saudi Arabia (although not uncritical), repeating that call.[5] Riyadh was angry at the Camp David accords, at the failure of the United States to fulfill defense equipment sales commitments to the kingdom and at U.S. suggestions for a Gulf security agreement which would allow American forces access to military facilities. The Saudis seemed to be responding to the Soviets; Foreign Minister Saud al-Faisal acknowledged the "positive stands adopted by the Soviet Union toward

---

[4]*As-Siyasah*, Jan. 31, 1979, in Foreign Broadcast Information Service, *Daily Report: Middle East* (hereafter cited as FBIS:ME), Feb. 2, p. C4.

[5]Agence France Presse, Dec. 30, 1978, in Foreign Broadcast Information Service, *Daily Report: USSR* (hereafter cited as FBIS:USSR), Jan. 3, 1979, pp. F11-12; *Literaturnaia Gazeta*, Jan. 31, 1979; *Za Rubezhom*, No. 21, 1979, in FBIS:USSR, May 31, 1979, p. H3; E. Primakov, *Beirut Monday Morning*, in FBIS:USSR, July 6, 1979, pp. 1-10.

Arab causes" and stated that Saudi Arabia recognized the USSR and its importance in international affairs.[6]

Nevertheless, even if Riyadh was seriously considering developing relations with the Soviets, events in the region forestalled the move. As Moscow was making its diplomatic advances, conflict broke out on the border between the two Yemens; South Yemen demonstrated its superiority, and the Saudis were unable to affect the outcome. This was clearly not the time to open the door to the Soviets. Moreover, in the summer of 1979 the Soviets signed a large arms deal with North Yemen, encouraging it in its aspirations to greater flexibility vis-à-vis Riyadh. In October 1979 South Yemen and the USSR signed a 20-year Treaty of Friendship and Cooperation. Coming on the heels of the Yemeni unity agreement which had been signed in Kuwait at the end of March, these moves must have been seen in Saudi Arabia not simply as guaranteeing Soviet positions in the southwest corner of the Arabian peninsula; rather, they must have looked like the deliberate application of Soviet pressure, or even as potential steps toward a Soviet client state which would be a potent force on the peninsula. These concerns were compounded in November by the seizure of the Grand Mosque in Mecca by religious fanatics.

Iranian-inspired disturbances in Bahrain and Kuwait in September 1979 finally convinced the Gulf Arab states to begin discussions on security cooperation; the need was underlined by Shiite disturbances in eastern Saudi Arabia in November. Interestingly, the Soviets barely commented. While theoretically the Soviet Union stands to benefit from unrest in the Gulf Arab states, by the end of 1979 Moscow must in fact have been wary of unrest inspired by Iran or Islamic fundamentalists. Iran, although satisfactorily anti-American, was showing no signs of responding to Soviet courtship. Meanwhile, Islamic fundamentalists in Afghanistan were threatening the existence of the Soviet puppet regime there, and preparations for the Soviet invasion were underway. The Soviets, of course, believed that successful revolutions in the Arab states would be another staggering blow to the United States and the West. However, unsuccessful efforts would push the governments into security measures (as they did) and into closer ties with the United States, which was already seeking access to military facilities in the region and bolstering its Indian Ocean naval presence. Premature Soviet public support for unsuccessful uprisings or for national liberation movements with no chance of success would only compound the problem.

---

[6]*Al-Hawadith*, Mar. 3, 1979, in FBIS:ME, March 5, p. C1. However, this was not the first such Saudi comment: cf. King Khalid's comment to the *Sunday Times*, quoted in FBIS:USSR, July 10, 1975, pp. F3-4.

Moscow had been somewhat insensitive to this fact at the beginning of 1979. A delegation representing the Popular Front for the Liberation of Oman (PFLO) arrived in Moscow in April for an "unofficial" but highly publicized visit. PFLO was by this time defunct as a fighting force, but with Iranian troops having been just withdrawn from Dhofar, the Soviets may have been trying to intimidate Sultan Qaboos to prevent him from increasing security cooperation with the United States. If this was their intent, the resurrection of the PFLO was counterproductive. Qaboos began to emphasize the communist threat and requested arms aid from Washington. He also began to urge the Americans to play a more active role in the region and in the late summer proposed to the other Arab Gulf states a security arrangement for navigation in the Strait of Hormuz which would have been linked to U.S. naval support.

Moscow reacted with bitter criticism of this proposal. However, when it saw that the other Gulf states were rejecting the Omani plan, it played up the differences, singling out Kuwait for its avowals of friendship with the Soviet Union and its rejection of U.S. military involvement in the Gulf.[7] Except for their personal attacks on Qaboos, the Soviets couched their propaganda in terms of the danger to the Gulf Arab states of increased U.S. Navy forces in the Indian Ocean and of reported American plans to create a rapid-deployment force to defend the oil fields. They reminded the Gulf Arabs about past American musings on occupying the oil fields and about the leading role the United States had played in the Camp David agreement and the Egypt-Israel peace treaty, both overwhelmingly unpopular in the Arab world. Occasionally, there were also hints that, because of its own vital security interests, the USSR would match increased U.S. military involvement, thereby dragging the Gulf into superpower confrontations.[8]

Hints such as these took on added significance at the end of 1979, when Soviet troops invaded Afghanistan, installed a new government and set out to crush Islamic fundamentalist and nationalist resistance. All of the Gulf states initially reacted with outrage and worry. All voted in the U.N. General Assembly to condemn the USSR's action. Saudi Arabia led the Islamic Conference Organization's condemnation, and Saudi Foreign Minister Saud al-Faisal seemed to be advocating an anti-Soviet struggle in his speech to that organization's foreign ministers:

> In the past, we expressed our appreciation for the Soviet Union's stand on the Palestinian issue. We hope that its stand and behavior in Afghanistan will not confront the Arab states in particular and the Islamic states

[7]*Literaturnaia Gazeta*, June 10, 1979, in FBIS:USSR, July 6, pp. H10-11; Moscow radio, June 29, 1979, in FBIS:USSR, July 2, p. H1.

[8]TASS, June 4, 1979, in FBIS:USSR, June 5, p. A2.

in general with the difficult choice—either to be subservient to it, obeying its desire, or to stand up against it and work to oppose it.[9]

However, prior to this, then-Crown Prince Fahd had struck a more realistic note about Saudi capabilities, and at the Islamic Conference meeting Kuwait's foreign minister took a more balanced position (though not one very much appreciated by Moscow), demanding the withdrawal of both the Israelis from occupied Arab territories and the Soviets from Afghanistan.[10] In mid-year Saud al-Faisal added an incentive, declaring that Saudi Arabia would consider establishing relations with the USSR should it pull out its forces.[11]

Recognizing these as encouraging signs, Moscow set out to limit the damage to its image by unleashing a blizzard of propaganda. Although it began with a crude equation of anti-Sovietism with pro-Zionism,[12] on the whole this campaign avoided direct attacks except in response to a direct criticism. It focused on two themes: that there was no contradiction between communism and Islam and (more successfully) that the Americans were using the USSR's "fraternal assistance" to Afghanistan as a pretext to build up their military presence and impose their will on the Gulf. It was the United States (so the message went) that, half the world away, had declared the Gulf to be "vital" to it and had long wished to control the Gulf's oil resources; the USSR had no need of the oil and had never sought to dominate the Gulf.[13] This was by no means a new message, but as before it struck a responsive chord in almost all the Gulf Arab countries, most particularly in Kuwait, where spokesmen on several occasions stated that the Soviet Union posed no threat to the Gulf.

The Soviets also attempted to deny the idea that the Gulf was an area of vital interest to the United States by calling for an all-European agreement on the "security of oil communications and equal commercial access to oil sources of the Persian Gulf region." In hindsight this must have been too redolent of the "superpower condominium" approach, and within a few days it had been changed to an "international conference on the Indian Ocean to guarantee supply lines."[14] However, even

[9]Saudi News Agency, Jan. 27, 1980, in FBIS:ME, Jan. 28, pp. A14-16.

[10]Qatar News Agency, Jan. 26, 1980, in FBIS:ME, Jan. 28, pp. C5-6; *Ar-Ray al-Amm* (Kuwait), Jan. 23, 1980, in FBIS:ME, Jan. 24, p. C3.

[11]Interview in *Beirut Monday Morning*, July 21-27, 1980, in FBIS:ME, July 28, p. C4.

[12]*Izvestia*, Jan. 26, 1980.

[13]*Pravda*, Feb. 2, 1980; Moscow radio in Arabic, Feb. 1, 1980, in FBIS:USSR, Feb. 4, p. H3.

[14]N. Portugalov, TASS, Feb. 29, 1980, in FBIS:USSR, Mar. 3, pp. G1-2; Moscow radio in English, Mar. 5, 1980, in FBIS:USSR, Mar. 10, pp. A5-6.

in this watered-down version the idea gained no support, and it sank from sight.

Never mentioned in Soviet propaganda, but weighing heavily on the minds of Gulf rulers, was the dramatic increase in the USSR's shadow of power by the spring of 1980. Over the previous three years the Soviets had strengthened their positions on the fringes of the Gulf, in Ethiopia, Afghanistan and South Yemen (although they had lost influence in Baghdad, as the Iraqi government began to look to the West for weapons and high technology). They had demonstrated their vastly improved capability to lift troops and equipment, not simply on relatively short hauls into Afghanistan but (more importantly to the Gulf) over longer distances. To these facts were added the overwhelming imbalance of Soviet forces over any others in southwest Asia and strategic parity with the United States, which many thought had paralyzed the reactive capabilities of Washington, still struggling with its post-Vietnam syndrome. Now Soviet forces were in Afghanistan, potentially a bare 350 miles from the Strait of Hormuz.[15] A prudent leader of a small state in a volatile region might well decide that accommodation with the Soviet Union would be the most effective guarantee of his government's security.

Gulf rulers (except Sultan Qaboos) did seem to be moving along this path, at least in their public statements. Not that they endorsed Soviet policies; they did not. However, they did adopt a declaratory policy that Gulf security was the responsibility of the Gulf states alone. Should this be rigorously applied, American forces would be excluded from the region, while Soviet forces (even after a withdrawal from Afghanistan) would be positioned on its edges. In view of the Gulf Arab states' military inferiority in relation to Iraq and Iran, of the reappearance of hostility between those two in early 1980 and of the potential for instability aroused by Iran's ideological proselytizing of Shiite minorities across the Gulf, this policy must have been seen in Moscow as a prescription for the continued weakness of the Gulf Arab states.

Nevertheless, any Soviet comfort from these developments was marred by countertendencies which it could not control and by its own actions, most notably, of course, its brutal behavior in Afghanistan. Iraq's adoption of the call for superpower disengagement from the Gulf, embodied in Saddam Hussein's Pan-Arab Charter in February 1980, did not bode well for a strong Soviet influence in Iraq. The broadcast by Radio Peace

---

[15]Keith Dunn has outlined the difficulties the Soviets would face in an attack toward the Gulf. Cf. Keith Dunn, "Soviet Strategy, Opportunities and Constraints in Southwestern Asia," *Soviet Union/Union Sovietique*, Vol. 11, Part 2 (1984), pp. 200-205. He also points out that existing airbases in Afghanistan are much farther away than 350 miles, at the outside edges of Soviet fighter operating ranges.

and Progress of a long piece praising the tiny and ineffectual Bahrain National Liberation Front in its struggle against "the Bahraini ruling clique"[16] would not have reassured other Gulf rulers. However, the most difficult development for the achievement of Soviet goals in the region was the resurgence of American resolve, exemplified by the Carter Doctrine, the U.S. naval buildup in the Indian Ocean and Gulf of Oman and the determination to proceed quickly with the establishment of the rapid-deployment force (RDF). All the rulers balked at basing the RDF or admitting they would cooperate in the venture even to the extent of allowing the United States to pre-position equipment. However, Oman did sign an agreement with Washington to allow U.S. forces access (although not automatic access) to the Masirah Island airfield and a number of other Omani military facilities in return for substantial military and economic aid. Although the other Gulf rulers publicly disapproved of this deal (especially after U.S. forces made unauthorized use of Masirah during the disastrous attempt to free the American hostages in Tehran in April 1980, a gaffe which the Soviets publicized effectively), they doubtless were not completely unhappy at a strong U.S. presence; not too visible, but not too far away.

These feelings were, if anything, made more acute by the Iraqi attack on Iran in September 1980. This fighting appeared to constitute a profound threat to the Gulf Arab countries no matter what its outcome or their stance toward it. They were forced along two paths. The first was closer cooperation among themselves in internal security and military matters. Desultory discussions picked up momentum in the fall and were given added impetus in November after Iranian planes fired missiles at two frontier posts in Kuwait. The attack underlined their vulnerability, as well as the need for more sophisticated air defense systems; Saudi Arabia's earlier request for four AWACS aircraft with American aircrew and technicians was vindicated, as was the second path: closer military ties to the West.

Moscow was understandably upset. It had not been consulted by Iraq, yet it was expected to support its erstwhile ally and incur even more hostility from Iran (a country which on most accounts was more important to it than Iraq). Yet, even if it followed this course it could have greater difficulty making inroads in the Gulf. As it happened, the Soviets compounded the problem by clearly tilting toward Iran in the early stages of the war. Nor would the Gulf rulers have appreciated Brezhnev's greetings in October to a conference supporting the national liberation movements of the Gulf. Faced with the collapse of its regional

---

[16]Radio Peace and Progress in Arabic, Feb. 16, 1980, in FBIS:USSR, Feb. 20, p. H9.

policies, Moscow reverted to a traditional Soviet tactic: the broad peace initiative. On December 10, while on a state visit to India, Brezhnev proposed an international agreement:

1. Not to create foreign military bases in the Arabian Gulf or on adjacent islands; not to deploy nuclear weapons of mass destruction there;
2. Not to use force or threaten the use of force against Arabian Gulf countries, and not to interfere in their internal affairs;
3. To respect the nonaligned status chosen by the Arabian Gulf states; not to draw them into military groupings to which nuclear powers are party;
4. To respect the sovereign right of the states of this region to their natural resources; and
5. Not to create any obstacles or threats to normal trade and the use of sea-lanes linking the states of this region with other countries of the world.[17]

The proposal met with mixed reviews in the Gulf. Only the national liberation movements, not a significant factor in Gulf politics, endorsed it. Kuwait gave it lukewarm approval, while Saudi Arabia and Oman rejected it for completely ignoring the presence of Soviet bases in South Yemen and Ethiopia and troops in Afghanistan. All the Gulf states recognized that it was an implied claim to a role in Gulf security and energy supply questions, a further indication that the superpower competition was spreading to the region. More voices within the Gulf expressed the desire for greater cooperation among the six countries.

THE GULF COOPERATION COUNCIL IS FORMED, A NEW ERA BEGINS

This movement came to fruition in February 1981 when the Gulf Arab foreign ministers agreed to the establishment of the Gulf Cooperation Council (GCC). To deflect criticism from radical and leftist circles, the participants stressed the economic, technical and cultural aspects of cooperation. However, all the GCC members were clearly preoccupied with defense and internal security. The Iran-Iraq war raged on; the Gulf Arab states were openly and materially siding with Iraq, and no one knew how Iran would respond. Oman, still pressing for a Hormuz security arrangement, was moving into a closer relationship with the United States; joint military exercises in communications were to be held in March, on Omani territory for the first time. Tension between Oman and the PDRY was rising as a result.

---

[17]*Current Digest of the Soviet Press*, Vol. 32, No. 50 (Jan. 14, 1981), p. 6.

Moscow's response to the GCC discussions was multifaceted and somewhat effective but also at times counterproductive. There were occasional harsh attacks on the idea;[18] but for the most part the Soviets muted their criticisms, in order not to play into the hands of those wanting closer military cooperation between the GCC and the West. They continued their campaign against the U.S. military buildup in the region and their Arabian Gulf proposals, which Brezhnev reiterated during the 26th Congress of the Communist Party of the Soviet Union in February.[19] (The publicity given to Gulf national liberation movements' support of the Arabian Gulf proposals and the high profile accorded to the delegate from the Bahrain NLF at the Congress were indicative of the Soviets' unhappiness at the Gulf Arab rulers' stance; on the other hand, the lack of publicity for the PFLO, even though the U.S.-Omani exercises took place during the Congress, demonstrated that they recognized the pitfalls in pushing the sultan too hard.)

Moscow also took heart from expressions of Gulf unhappiness over American policy in the Gulf and Middle East and from Saudi Arabia's anger over the bruising battle in the U.S. Congress over the sale of AWACS aircraft and F-15 enhancements. At the same time, Moscow saw these purchases as a setback, possibly a step toward official U.S.-Saudi military links and pre-positioning for the RDF. However, again Soviet criticism was muted, and they concentrated on their assets, mainly Kuwait's overriding belief that its interests can only be protected by nonalignment and the exclusion of the superpowers from the Gulf. Kuwait's Foreign Minister Sheikh Sabah al Ahmad al Jaber al Sabah visited Moscow at the end of April 1981 for talks with Andrei Gromyko. Although both sides agreed that the Gulf states should be responsible for their own security and that foreign military bases should be excluded from the region, the talks were not a complete success. Sheikh Sabah did endorse Brezhnev's Middle East peace proposals; moreover, the mere fact of his visit demonstrated the lack of unity of the conservative Arab opposition to Soviet moves in Afghanistan and was an effective counterpoint to Alexander Haig's just-completed tour of the Middle East seeking a "strategic consensus" against the Soviet Union. However, the wording of the communique ("detailed exchange of opinions," "the proximity of the sides' views"[20]) indicated considerable disagree-

---

[18]TASS in English, Dec. 31, 1980, in FBIS:USSR, Jan. 2, 1981, p. CC7; V. Peresada, "On a Dangerous Course," *Pravda*, Feb. 10, 1981, in FBIS:USSR, Feb. 13, pp. H1-2.

[19]Brezhnev's arresting, although ultimately insubstantial offer in his Congress address to link the Afghanistan question with Gulf security was also an attempt to disarm Gulf resistance to the USSR.

[20]FBIS:USSR, Apr. 29, 1981, pp. H3-5.

ment. The Kuwaiti foreign minister did not endorse Brezhnev's Gulf proposals, expressed opposition to the Soviet occupation of Afghanistan and urged Moscow to pressure the PDRY to come to terms with Oman. He also argued that the GCC was not aimed at the Soviet Union or any other country. Gromyko demurred, pointing to Oman's agreement with the United States on access to its military facilities. Sabah then argued that if the PDRY lowered tensions with Oman, Oman could be persuaded to abrogate its agreement with Washington.[21] The Soviets did not believe this (nor did Sultan Qaboos give them reason to) but implied that they might apply pressure to the PDRY if the GCC states established relations with the USSR.[22]

The GCC states remained unconvinced. The Soviet case was not helped by an interview given by Leonid Zamiatin (chief of the CPSU Central Committee's International Information Department) to the Kuwaiti paper *As-Siyasah*, in which he advocated a conference on Gulf security with places for both the Soviet Union and the United States; this was seen by many as a return to the "superpower condominium" idea.[23] Nor was a Soviet naval visit to Aden (unusual for the publicity accompanying it) during the GCC's founding summit meeting appreciated. Nevertheless, the visit (which may have been at the insistence of the PDRY) did not prevent the GCC from again rejecting the Omani call for coordinated military planning with the United States. Apparently encouraged, the Soviets were rumored to be pursuing relations with Saudi Arabia and the UAE.[24] The latter, toward which the Soviets had made commercial overtures in March, appeared to be more receptive; Sheikh Zayed Al-Nahayan, the president of the UAE, referred on one occasion to the entry of Soviet forces into Afghanistan "at the official invitation" of the country's government.[25]

Nevertheless, if there had been any prospects for relations, they were dissipated by events in the second half of 1981. More Iranian air attacks on Kuwait in June and October made that country more interested in a Gulf air defense plan; the approval of the AWACS purchase made it likely that those aircraft would form the basis for any plan. The signing of the Tripartite Alliance (South Yemen, Ethiopia and Libya) in August,

[21]*Al-Hadaf* (Kuwait), May 7, 1981, in FBIS:ME, May 13, p. C6.
[22]This was reported by Saud al-Faisal in an interview with *Ukaz*, May 26, 1981, cited in A. Yodfat, *The Soviet Union and the Arabian Peninsula* (New York: St. Martin's Press, 1983), p. 137.
[23]FBIS:USSR, May 13, 1981, p. H7.
[24]*As-Siyasah*, June 4, 1981, and Qatar News Agency, June 8, 1981, in FBIS:ME, June 8, pp. C1-2.
[25]Gulf News Agency, June 8, 1981, in FBIS:ME, June 9, p. C5.

with the reported collusion of the Soviets,[26] again aroused the concern of Oman and Saudi Arabia and may have led to pressure on Kuwait not to go ahead with its intended purchase of Soviet air-defense weapons.[27] Moscow attempted to recoup by supporting Crown Prince Fahd's Middle East peace plan but was undermined by Syria's rejection of it and by Soviet criticism of the AWACS purchase and Saudi oil-pricing policies.[28] There was a brief flurry of excitement in the Soviet media as Moscow radio reported that the Saudi foreign minister had endorsed the idea of an international conference, with the participation of the Soviet Union, as the best way to safeguard permanent peace in the Middle East.[29] Shortly thereafter, the same source reported that the GCC members had offered large-scale aid to Oman if it abrogated its facilities agreement with the United States.[30]

However, Gulf attention was abruptly switched away from foreign affairs issues to internal security by a foiled coup in Bahrain in December, reported to be only one of a series in the Gulf planned by Iran.[31] In its wake, Saudi Arabia quickly signed bilateral security agreements with the other GCC members (except Kuwait), and the first public call came (from Bahrain's interior minister) for a GCC rapid-deployment force which would be capable of helping Gulf states to deal with internal unrest.

Acceptance of this proposal and of the idea of creating an early warning system based on the AWACS gained momentum, especially after the Gulf war changed course with Iran's invasion of Iraq in July 1982. There was little Moscow could do initially to halt the GCC's slide into closer ties with the United States except continue its existing policies. The Soviets raged against American plans to intervene in the Gulf; they focused on the visit of U.S. Defense Secretary Caspar Weinberger, who was said to be trying to use Saudi Arabia and Oman to turn the GCC into a "closed military bloc" (i.e., excluding the USSR) serving the interests of American imperialism.[32] Oman was subjected

---

[26]Cf. Michael C. Dunn, "Soviet Interests in the Arabian Peninsula: The Aden Pact and Other Paper Tigers," *American Arab Affairs*, No. 8 (Spring 1984), pp. 92-98.

[27]A Kuwaiti military delegation was to visit the Soviet Union in September to shop for weapons after Kuwait turned down a U.S. offer to sell ground-to-air missiles; it did not.

[28]*Pravda*, Sept. 6, 1981, in FBIS:USSR, Sept. 16, pp. CC6-7; Radio Peace and Progress, Oct. 30, 1981, in FBIS:USSR, Nov. 12, pp. H1-2.

[29]Moscow radio in Arabic, Nov. 5 & 6, 1981, in FBIS:USSR, Nov. 6, p. H1.

[30]Moscow radio in Arabic, Dec. 3, 1981, in FBIS:USSR, Dec. 4, p. H1.

[31]WAKH (Manama), Dec. 13 & 16, 1981, in FBIS:ME, Dec. 14, p. C1, and Dec. 16, p. C1. Doubt was cast on the extent of the conspiracy by Eric Rouleau in *Le Monde*, Apr. 4, 1982.

[32]Radio Peace and Progress in Arabic, Feb. 10, 1982, in FBIS:USSR, Feb. 11, p. H1.

to particularly strong Soviet media attacks despite (or perhaps because of) its agreement to negotiate an end to hostile relations with the PDRY. In this negative mode, however, Moscow used Radio Peace and Progress, an "unofficial" Soviet station. This practice (more noticeable with regard to the Gulf after the formation of the GCC) gave Moscow official deniability, while allowing it to quote national liberation movements or to attack Saudi Arabia for supporting the Afghan *mujaheddin*.

The positive side of Soviet policy continued as well. The Bahrain coup attempt was given little publicity in the Soviet media, as was Bahrain's decision to buy U.S. fighter aircraft. Soviet spokesmen made periodic attempts to convince Saudi Arabia and other Gulf states that it would be advantageous to establish relations. The modest commercial initiatives of the USSR and East European countries continued. To these various moves the response was as before: Kuwait supported them, Oman decried them and the others made a few encouraging sounds, most likely with an eye to keeping Moscow and Washington off balance. (The UAE interior minister did go to Moscow for a private visit for medical treatment. Even if no official contacts took place, this was an indication that normal relations were not out of the question.)

These Soviet tactics were a holding action such as Moscow has been forced to conduct much of the time in this region. However, as before, regional events allowed the Soviets to make a little headway. Israel's invasion of Lebanon in June and the siege of West Beirut caused an outburst of anti-American outrage in the Gulf. Nevertheless, Moscow was hampered in its propaganda by the widespread criticism it received for its failure to intervene on behalf of the Palestinians and for the poor performance of its weapons in Syrian hands. Frustrated, the Soviets lost some ground by lashing out at Arab countries for their disunity and the oil states in particular for their refusal to use their oil weapon.

In addition, in the spring of 1982 the Soviet Union was being accused by the GCC (led by the Saudis) of throwing its "full weight" behind Iran after that country had moved onto the offensive against Iraq.[33] However, Iran had shown no sign of allying itself to the Soviet Union, and Moscow had every interest in preventing a clear-cut Iranian victory which might bring the United States into the Gulf by consent. Thus, to the relief of the Gulf Arab states the Soviet Union resumed sales of weapons (halted shortly after the war began) to Iraq.

The improvement in relations between Oman and the PDRY, which led to their normalization agreement in October 1982, also improved Soviet prospects in the Gulf, although Oman had not been obliged to

---

[33]KUNA, May 15, 1982, in FBIS:ME, May 17, p. C5; Radio Monte Carlo, May 30, 1982, in FBIS:ME, June 1, pp. C1-2.

reduce its close ties with the United States. The available evidence suggests that Moscow was not consulted by Aden and did not approve.[34] Nevertheless, the favorable fallout in the Gulf from the PDRY-Oman deal and a subsequent friendly PDRY-Saudi meeting did enhance Moscow's acceptability among the Gulf states. The Soviets tried to take advantage with a minor overture to both Qatar (for the first time) and Saudi Arabia and a major attack on U.S. activities in the Indian Ocean.

The Andropov months (November 1982 to February 1984) seemed to involve less public attention and on the whole a tougher approach toward the GCC countries. The Saudi foreign minister visited Moscow in December as part of an Arab League delegation (the first Saudi official visitor since 1932), and his talk with Gromyko was said in Arab reports to be cordial, "concerning possible restoration of relations . . . in the near future."[35] However, the Soviet media made no attempt to capitalize on it. In April King Fahd made an unprecedented appeal to Andropov to exert his efforts to help in ending the Iran-Iraq war; again the Soviets barely responded. At the same time, on several occasions during Andropov's brief tenure, several propaganda attempts were made to undermine Saudi Arabia. Soviet propaganda was completely counterproductive to the apparent Soviet desire to establish good relations with Riyadh. Its appearance in *Pravda* February 24, 1983, therefore, is a mystery, perhaps even relating to the succession maneuverings in Moscow.[36]

Soviet inattention was largely due to the paralysis engendered by Andropov's health and by other much greater concerns in domestic and foreign policy. The tougher line may have been a spillover from the Soviets' sense that they were on the defensive in the Middle East, what with a stalemate in the Gulf war (for which Kuwait's foreign minister blamed both the United States and the Soviet Union[37]), the arrest of the Tudeh leaders and expulsion of Soviet diplomats from Tehran, the Soviet Union's inability to control Syria in its attempt to undermine PLO Fatah leader Yassir Arafat and the stationing of U.S. and other Western forces in Lebanon. Add to these the continuing apparent close linkage between the United States and a much enhanced GCC defense through AWACS, arms sales to Saudi Arabia and the facilities agreement with Oman (which the GCC apparently was no longer trying to cancel[38]). It was small wonder that Moscow appeared to downgrade its interest in improving relations with GCC countries. (However, the

---

[34]Stephen Page, pp. 146-47.
[35]KUNA, Dec. 3, 1982, in FBIS:ME, Dec. 6, p. H3.
[36]*Yearbook on International Communist Affairs 1983*, p. 40.
[37]KUNA, Jan. 3, 1983, in FBIS:ME, Jan. 7, pp. C2-3.
[38]Radio Monte Carlo in Arabic, Aug. 24, 1983, in FBIS:ME, Aug. 25, p. C1.

Omanis revealed in 1985 that it was during Andropov's time that the contacts began which culminated in the establishment of relations between Oman and the Soviet Union.)[39]

Following Andropov's death in February 1984, regional events during Konstantin Chernenko's year in office once again encouraged the Soviets to pay more attention to the Gulf, although the state of his health and the continuing succession struggle in the Kremlin militated against major initiatives. At the same time (perhaps partly due to this lack of activism) the GCC grew less wary of the idea of relations with the USSR.

The U.S. commitment of Marines to Beirut from September 1982 until February 1984, evidence of "a starkly bipolar [interpretation of] Lebanon's complex political realities" and an "exaggerated belief in the efficacy of military force,"[40] was seen in the Gulf as a policy supporting Israeli aggression. This had aroused further concern as to Washington's ability to respond appropriately to Gulf needs. Paradoxically, Gulf leaders also worried that the forced withdrawal of the Marines was yet another example of Washington's unreliability in a crisis. These concerns became urgent as the Gulf war heated up again in the spring of 1984, with attacks on shipping and Iranian threats to close the Strait of Hormuz. Saudi Arabia and the UAE joined Kuwait in criticizing U.S. policy in Lebanon, while Oman seemed to back slightly away from its relationship to the United States.[41] The Saudi ambassador to the United States made several widely publicized feints in the direction of Moscow.[42] The Reagan administration defused some of this criticism by agreeing to the sale of Stinger antiaircraft missiles to Saudi Arabia, while the role of the AWACS in the Saudi downing of an Iranian plane in June also helped U.S. prestige in the Gulf. However, the refusal of Congress, under pressure from the Israeli lobby, to approve the sale of Stingers to Kuwait again cast doubt on Washington's reliability.

Moscow made what it could of the situation. It abandoned its open criticism of Oman and again courted Saudi Arabia, praising Riyadh for its role in the abrogation of the U.S.-backed agreement between Israel and Lebanon.[43] It continued to develop commercial ties with the UAE. It supported the GCC-sponsored resolution in the U.N. Security Coun-

---

[39]Qatar News Agency, Sept. 27, 1985, in FBIS:ME, Sept. 30, p. C2.

[40]T. L. McNaugher, "Southwest Asia: The Crises that Never Came," in B. M. Blechman and E. N. Luttwak, eds., *International Security Yearbook 1984/85* (Washington, DC: Center for Strategic and International Studies, 1985), p. 156.

[41]ANSA (Rome), Mar. 15, 1984, in FBIS:ME, Mar. 16, p. C1.

[42]KUNA, Apr. 16, 1984, in FBIS:ME, Apr. 16, p. C1; *Ar-Riyadh*, Apr. 12, 1984, in FBIS:ME, Apr. 19, p. C8.

[43]Moscow radio in Arabic, Feb. 17, 1984, in FBIS:USSR, Feb. 23, pp. H10-11; Moscow radio in Arabic, May 6, 1984, in FBIS:USSR, May 8, p. H1.

cil against Iran's attacks on Gulf shipping. It conducted a propaganda campaign throughout the spring and summer of 1984, insisting that the United States was about to use the attacks against shipping as a pretext for military intervention and seizure of the oil fields. Perhaps more important, the Soviet Union quickly offered to sell Kuwait the antiaircraft missiles it was seeking and indeed to "satisfy all Kuwait's needs for various weapons."[44]

Relations between the GCC and the United States did not decline further, partly because the Gulf conflict subsided but also because of Washington's low-key response both to the Kuwait arms deal and to the conflict itself. These same facts (Soviet arms sales and U.S. low-key responses, as well as the usual anger over the strong U.S. ties with Israel) probably also encouraged GCC members to proceed with normalization of relations with the Soviet Union. Reports appeared on several occasions in the fall of 1984 of Saudi and UAE contacts with Soviet officials and of lower Saudi resistance to relations between the USSR and the UAE. These reports were buttressed by the establishment of diplomatic relations between the UAE and China (not an event which would please Moscow, but nevertheless one which indicated less resistance to communist countries). The resumption of relations between Washington and Baghdad in December also contributed to the move toward GCC-Soviet relations by lowering the level of ideological and superpower competition.

GORBACHEV AND DIPLOMATIC ACHIEVEMENTS

Thus, in retrospect it is evident that by the time Mikhail Gorbachev came to power in March 1985 the prospects for advances in the Gulf were much improved. Expressions of antagonism toward Soviet occupation forces in Afghanistan were muted. In December 1984 the Islamic Conference Organization had barely mentioned Afghanistan and had not referred to the USSR, while it had attacked the United States. Saudi Arabia, it is true, continued to support the *mujaheddin* financially, but on the whole the GCC states seemed to have decided that Soviet activities in Afghanistan did not threaten them. Likewise, the sultan of Oman appeared to have accepted that PDRY moderation was genuine and that the Soviets could and would help to keep it that way. He abandoned the anti-Soviet rhetoric of previous years and appeared to put greater restrictions on U.S. access to Omani facilities, making it contingent upon the request of the majority of the GCC.[45] In the Gulf the main external threat was perceived to be Iran. Moscow had succeeded in

---

[44]KUNA, July 10, 1984, in FBIS:USSR, July 10, pp. H4-5.
[45]Middle East News Agency, Apr. 4, 1985, in FBIS:ME, Apr. 5, p. C3.

dissociating itself from the Islamic Republic both by propaganda attacks on it and by arms sales to Iraq and Kuwait. The United States promised more active support against Iran, but its reliability as an arms supplier was in great doubt due to the Israeli lobby's influence on Congress, and its acceptability as a partner was problematic; some balance (even if only superficial) in relations with the superpowers might offset continuing ties with Washington. Good relations with the Soviets might also give them some stake in the existing Gulf regimes.

Reported Soviet contacts with Gulf countries increased in the spring and summer of 1985. Semiofficial visits by a Saudi sports delegation to Moscow and by a Soviet tourism delegation to Bahrain (the first visit by a Soviet government delegation) indicated that the barriers were dropping. Other behind-the-scenes contacts were reportedly conducted in an effort to find an end to the Gulf war. The Soviet media played up U.S.-Saudi differences, particularly over arms sales and the Palestinian question, but they also published articles critical of Saudi foreign and domestic policies,[46] evidence perhaps of differences of opinion in Moscow about normalization of relations.

It came as a surprise, however, that the diplomatic breakthrough in September was with Oman, which for all its moderation in the past year was still the most openly anti-Soviet country in the GCC. It was followed two months later by the UAE. (Bahrain, which had advocated in June that GCC members reconsider their lack of relations with the USSR, announced in November that it would not do so.)

Sultan Qaboos tried to portray his decision in a matter-of-fact manner, saying that it "was as good a time as any, with new faces in the Kremlin, to start a new chapter."[47] His minister of foreign affairs referred to a new trend in Soviet policy "toward enhancing stability in the Arabian Peninsula,"[48] without being more specific. Other comments by Qaboos made it clear that he intended to keep the Soviet presence in Oman strictly controlled.

The intentions of the UAE were not made clear, although the trade and cultural contacts made before diplomatic relations were established make it likely that the Soviets will have a greater presence there. Whatever the practical consequences of the diplomatic ties, the Soviets regard them (rightly) as a psychological victory. Commentators pointed out that even though this is a region which Washington has declared to be a zone of its national interests, "the moderate Arab countries do not

[46]*Izvestia*, Feb. 22, 1985; *Pravda*, July 18, 1985; *Pravda*, Sept. 23, 1985.
[47]*Middle East Economic Digest*, in FBIS:ME, Dec. 16, 1985, pp. C2-3.
[48]Muscat radio, Sept. 28, 1985, in FBIS:ME, Sept. 30, p. C2.

believe U.S. propaganda about a Soviet threat."[49] A *Pravda* report claimed that diplomatic relations with Gulf countries are "a perceptible blow at the calculations of those western countries who want to distance the USSR from participation in a solution of Middle Eastern problems and to turn the region into a preserve of imperialist domination."[50] Particularly prized are endorsements of the idea of an international conference on the Middle East conflict with Soviet participation; Oman's was given at the GCC summit in November 1985. Karen Brutents (deputy head of the CPSU Central Committee's International Department) perhaps summed up Moscow's enthusiasm at the breakthrough when he pointed to it as a refutation of the late Anwar Sadat's judgment that the United States holds 99 percent of the cards needed to settle the Middle East problem.[51]

The only fly in the ointment is Saudi Arabia's refusal to cooperate despite its growing commercial connection; the Saudis, apparently using their oil to pay for Iraqi arms purchases, are now the Middle East's third-largest oil exporter to the USSR.[52] Riyadh has declared that it has no immediate plans to resume relations with the Soviet Union but has repeated its earlier assertion that the future of relations "depends on the extent of the Soviet leadership's response to Islamic causes in Afghanistan or elsewhere."[53] (This may be a factor in recent attempts to broaden the base of Afghanistan's puppet regime.) As the period under review ended, Igor Beliaev made yet another appeal in *Literaturnaia Gazeta* for renewed relations, adding a new claim that the Soviet Union had once guarded Saudi Arabia "from the intrigues of the English colonialists and the Nazis."[54]

The calm public response of the GCC members to the coup in the PDRY in January 1986[55] appears to bear out the greater self-confidence with which the GCC is looking at regional affairs,[56] and possibly its greater confidence in the nonaggressive intentions of the Soviet Union.

---

[49]Moscow television, Nov. 20, 1985, in FBIS:USSR, Nov. 22, pp. H4-5; Moscow radio in French to the Maghreb, Nov. 18, 1985, in FBIS:USSR, Nov. 20, p. H5.

[50]*Pravda*, Nov. 18, 1985.

[51]*Al-Watan* (Kuwait), Jan. 6, 1986, in FBIS:USSR, Jan. 9, pp. H3-15.

[52]*Middle East Economic Digest*, No. 48 (Nov. 30-Dec. 6, 1985), p. 11.

[53]Defense Minister Prince Sultan, quoted in SPA, Dec. 17, 1985, in FBIS:ME, Dec. 18, pp. C2-3.

[54]Igor Beliaev in *Literaturnaia Gazeta*, March 12, 1986, in *The Soviet Union and the Middle East*, Vol. 11, No. 2 (1986), p. 14.

[55]For a brief analysis of the PDRY coup and the Soviet reaction to it, cf. Stephen Page, "Patterns of Soviet Activity in Southwest Asia," *International Journal*, Spring 1986.

[56]It should be noted, however, that *Ar-Ray al-Amm* reported a demand at the highest GCC levels for a freeze in Soviet-UAE and Soviet-Oman relations before they develop further. FBIS:ME, Feb. 5, 1986, p. C1.

Gulf rulers are probably not happy about the departure of Ali Nasir Muhammad, whose policies toward them since 1980 had been moderate. Nevertheless, the disappearance of virtually all the old radical figures from the Aden regime, the reported crippling of the armed forces and the PDRY's desperate need for economic assistance presages a continuing period of moderation, confirmed by the new regime's endorsement of the old foreign policy line. Moscow's apparent support of Haydar Abu Bakr al-Attas, a moderate, to be part of the collective leadership, was appreciated in the Gulf, as was its strong stand against foreign intervention and its apparent nonparticipation (at least until the issue was decided[57]).

CONCLUSION

How far has the Soviet Union moved toward fulfilling its goals in the Gulf region after 15 years of effort? The Gulf states are not likely to allow the United States to use their military facilities against the USSR. This, however, is only a net gain in the case of Iran (albeit an extremely important one); the other Gulf states were never likely to allow this because of their perceptions of their own interests. On the other hand, the Soviets have not succeeded in expelling or even neutralizing Western naval presence in the Indian Ocean. U.S. influence has declined in a number of significant ways. However, the United States (although to an increasingly lesser extent) and other Western countries still provide the bulk of foreign input into the GCC, whether cultural, technological, economic or military.

Oil has been used as a weapon with divisive results in the West, and price increases (and decreases as well) have been disruptive of Western economies. This has been a positive factor for the Soviet Union, both for the economic trouble it has caused the West and for the increased hard currency it has generated for Soviet oil exports; but Moscow has not gained any influence over Gulf oil matters, nor does it appear poised to gain concessionary rates for its East European clients.

While the Soviets have been unable to effect a decrease in Western influence, they have seen an increase in their own presence (in limited numbers thus far) and prestige, and to some extent their influence. The GCC countries have begun to come to terms with some measure of Soviet involvement. This is partly due to the Soviet military preponderance in the region and the GCC's greater military and political self-

---

[57]Some Soviets did apparently participate in the fighting, and there were reports of Soviet ships giving communications assistance to the anti-Muhammad forces. I have not been able to discover whether this support was organized or (as seems more likely in the heat of the battle) was given by individual units on the spur of the moment.

confidence. However, it is more particularly due to the respective Soviet and American positions on the Arab-Israeli conflict.[58]

To the extent that Moscow's policies have been responsible for the improvement in its relations with the Gulf states, this has been a result of its pursuit of state-to-state relations; its support of national liberation movements, to the meager extent that it has occurred, was counter-productive.[59] As in other parts of the world where conditions are not ripe for revolutionary change, the Soviets have accepted the limitations of local and regional conditions and also the opportunities provided by them. Without major assets to protect in the GCC countries, the Soviets have probed for incremental gains on which they can build, without risking a major confrontation with the United States or regional countries which could throw the two together. This course of action will likely be maintained. One must note, however, that the uncertainties in the region are still great, and the outcome of the Iran-Iraq war or further radical change in Iran could prompt changes in Soviet policy toward the GCC.

---

[58]The recently reported [November 1986] U.S.-sponsored Israeli arms shipments to Iran are likely to erode further the credibility of the United States in the Gulf.

[59]The Soviets may be in the process of accepting this. The 1985 Draft Program of the CPSU downgrades solidarity with national liberation movements to bottom place in the list of foreign policy aims.

Chapter 8

THE GCC AND REGIONAL SECURITY

J. E. Peterson

Dr. Peterson is an author and consultant on Middle East affairs in
Washington, DC. His latest book is Defending Arabia *(New York: St.
Martin's Press, London: Croom Helm, 1986).*

THE GCC SECURITY ENVIRONMENT

For the Arab states of the Gulf, the close of the 1970s began a period
of apprehension. The situation prior to 1971 and through much of the
1970s was relatively benign. The British political and military presence
provided a regional security umbrella, much as it had for the previous
century or more. Iran, the Gulf state with the greatest power potential,
was kept in check first by direct British pressure and then by American
influence. The real threat to the Arab littoral came not from potential
invasion but from the ideology of radical Arab nationalism, with Iraq
(after its revolutions in 1958, 1963 and 1968) serving as a source of
worry.

As long as the British remained in the Gulf, the Arab monarchies
seemed to have little reason to fear external threats. Even the Iraqi
claim on Kuwait in the sixties was deterred in part by a continued
British security umbrella. But the security situation did not seem to
deteriorate significantly even after British withdrawal in 1971. The smaller
Gulf states eased into independence smoothly, the radical Arab threat
paled, Iraq moved from confrontation to coexistence, and the only
serious internal threat, the rebellion in Dhofar, was put down by 1975.
Only a few clouds intruded on the bright security horizons of the conservative peninsula states.

The year 1979 marked a watershed in perceptions of Gulf security
and set in motion a train of events that has yet to abate. Indications of

a gathering storm began to attract worried concern in Riyadh and neighboring capitals. The Soviet menace had abated earlier in the decade and differences had even cropped up between Baghdad and Moscow. But events in Africa, particularly the revolution in Ethiopia and subsequent fighting in the Ogaden, and the ever more radical regime in Aden all increased the wariness of the Gulf rulers. Finally, the downfall of the shah seemed to remove the most important part of the bulwark between Soviet expansion and the Gulf. The period from 1979 through the mid-1980s was an era of heightened concern for the security of the Arab littoral states from external, regional and internal threats. While the specter of the Soviet Union has been an Arab concern, though not as looming as in the United States, it has been overshadowed by developments in Iran, which seemed to present a more immediate and insidious danger.

The Iranian revolution presented the Arab states with three causes for worry. First, it removed one of the Gulf's most stalwart opponents of Moscow, and probably the most formidable regional deterrent to a Soviet advance on the Gulf. The vulnerability of the new and intolerant successor regime seemed initially to create fertile ground for Soviet intrigue. Second, the upheaval excited passions on both sides of the Gulf and raised the possibility of political agitation and even revolutionary sentiment among the population, especially the Shia elements, of the Arab littoral. Third, it seemed likely that the new Iranian regime would act aggressively against the other states of the Gulf, either in directly engaging in subversive acts, as in fact occurred in Iraq and later in Kuwait, or by supporting indigenous dissidents, as demonstrated in Bahrain in late 1981. There was a parallel to the Russian revolution of 1917, in that the goal of Tehran's new leaders was the overthrow of all governments in Islamic countries and not just Iran.

The outbreak of war between Iran and Iraq seemed to confirm these fears. For the first time in modern history, two of the Gulf's states were engaged in a full-scale war which threatened to involve the remaining littoral governments. The potential Soviet threat from over the horizon had been superseded by a more immediate regional threat, requiring caution and diplomacy as an appropriate response rather than activation of armed forces and reliance on outside military assistance. Somewhat ironically, the war produced the conditions enabling the creation of the long-discussed Gulf Cooperation Council (GCC).[1]

---

[1]For background on security issues within the GCC, see Abdullah Fahd al-Nafisi, *Majlis al-Taawun al-Khaliji: al-itar al-siyasi wal-istratiji* [The Gulf Cooperation Council: The Political and Strategic Framework] (London: Taha Publishers, 1982); Anthony H. Cordesman, *The Gulf and the Search for Strategic Stability* (Boulder,

Talk of a security pact among the Gulf's eight littoral states had been circulating since the early 1970s. Such a pact, it was argued, would provide a joint defense network against external threats, help prevent disputes from flaring into hostilities, and possibly constitute an initial step toward turning the Gulf into a zone of peace. Despite the expressed approval of such a pact by all eight states, putting words into action proved impossible. The attempt to write a security pact at the foreign ministers' meeting in Muscat in December 1976 came to an abrupt end when it was realized that all eight states could not agree on a common formula.

Essentially, the problem was Iraq and Iran: without these two states, the other six formed a very compatible group. Iraq, however, was a source of mistrust in the early seventies because of its pan-Arab socialist ideology. Iran was suspect because it was non-Arab, and suspicions lingered of centuries-old perceived efforts at Persian hegemony in the Gulf. Furthermore, the other seven Gulf leaders were particularly wary of the goals and personal ambitions of Muhammad Reza Shah. It was not until the Iran-Iraq war removed these two countries from consideration for participation in a security pact that the foundations of the GCC could be laid.

The remaining six states formed a cohesive group. Not only did they share close ties to the West and a common mistrust of both Iran and Iraq, but they exhibited numerous similarities in their political, economic and social systems. It was not unreasonable to assume that any organization built around these six states conceivably could entail far more cooperation than a security pact to which all eight might adhere. There were, after all, many antecedents for cooperation in the political, economic and security spheres.

All six had maintained close ties since the early 1970s—far earlier in most cases—and a number of the ruling families were interrelated. Federation talks had taken place between the seven Trucial States (later the UAE) as well as Bahrain and Qatar in the late 1960s. While an

---

CO: Westview Press, 1984); Robert G. Darius, et al., eds., *Gulf Security into the 1980s* (Stanford, CA: Hoover, 1984); Shireen Hunter, ed., *Gulf Cooperation Council: Problems and Prospects* (Washington: Georgetown University CSIS, 1984); Thomas L. McNaugher, *Arms and Oil: U.S. Military Strategy and the Persian Gulf* (Washington: Brookings Institution, 1985); Joseph A. Kechichian, "The Gulf Cooperation Council: Search for Security," *Third World Quarterly*, Vol. 7, No. 4 (Oct. 1985), pp. 853-81; Mazher A. Hameed, *Arabia Imperilled: The Security Imperatives of the Arab Gulf States* (Washington: Middle East Assessments Group, 1986); and J. E. Peterson, *Defending Arabia* (London: Croom Helm; New York: St. Martin's Press, 1986).

abundance of needless competition seemed to outweigh cooperation in the economic arena, a number of joint projects had been initiated under the aegis of the Organization of Arab Petroleum Exporting Countries (OAPEC, to which all but Oman belonged), not to mention the tradition of bilateral aid provided by the richer (and earlier oil producers) to the poorer states. Saudi Arabia had contributed forces to the defense of Kuwait during the 1961 and 1963 Iraqi threats. The Saudis also provided financial aid and transferred some small arms to Oman during the Dhofar rebellion; the UAE's contribution to that effort included money and border patrols in northern Oman to release Omani forces for duty in Dhofar. In addition, there had long existed an informal intelligence-sharing network among the smaller Gulf states, originally because of ties among the states' British intelligence officers.

It is not surprising then that the leaders of the six states should have entertained hopes of building a formal structure on these bases. In May 1976 Sheikh Jaber al Ahmad al Sabah (then prime minister of Kuwait and the ruler since 1978) formally called for "the establishment of a Gulf Union with the object of realizing cooperation in all economic, political, educational and informational fields . . . ."[2] This sentiment was stymied by the inconclusive results of the Muscat conference later that year, and the issue remained moot until the Iran-Iraq war provided a welcome opportunity and galvanized the remaining six into action. On February 4, 1981, the six foreign ministers met in Riyadh to set down the text of the GCC charter. The document was signed by all the heads of state at Abu Dhabi on May 25, 1981, thus bringing the Cooperation Council of the Arab States of the Gulf into formal existence.[3]

From the beginning, the members of the new Council differed in their conceptions of what the GCC should be doing. Kuwait saw the organization as a vehicle for economic integration and resisted security cooperation. On the other hand, Oman feared economic penetration by the other states' larger and more sophisticated economies, yet its experience in the Dhofar war and location astride the vital Strait of Hormuz forced it to regard security cooperation as a top priority. By 1982, two initiatives firmly planted the imperative of a security dimension in the GCC. Recognition of the need for military cooperation was first prompted by the threat to Oman posed by South Yemen. The November 1981

---

[2] *Cooperation Council for the Arab States of the Gulf: On the Occasion of the Second Anniversary, May 25, 1981-May 25, 1983* (London: Gulf Information and Research Centre, 1983) (hereafter cited as "Cooperation Council").

[3] See p. 217 for the text of the Charter. While the Iran-Iraq war enabled the creation of the Council, the takeover of the Great Mosque in Mecca in late 1979 pointed out the need for better cooperation on internal security matters and spurred some planning for what was to become the GCC.

GCC summit ordered a military mission to Oman to determine the sultanate's situation, and as a consequence the six defense ministers met for the first time in January 1982 to discuss the mission's report and military cooperation. The second initiative involved internal security coordination. It was prompted by the attempted coup d'etat in Bahrain in late 1981 and resulted in the first meeting of the GCC's interior ministers in February 1982.

A large number of potential security threats confront the GCC states. Most pressing, of course, is the Iran-Iraq war, now in its seventh year. While the war's developments in 1986 have been contained, they remain worrying. Most prominent among these has been Iraq's inability to dislodge the Iranian invaders from the strategic Faw peninsula (as well as several other smaller Iranian encroachments on Iraqi territory farther north). It inevitably raises the question of Iraq's military capability and/or political will in the face of a seemingly unending series of Iranian offensives. A second development was a new twist in the continuing tanker war, as Iran began to use oil platforms near the entrance to the Gulf to strike Arab-bound shipping off the coast of the UAE. The expansion of the war to the southern part of the Gulf was dramatically underscored when Iraqi aircraft used mid-air refuelling to attack Iran's new oil terminal on Sirri Island.

These developments reinforce the unpredictable nature of the course of the war and its interminability given Iran's refusal to countenance peace negotiations. While on the one hand the GCC states have learned to live with the war as it is, they are not prepared to assume the role of defensive combatants should hostile Iranian policy turn directly against them.

While Iran is the only source of recurrent active hostility within the region, the GCC must also prepare contingencies against other regional threats. Most prominently, these are Israel to the northwest and the Yemens to the south. The specter of a direct Soviet threat, which prompted the formation of the U.S. Rapid Deployment Force and its successor, the U.S. Central Command, has receded. It has not entirely disappeared, however, and the GCC states must develop contingency plans for this threat, not only collectively but especially in cooperation with friendly outsiders.

The possibility of internal subversion and/or sabotage forms a final category of security threats. These tend to be the most nebulous and difficult to defend against. It must be stressed that, despite Western apprehensions, the internal stability of all six GCC states is remarkable. Nevertheless, there are significant internal social divisions and large immigrant populations that pose risks to public order. The following sections assess the security capabilities of the GCC states individually and then the progress of collective security efforts.

SAUDI MILITARY CAPABILITIES

Of all the armed forces of the Arabian peninsula, those of Saudi Arabia are the most formidable, both in terms of number of personnel and extent and sophistication of its arms and equipment (see table). With more than 52,000 men under arms (not including the National Guard) and defense expenditures of over $17 billion, the kingdom is easily the dominant force within the GCC. Oman's armed forces, perhaps the most competent and certainly the most battle-hardened, are estimated at only 21,500. While the UAE ranks second in total numbers at 43,000, its armed forces were merged formally from a number of separate forces only a few years ago, and the individual commands remain essentially autonomous. In addition, while Oman ranks second in defense expenditures at $2.076 billion, that figure amounts to about 12 percent of the Saudi total. At the same time, however, it should be kept in mind that the size of these armed forces pales beside those of their other Middle Eastern neighbors.[4]

TABLE
Gulf Cooperation Council:
Military Capabilities

Country	Pop. (millions)	Total No. of Armed Forces	GDP ($ billions)	Defense Expenditures ($ billions)
Bahrain	.40	2,800	4.628	.279
Kuwait	1.80	12,000	21.269	1.430
Oman	1.00	21,500	7.962	2.076
Qatar	.29	6,000	5.788	.166
Saudi Arabia	10.00	52,500	108.349	17.777
UAE	1.40	43,000	27.595	2.043
TOTAL	14.89	137,800	175.591	23.771

SOURCE: *The Military Balance, 1985-1986* (London: International Institute for Strategic Studies, 1985), pp. 69-88.

---

[4]For example, Iraq has 600,000 men under arms (1.25 million if the Popular Army is included) while Iran totals 555,000 regular troops and Pasdaran, with an additional several million paramilitary forces. Of course, these figures represent countries at war, but even Israel maintains a standing army of 142,000, with an additional 370,000 reservists. These figures are from *The Military Balance, 1985-1986* (London: International Institute for Strategic Studies, 1985), pp. 69-88.

Like the other GCC states (except for Oman), the development of Saudi Arabia's military capability has been quite recent, and the enormous defense expenditures over the past decade will require considerable time to digest. Even the organizational structure is relatively new, and there exists wide disparity in the capability of the various components of the armed forces. Furthermore, the kingdom faces serious difficulties in recruiting and retaining competent personnel. For the foreseeable future, the Saudi armed forces will be heavily dependent on foreign assistance in training and the operation of equipment.[5]

Formally, the High Defense Council (established in 1961) determines policy, although in practice the king's decisions are final. The minister of defense and aviation (the office has been occupied since 1962 by Prince Sultan bin Abd al-Aziz, second in line to the throne) controls the army, air force and navy, while the National Guard (commanded since 1963 by Crown Prince Abdullah bin Abd al-Aziz) theoretically falls under the control of the minister of the interior, along with the Frontier Force, the Coast Guard and internal security forces. In practice, however, the National Guard is answerable only to Prince Abdullah and, through him, the king.

SAUDI AIR FORCE

The last two decades have seen dramatic changes in the structure and capabilities of all components of the Saudi armed forces. The air force has undergone perhaps the most spectacular transformation. The improvement of air-defense capability has been given top priority for a variety of reasons. One of these is geography: the fact that the kingdom is bordered by the Arabian Gulf, the Red Sea and wide deserts to the north and south means that attacks on the kingdom would necessarily have to come through the air. This logical assumption is confirmed by the experience of Egyptian air maneuvers during the Yemen civil war, the separation of Saudi Arabia and South Yemen by the Rub al Khali desert, Israeli overflights of Saudi territory and most recently by the Iranian-Saudi dogfight in June 1984. The sheer size of the country and its long frontiers makes reliance on land-based defense nearly impossible, even if it were not for the manpower restrictions faced by the kingdom. The Saudis cannot hope to match the armies of Israel, Jordan,

---

[5]On background to the Saudi armed forces, see J. C. Hurewitz, *Middle East Politics: The Military Dimension* (New York: Praeger, 1969), pp. 241-52; John Keegan, *World Armies*, 2nd ed. (Detroit: Gale Research, 1983), pp. 506-13; Cordesman, especially chapters 3-10; Richard F. Nyrop, ed., *Saudi Arabia: A Country Study*, 4th ed. (Washington: GPO, 1984); Thomas L. McNaugher, "Arms and Allies on the Arabian Peninsula," *Orbis*, Vol. 28, No. 3 (Fall 1984), pp. 489-526; McNaugher, *Arms and Oil*; David E. Long, *The United States and Saudi Arabia: Ambivalent Allies* (Boulder, CO: Westview Press, 1985), pp. 33-72; and Peterson, pp. 191-203.

Syria, Egypt, Iraq, or Iran in either personnel or firepower. But these disparities can be offset to a certain degree by an air force with highly trained personnel and highly sophisticated equipment.

As with the other Saudi services—and to an even greater degree than the army—U.S. guidance and assistance have shaped the development of the Royal Saudi Air Force (RSAF). But the U.S.-RSAF relationship has been plagued increasingly in the last decade by complications arising from the close ties between the United States and Israel, and the latter's ability to influence and even prevent many U.S. arms sales to Arab states. The Saudis had long been interested in the F-4 as a front-line fighter but were discouraged from asking for it because of its offensive potential *vis-à-vis* Israel; later, they were turned away from the F-14 and the F-16 at least partially for the same reason (in addition, the RSAF is wary of single-engined aircraft). Instead, the Saudis purchased 60 F-15 aircraft. While the F-15 is principally an air-superiority fighter and not an attack aircraft, it was deemed suitable for Saudi needs and the sale could not be effectively opposed by Israel, which was also receiving it.[6] The United States also had a prominent role in the development of Saudi Arabia's Peace Shield program, a $4 billion project to create the most technologically advanced integrated air-defense system outside of NATO and the Soviet bloc. The first major contract for the Peace Shield system, scheduled to become operational in 1992, was awarded to Boeing in early 1985.[7]

The 1981 request for five E-3A Airborne Warning and Control Systems (AWACS) aircraft was a logical follow-on to the acquisition of the interceptor force. The United States had briefly operated an AWACS watch out of Riyadh during the two Yemens' border war in early 1979, and they returned to Saudi Arabia after the Iranian seizure of U.S. hostages in Tehran. The permanent stationing of the E-3As over Saudi skies meant that the sale of the new AWACS to Saudi Arabia would have little effect beyond the change in ownership. But the furor and negative publicity over congressional approval of the AWACS sale, and the close vote, proved to be far more important (as well as troublesome for both parties) for its political ramifications than for its military implications. The first Saudi AWACS was delivered in mid-1986.

The bruising battle in Congress over the AWACS sale, stimulated by opposition from the pro-Israel lobby and fears over potential compromise of U.S. military technology, contributed strongly to the Reagan administration's reluctance to push further aircraft sales through Congress. The 60 F-15s in the Saudi inventory as a result of the earlier sale

---

[6]Cordesman, pp. 205-27.

[7]*New York Times*, May 19, 1985. See also the *Middle East Economic Digest*, May 11, 1984, Dec. 14, 1984, and Feb. 1, 1985.

were too few to allow the RSAF to maintain a 24-hour combat watch over all vital installations and, as expected, Riyadh formally requested the purchase of an additional 40 to 48 F-15s at the beginning of 1985. But the U.S. government continued to prevaricate through the first half of the year and in September Saudi Arabia announced that it would purchase 48 Tornado interdictor/strike aircraft from the British-German-Italian Panavia consortium instead and finance the sale at least partly through an oil barter arrangement. The first six planes were delivered in 1986 and a further batch of 18, diverted from the RAF assembly line, was promised for 1987. The sale also included spare parts, training and 30 Hawk advanced fighter-trainers and 30 PC-9 basic trainers, as well as the buy-back of Saudi Arabia's aging Lightnings.[8]

Of all the components of the Saudi armed forces, the air force is generally regarded as the most advanced and capable. Service with the RSAF carries more prestige than the other branches, as reflected in the number of Al Saud family members who have made their careers in the air force. Some have noted that U.S. assistance has been steadier and more professional than elsewhere, and RSAF personnel reflect a higher degree of professionalism. In the air force, as throughout the Saudi armed forces, reliance on expatriates for training on equipment and support services is likely to continue indefinitely. Nevertheless, the RSAF undoubtedly is better placed to carry out its assigned mission than the other branches, as well as to provide cover for other GCC states.

SAUDI ARABIA LAND FORCES

While the emphasis, both in Saudi planning and the American military connection, has been on strengthening the air force, considerable effort and expense have been devoted to modernization of the other Saudi services, particularly the Saudi Arabian Land Forces (SALF). Despite being created after the 1934 Saudi-Yemeni war and benefiting from American training teams and modest arms transfers since the late 1940s, the army remained smaller and less important than the National Guard

---

[8]There had long been speculation that the Saudis might purchase either the Tornado or the French Mirage 2000 if it could not get the F-15. There was also speculation that the sale was a setback for the Israeli lobby in the United States, since the Europeans were unlikely to impose any restrictions on the basing of the Tornados, unlike U.S. prohibition of F-15 basing at Tabuk air base. It would also mean the loss of a considerable amount of export revenue for U.S. manufacturers and could possibly lead to other non-U.S. arms purchases by the Saudis. *Washington Post*, Sept. 15 and 17, 1985; *New York Times*, Sept. 16, 1985; *Jane's Defence Weekly*, Sept. 28, 1985; *Middle East Economic Digest*, June 21, 1986. For a gossipy account of the background to the sale, see John Newhouse, "Politics and Weapons Sales," *New Yorker*, June 9, 1986, pp. 46-57, 60-69.

until expanded and modernized in the 1960s (including incorporation of the hitherto-autonomous Royal Guard battalion in 1964).

The modernization process in the army has been more problematic than in the air force for several reasons. One early problem involved the predominance of Saudis from the Najd province, particularly in the officer corps, at the expense of personnel from other areas of the country, especially Hijaz (this was even more acute for the air force, where technical skills are at a premium). It was not until after a number of military personnel were arrested in 1969 that steps were taken to improve discipline and professionalism. A second complicating factor arose out of the decision to divide the army into two parts, one equipped and trained by the United States and the other by France. Prominent among French purchases have been 300 AMX-30 light tanks, as well as armored cars, infantry carriers and antiaircraft guns.[9]

Since the late 1970s, the United States has stepped up its assistance to the SALF, with the provision of 150 M-60 tanks, 16 Improved Hawk SAM batteries, TOW missiles and various other items. At the same time, the U.S. Army Corps of Engineers has been heavily involved in army construction, particularly in the building of major facilities at Khamis al-Mushayt, Tabuk and Sharura, and the King Khalid and Asad military cities. These bases have helped to expand SALF strength from its older bases at Jeddah, Dammam and al-Taif to strategic points closer to potential threats.[10]

The higher priorities given to the air force, its smaller size and prestige status inevitably mean that the army will lag behind the RSAF in modernization and competence for some time to come. It has experienced some difficulties in recruitment and training, in coordinating brigades that have received either American or French equipment and an inability to cover all sections of the expansive kingdom. Perhaps most severe in the long run is the small population base of the kingdom and the manpower crunch. Not only will it be impossible for the Saudis to field anywhere near the number of men that Iraq or Iran can, employment

---

[9]The government has sought to redress the problem of incompatible equipment and training by concentrating the French-supplied units at Tabuk in the northwest, a move that may also strengthen Saudi requests for future arms purchases from the United States by reducing the chances for their use against Israel. See Cordesman, pp. 170-73. The subsequent purchase of British arms added another layer of complications to the army's effectiveness.

[10]Khamis al-Mushayt is located in the southwestern province of Asir, just north of Yemen; Tabuk is situated just south of the Jordanian border and near the Gulf of Aqaba; Sharura is on the edge of the Rub al Khali desert near the intersection of Saudi borders with both North and South Yemen; King Khalid Military City is located at Hafr al-Batin, just south of the Iraq-Saudi Arabian Neutral Zone; and Asad Military City is at al-Kharj, south of Riyadh.

opportunities elsewhere within the kingdom make recruitment for even a smaller army particularly difficult without turning to expatriates.

Modernization of the National Guard has involved even more problems than the army. This has been largely due to the traditional mission of the guard: internal security as opposed to the army's task of defending the kingdom from external threats. As the security of the state has been inseparable from the security of the royal family, composition of the guard has always been based on loyalty to the family. The White Army, Abd al-Aziz's instrument for downing the Ikhwan rebellion in the late 1920s, provided the nucleus of the present guard, which has always been a tribal force, drawing on the Al Saud's Najdi allies, with some personnel classified as "regulars" and the others as "reserves." The estimated total figure of 25,000 men is misleading, since many guardsmen are either part-time or pensioners from the earlier days of Abd al-Aziz's expansionary moves.

While the guard served well as the instrument of the king's power in the first half of this century, it has become increasingly clear that its orientation is unsuitable to such newer tasks as preventing sabotage in the oil fields, countering terrorism, handling civil disturbances and backing up the army in matters of national defense. One observer, however, contends that the guard is "more a means through which the royal family allocates funds to tribal and bedouin leaders than a modern combat or internal security force. . . . The Guard is politically vital but it has not found a clear military mission."[11] Other assessments point to the extensive modernization and professionalization that the National Guard has undergone in recent years.

A National Guard modernization program was initiated in 1972 with the goal of converting the tribal basis of the guard into a more professional/modern light infantry force with several mechanized battalions. Once again, considerable U.S. input was solicited and provided for the Saudi Arabian National Guard Program (SANG). In true Saudi style, an ambitious armament program was undertaken, which included the acquisition of over 700 Commando APCs, large numbers of self-propelled Vulcan antiaircraft guns, M-102 howitzers, and TOW antitank guided missiles. In addition, the guard has built its own military cities

---

[11]Cordesman, p. 365. In addition, the overall effectiveness of the Guard has been limited in the past by its role as a counterweight to potential opposition within the other military branches and as a power base for Crown Prince Abdullah within the ranks of the Al Saud (and particularly in balancing the power of the so-called "Sudayri Seven," whose ranks include King Fahd and Prince Sultan, the minister of defense and aviation). David Long also notes the role played by the National Guard in facing King Saud's supporters in 1964 and helping to ensure a peaceful abdication. Long, p. 52.

at al-Hasa in the Eastern Province and at Qasim in the central Najd, along with a new headquarters and academy in Riyadh.

This program, however, has encountered greater difficulties than its equivalent for the army. On the one hand, the bedouin background, widespread illiteracy and lack of discipline and training endemic to the majority of the guard's personnel inevitably have meant that training efforts must be more basic and slower to be effective. On the other hand, external assistance to the army has been better in terms of quantity and quality and has had more time in which to show positive results. Despite a decade of modernization, questions still remain about the guard's ability to handle new and complicated tasks. The National Guard's effectiveness is of particular concern because it has the assigned role of defending Saudi oil fields.[12] Nevertheless, gradual improvement is discernible, particularly in the more prestigious mechanized units.

ROYAL SAUDI NAVY

The Royal Saudi Navy (RSN) is the last of the Saudi armed forces to emerge—and consequently it remains the least developed. Formed as an adjunct of the army in 1957, it received its first naval officer as commander in 1963 and only began functioning as a separate force in 1969. In conjunction with the bold schemes advanced for the other services, the Saudi Naval Expansion Program (SNEP) was launched in 1972, again with American assistance and with overly ambitious plans for a 20-30 ship navy that included major bases at Jubail on the Gulf and Jeddah on the Red Sea, a repair facility at Dammam on the Gulf and a naval headquarters complex in Riyadh.

Even though plans were scaled back several times, serious problems continued to arise due to the lack of Saudi manpower and the U.S. Navy's inability to provide the proper supervision and training personnel. One result was Riyadh's appeal to France for help, thus once again complicating the picture with competing and often-incompatible equipment, concepts and training methods. Fortunately, SNEP's slow prog-

---

[12]Thomas McNaugher charges that "provisions for the protection of oil fields have apparently changed little since 1979. There are no additional barriers, no hardening of key technologies or port facilities, and no electronic surveillance technologies to scan for intruders. Indeed, U.S. personnel knowledgeable about the oil fields suggest that rigs, pumping stations and other equipment have deteriorated somewhat since 1973 and that the fields lie fairly open to attack." *Arms and Oil*, p. 131. But a U.S. Senate staff team in July 1984 reported that "ARAMCO has already taken many precautions to stop saboteurs and is currently spending millions more to enhance internal security. . . ." U.S. Congress, Senate, Committee on Foreign Relations, Staff Report, *War in the Gulf* (Washington: GPO, 1984), p. 29. The report also notes that, because it is impossible to protect all oil facilities from sabotage, the Saudi government relies on harsh punishment and redundancy within the oil sector to protect the flow of oil.

ress has been ameliorated by the weakness of potential naval threats from Saudi Arabia's neighbors in the Red Sea and Gulf, especially since the Iranian revolution severely crippled the navy built up by the shah. Nevertheless, Saudi patrols in the Gulf are said to have increased only slightly in recent years, for fear of provoking Iranian attacks.[13]

The effectiveness of the Saudi armed forces forms the key to the GCC's defensive capabilities. The kingdom is the largest and most powerful of the six GCC states, and its oil reserves vastly dwarf those of its neighbors. Its wealth makes it an important actor in Arab, Islamic and Third World arenas. More important, its geographic sprawl places it in potential confrontation with many possible enemies.

RELATIONS WITH THE YEMENS

Saudi Arabia is the only GCC state that borders both Yemens, and a major focus of Saudi security concern has centered on threats from this corner of the Arabian peninsula since Egypt became involved in the North Yemen civil war of the 1960s. In part, Riyadh has responded to the Yemeni threat by building major bases at Khamis al-Mushayt in Asir and at Sharura deep in the Rub al Khali desert, as well as maintaining large numbers of troops there. In terms of total troops, the two Yemens have more military personnel on paper than Saudi Arabia, but the quality of many of their troops, particularly in the Yemen Arab Republic (YAR), is questionable, and neither North nor South Yemen has been able to acquire weaponry of the level of Saudi Arabia's. The ability of both Yemeni states to act in concert against Saudi Arabia is even more doubtful. The long distance between the Yemeni borders and Saudi centers of population, capital and oil reduces the impact of even a direct, combined Yemeni attack against the kingdom to relatively localized hostilities in the southern province of Asir.

Such a direct Yemeni threat is unlikely, and military engagement between Saudi Arabia and its southern neighbors more probably will be limited to the kinds of border skirmishes that have occurred periodically for a number of years. Ever since the 1960s, Saudi Arabia has sought to minimize the Yemeni threat through nonmilitary means. Riyadh has maintained significant influence with the North Yemeni government through varying techniques such as extensive budget subsidies, pressure on its rulers, intrigues with both military officers and civilian politicians in Sanaa, as well as subsidies to the northern Yemeni tribes

---

[13]*Washington Post*, Aug. 21, 1986. Brief mention may be made of two other auxiliary forces. The Frontier Force and the Coast Guard, with 8,500 men, both fall under the purview of the Ministry of the Interior (as does a helicopter-equipped counterterrorist unit). Their duties include policing the bedouin, civil defense duties and maintaining border and port security.

and sheikhs. While the nearly one-half-million Yemeni workers in Saudi Arabia are often cited as a potential security threat to the kingdom, the loss of their remittances would cripple the YAR's economy.[14]

At the same time, Riyadh generally has sought to isolate the Marxist government in Aden and has in the past supported dissident movements against South Yemen. While the Saudis displayed considerable reluctance to pursue rapprochement when favorable occasions presented themselves in 1978 and 1980, they apparently have approved of Kuwaiti and UAE development assistance and reconciliation efforts between South Yemen and its North Yemeni and Omani neighbors. More recently, they have gone out of their way to strengthen ties to the new leadership in Aden, arising out of the January 1986 civil war, and welcomed new President Haydar al-Attas to Riyadh in the summer of 1986. The surprising stability of the Ali Abdullah Salih government in Sanaa has meant that YAR-Saudi relations have remained on an even keel, even if sometimes strained. As a result, the Saudi policy of diplomacy, rather than military confrontation, has paid off in the case of the Yemens.

ISRAEL, IRAN AND IRAQ

In the case of potential threats to the kingdom from the northwest (Israel) and the northeast (Iran or Iraq), Saudi Arabia once against must rely basically on nonmilitary means to deter attack. No amount of military buildup would put the Saudis on an equal footing with any of these countries. At the same time, it is unlikely that any of the three would try to invade the kingdom in the foreseeable future. Despite the protestations of Israel's supporters in the United States, Saudi Arabia is not and never will be a military threat to Israel, and confrontation between them will continue to be played out politically through third parties, particularly the United States. At most, Saudi Arabia can hope through its military buildup to deter Israeli aerial and naval violations of Saudi territory without provoking the kinds of raids Israel has carried out against Baghdad and Tunis.

As far as the Gulf is concerned, the threat is far greater to Kuwait than to Saudi Arabia, which once again benefits from its strategic depth.[15] Saudi military options are largely limited to its air-defense capabilities, as demonstrated in June 1984, although the King Khalid Military City at Hafr al-Batin, near the Iraqi and Kuwaiti borders, provides a base

---

[14]On Saudi-Yemeni relations, see Saeed M. Badeeb, *The Saudi-Egyptian Conflict over North Yemen, 1962-1970* (Boulder, CO: Westview Press, 1986; copublished with the American-Arab Affairs Council).

[15]Thomas L. McNaugher acknowledges Saudi Arabia's "geographic buffers" and postulates that they encourage " 'two-stage' attacks in which external antagonists acquire a position anywhere on the Peninsula and then seek to exploit it in ways unhampered by geography." "Arms and Allies," p. 497.

for modest ground forces capability. Still, a build-up of SALF forces at Hafr al-Batin inevitably will mean starving the other frontline bases at Tabuk and Sharura. As long as the war between Iran and Iraq lasts—and that still looks like a very long time—a direct Iranian attack on the Arab side will have only nuisance value.

The Iraqi threat continues to recede. Because of the war, the Saddam Hussein regime has become dependent on Saudi and other GCC financial assistance, Saudi willingness to transship Iraqi oil across the kingdom and sell Saudi oil on Iraq's behalf and—especially at the beginning of the war—the Saudi role as a middleman between Baghdad and Washington. Iraq's oil reserves are second only to Saudi Arabia's in the Middle East, and it has no reason to covet Saudi fields. Rather than military confrontation (or even subversion), the potential Iraqi threat to Saudi Arabia in the future would appear to consist of disputes over oil-pricing and production quotas due to competition in a stagnant world oil market.

Assuming a worst-case scenario—that Iran emerges victorious against Iraq, rearms and still desires to carry the war forward into the GCC—Saudi Arabia's only option is virtually the same as it would be in the case of a direct Soviet attack. It can use its early-warning system and interceptor aircraft to delay an enemy attack until help arrives from outside. Militarily, Saudi Arabia is and will remain vitally dependent on outside assistance. In direct terms, Saudi Arabia depends on the approximately 1,700 American military personnel now stationed in the kingdom, as well as the several thousand personnel employed by more than 40 U.S. military contractors.[16] Over 4,000 French and 2,000 British expatriates work in similar capacities, and more than 10,000 Pakistanis serve in the Saudi armed forces.[17] Pakistanis are particularly noticeable in the officer and enlisted ranks of all the GCC naval forces.

While the Saudis have relied heavily on arms purchases from the United States,[18] they have also bought from other Western European

---

[16]*New York Times*, May 19, 1985.

[17]Some estimates put the number of Pakistani troops in Saudi Arabia as high as 20,000, and it is conjectured that entire Pakistani units have been loaned to the Saudi armed forces. Saudi Arabia and Pakistan are bound by a military cooperation pact signed in 1967 and renewed in 1980, which covers training for Saudi soldiers and the exchange of experts. *Arab News*, May 22, 1984. Some Pakistanis were alleged to have been captured by YAR troops during a 1984 border incident. *Washington Post*, Nov. 25, 1984.

[18]Between 1950 and 1964, total sales agreements between Saudi Arabia and its principal supplier, the United States, totalled $87 million. In 1965 alone, they equalled $342 million. A decade later, the total was over $2 billion and by 1980 reached $35 billion. U.S. Congress, House, Committee on Foreign Affairs, Subcommittee on Europe and the Middle East, Report, *Saudi Arabia and the United States: The New Context in an Evolving "Special Relationship"* (Washington: GPO, 1981), p. 54.

countries, as well as Brazil and South Korea. The January 1984 agreement with France for the $4 billion Shahine ground-to-air missile system represented France's biggest arms sale ever. The French have also been prominent in the development of the Saudi navy, and the Mirage 2000 reportedly was being considered along with the F-15 and the Tornado for the 1985 Saudi interceptor purchase. The Tornado sale announced in September 1985 could not have come at a more propitious time for Britain, given the aircraft's enormous development costs. The purchase may also represent a deepening Saudi desire to diversify arms purchases to lessen dependence on any one country, particularly given the widespread opposition fomented against Saudi Arabia by the pro-Israel lobby in the U.S. Congress.

At a more indirect but even more important level, the ultimate Saudi defense—and therefore the defense of all the GCC nations—must come from the United States, although at the direct request of the kingdom and the GCC. While the Saudis have consistently refused to allow the stationing of American military forces in the kingdom and do not cooperate with the United States in any military exercises (in part due to the special security relationship between the United States and Israel), the overstocking built into their weapons and equipment purchases strongly indicates that they recognize that full cooperation with a prompt deployment of USCENTCOM forces is necessary in the case of severe threats, as from the Soviet Union.[19] At the same time, however, it should be remembered that the effectiveness of U.S. military support applies to only a few, relatively unlikely situations. Saudi Arabia's security is most dependent on the skillfulness of its foreign policy and the astuteness of its leaders in adapting to and complying with the demands of its citizenry. Additionally, USCENTCOM policy is based upon a requisite GCC request for assistance prior to deployment of U.S. forces.

OTHER GCC DEFENSE CAPABILITIES

Oman

Oman's armed forces have perhaps the longest history of any in the peninsula states.[20] Several small forces, organized with British help,

---

[19]In this vein, a secret Reagan administration policy study provided to Congress in mid-1985 announced that "Although the Saudis have steadfastly resisted formal access agreements, they have stated that access will be forthcoming for United States forces as necessary to counter Soviet aggression or in regional crises they cannot manage on their own." Quoted in the *New York Times*, Sept. 5, 1985.

[20]For background on the military in Oman, see J. E. Peterson, *Oman in the Twentieth Century: Political Foundations of an Emerging State* (London: Croom Helm; New York: Barnes & Noble, 1978), pp. 90-96; J. E. Peterson, "American Policy in the Gulf and the Sultanate of Oman," *American-Arab Affairs*, No. 8 (Spring 1984), pp. 117-30; and Peterson, *Defending Arabia*, pp. 204-07.

were reorganized into the Sultan's Armed Forces (SAF) in 1958, with the foundations of the Sultan of Oman's Air Force (SOAF) and the Sultan of Oman's Navy (SON) laid soon after. The subsequent rebellion in Dhofar provided the major spur to the extensive buildup and modernization that Oman's armed forces have undergone since the late 1960s. In addition, considerable progress was made during the 1970s to add capability in such specialized areas as training facilities, artillery units, engineering and air and coastal patrols. Just as important, the SAF benefited from a considerable number of seconded officers and even more contract personnel, both civilian and ex-military. The chief of the general staff and the commanders of the air force and navy remained British seconded officers through the mid-1980s. With the guidance and manifold assistance provided by Britain, the SAF has been molded into probably the most professional and capable military organization in the peninsula.[21]

The SOAF has received the lion's share of arms and equipment purchases over the past decade or two, and currently boasts nearly two dozen Jaguars and a dozen aging Hunters among its combat aircraft, as well as a helicopter squadron equipped mainly with Augusta Bells and a Rapier SAM system. In June 1985 Oman committed itself to the purchase of a half-dozen Tornado air defense variant (ADV) aircraft, choosing the West European consortium's aircraft over the U.S. F-20A Tigershark. Severe budgetary constraints, however, soon postponed the sale to the 1990s and have probably cancelled it. In addition to its headquarters, adjacent to al-Sib International Airport (outside of Muscat), the SOAF operates out of the former RAF bases on al-Masira Island and at Salala, strategically located bases at Thamarit (Dhofar) and Khasab (Musandam), as well as from a dozen other airstrips.

The Sultanate of Oman Land Forces (SOLF), with approximately 16,500 men (or nearly 80 percent of the total armed forces), utilizes several dozen Chieftain tanks (and a few M-60s), Saladin armored cars,

---

[21]In addition to the British, seconded Jordanian and Pakistani administrative personnel, engineers and NCOs have all been a feature of the SAF's past. The heavy preponderance of Baluch soldiers in the ranks, many of whom had been recruited from Oman's former possession of Gwadur in Pakistan, was gradually reversed in favor of an Arab majority among the more than 20,000 troops in the military today. Since the great majority of recruits were illiterate, sophisticated training had to await implementation of basic educational programs. Over the past decade, though, the infusion of more educated Omanis has helped to raise standards and enable Omanis to move into slots as regimental commanders and pilots. Because of the large numbers of expatriates at all levels of the armed forces, considerable emphasis has been placed on Omanization. By the end of 1985, there were five Omani major-generals, including the commander of SOLF, and it was expected that command of SOAF would be turned over to an Omani soon.

TOW antitank missiles and Blowpipe SAMs. Considerable progress has been made by the SON, which now has eight fast attack craft (six equipped with Exocet missiles), a half-dozen smaller patrol boats and various support craft, and has beefed up its presence in the Omani territorial waters around the Strait of Hormuz. Al-Ghanam Island (on the Gulf side of the strait) has been made into a naval base, thus complementing the main base at Muscat, the naval training center at Sur and facilities at the Dhofar port of Raysut; a new base is under construction at Wudam Alwa along the Batinah Coast. In addition, the Royal Oman Police has been built up as a major gendarmerie and frontier force, and several thousand Dhofari irregulars belong to the *firqa* units formed from surrendering rebels. While the *firqas* have been regrouped into regular army units, they still have not been assigned a mission, presumably because of questions of their military suitability.

The traditional lines between the predominantly American tutelage of the Saudi armed forces and British guidance of the Omani military have broken down in recent years, in large part because of British economic decline and military retrenchment. While Oman may still lie within a "British sphere of influence" through the organization, armament and expatriate personnel in its forces, recent American perceptions of a deteriorating security situation in the Gulf and emphasis on developing a "go-it-alone" military capability have led Washington to upgrade its ties to Muscat. The sultanate's apparent willingness to cooperate more fully with the United States than its neighbors would like is in part based on its perceptions of vulnerability to external threats and in part on its financial needs. As a consequence, the United States has provided development assistance and some military grants in return for the use of Omani military facilities in emergency and some routine situations, and has even undertaken the physical improvement of these facilities. U.S. military spending in Oman has totaled more than $300 million, with half of that on the strategic air base on Masira Island.[22] By 1984, however, the Omanis had become noticeably less enthusiastic about the emerging relationship with the U.S. government.[23]

---

[22]For a recent overview of the Omani armed forces, the extensive Rad exercises carried out in early 1985, and the U.S. military role in Oman, see Jean-Loup R. Combemale, "Oman: Defending the Sultanate," *Journal of Defense and Diplomacy*, Vol. 3, No. 6 (June 1985), pp. 42-45.

[23]"The United States cannot expect an automatic hand from Oman in an intervention to stop Iran from blocking off the Strait of Hormuz," Sultan Qaboos was quoted, making it clear that his government would not support any American operation in the region unless it had the backing of all other Arab nations in the Gulf area. ANSA (Rome) in English, Mar. 15, 1984 (FBIS, Mar. 16, 1984). Oman's attitude toward continued U.S. Central Command use of Omani facilities was considerably tougher during the early 1985 negotiations to renew the 1980 agreement. Omani

Despite their high degree of professionalism and combat experience, the Omani armed forces remain too small and underequipped for the multitude of security tasks they face. While the navy has beefed up its surveillance activities in the Strait of Hormuz (the shipping lanes in the strait run through Omani territorial waters), its ability to handle threats to shipping remains limited to minor hit-and-run attacks using speedboats. Even in the case of mining, Oman would have to call on NATO assistance. The SAF has proven its ability to deal with internal threats of subversion and rebellion on various occasions in the last quarter-century. With considerable outside help, the SAF was successful in putting down the rebellion in Dhofar, and it could probably hold its own against a South Yemeni attack, since the PDRY superiority in tanks would be negated by the rugged terrain. Oman is more vulnerable to an Iranian attack, since its air force is very small and its ground forces basically consist of light infantry. It faces the same manpower problems as the other GCC states and is further constrained by the lack of funds for defense expenditure.

Given these limitations and its extreme exposure, it is not unexpected that the Omani government, of all the GCC states, has displayed the most military cooperation with the West. Similarly, it is not surprising that the Omanis have placed considerable emphasis on diplomacy as a tool to enhance their security. Diplomatic relations with the PDRY were established for the first time in 1984, with the help of Kuwaiti and UAE mediation, and nonresident ambassadors were exchanged in 1985.[24] Relations with revolutionary Iran have been superficially good, especially in light of the close ties between the shah and Sultan Qaboos. Despite China's involvement in the early stages of the Dhofar rebellion, Oman recognized the PRC in 1975. A similar pragmatic strategy may have been at work when the intention to establish diplomatic relations with the Soviet Union was announced in September 1985.[25] In sum, Oman is capable of providing for its own security in most threat scenarios but must call for outside assistance in case of an all-out Soviet or Iranian attack. Only Oman can join Saudi Arabia in providing out-

---

pique over American demands in these negotiations and U.S. media reports of CIA influence in the sultanate may have contributed to the decision in September 1985 to open talks with the Soviets.

[24]The fighting in Aden in January 1986 did not seem to harm relations. The Omani minister of state for foreign affairs visited Aden in June 1986, and plans were laid for further discussion on border disputes and the 1987 opening of embassies. There was also some talk of economic aid.

[25]The announcement came as a surprise, although Omani-Soviet discussions, with the assistance of Jordan, had been going on for several years. Nonresident ambassadors were exchanged in July 1986. A third GCC state, the UAE, also announced its intentions in November 1985 of establishing relations with Moscow.

of-area assistance to the GCC, but its capabilities in this regard are considerably less than those of the Saudi armed forces.

Kuwait

The other four GCC members have little of the military potential of Saudi Arabia and Oman, and—for the most part—began to build armed forces at a far later date and for more modest purposes.[26] These smaller states exhibit basically identical problems in self-defense, differentiated by minor details. At the northern end of the Arab littoral, Kuwait is confronted by the inescapable fact that its power inherently is limited by its small population and territorial size, even as its central location and long exploitation of oil makes it a desirable and highly visible target. At the same time, it faces a number of serious potential threats, externally from its larger neighbors—Iran, Iraq and possibly Saudi Arabia (in the form of pressure rather than aggression)—and internally from a population composed in the majority of non-Kuwaitis, as well as from its Shia and Persian minorities.

The ruling Al Sabah family has sought to deal with these threats with diplomacy and an even more viable means, financial assistance. An extremely large proportion of the oil income has long been distributed as foreign aid, regardless of the recipient's politics. Well before the Iran-Iraq war, Kuwait provided Iraq with generous loans, and the Palestinian cause has been the recipient of both financial and verbal support for decades. Internally, oil income has been evenly distributed among the native population, although the country faces a major dilemma regarding expatriates. They are not covered under most benefits of the extensive state welfare system and with few exceptions are not eligible for citizenship, which is particularly rankling to many Palestinians who have spent most or all of their lives in Kuwait.

Kuwait's armed forces have been capable of little more than border protection and internal security. Between independence in 1961 and British withdrawal from the Gulf in 1971, Kuwait could rely on British protection through a treaty negotiated at independence. Since 1971, however, Kuwait has sought to expand its defense capability, increasing

---

[26]On the military background to the four states of Kuwait, UAE, Bahrain and Qatar, see Richard F. Nyrop, ed., *Area Handbook for the Persian Gulf States* (Washington: GPO, 1977; American University, Foreign Area Studies); Alvin J. Cottrell, Robert J. Hanks and Frank T. Bray, "Military Affairs in the Persian Gulf," in Alvin J. Cottrell, gen. ed., *The Persian Gulf States: A General Survey* (Baltimore: Johns Hopkins University Press, 1980), pp. 140-71; Keegan; Cordesman; U.S. Congress, House, Committee on International Relations, Report, *United States Arms Policies in the Persian Gulf and Red Sea Areas: Past, Present and Future*; (Washington: GPO, 1977); U.S. Congress, Senate, *War in the Gulf*, pp. 28-33; and Peterson, *Defending Arabia*, pp. 207-13.

the number of men under arms by about 50 percent and authorizing over $7 billion in military expenditure. Not surprisingly, the bulk of the armed forces is found in the army, with about 10,000 men, largely drawn from the bedouin tribes of the area shared by Kuwait, Iraq and Saudi Arabia. In the years since 1971, it has been equipped with Chieftain tanks, Saladin armored vehicles, Saracen APCs, Ferret scout cars, AMX self-propelled howitzers and TOW antitank missiles. The air force boasts about 70 combat aircraft, mostly A-4 Skyhawks and Mirage F-1 interceptors. In addition, there are three helicopter squadrons equipped with Gazelles and Pumas and several batteries of I-Hawk SAMs. The navy is the least developed of the services, essentially consisting of a coast guard with a few armed patrol craft and some Exocet missiles.

Traditionally, Kuwait has looked to Britain as its principal military supplier, but it has turned increasingly to the United States and France in recent years.[27] For political reasons, Kuwait concluded a highly publicized deal with the Soviet Union in 1977 for SA-7 missiles, purchasing more missiles the following year, and then turned again to Moscow in 1984 in a multimissile deal worth over $300 million.[28] It should be emphasized that these token transactions underscore Kuwait's long striving for neutrality, as well as policy differences with the United States, rather than any fundamental shift in foreign policy. For example, the 1984 arms deal with the Soviet Union was initiated only after rejection of a Kuwaiti request to the United States for Stinger missiles to defend Kuwaiti oil tankers against Iranian air attacks and fears that future arms requests would become entangled in U.S.-Israeli relations. Kuwait continues to rely upon Britain, the United States, Pakistan, Jordan and Egypt for military assistance and training, and that orientation is unlikely to change.

Despite its expansion program, Kuwait's defense situation is not much changed from the 1960s, when British troops and a symbolic Arab League presence were felt necessary to deter Iraqi encroachment. As a small state surrounded by much larger ones, Kuwait's basic strategy necessarily entails keeping on good terms with its neighbors and relying on the collective capabilities of the GCC for protection. The country does not have the strategic depth of its neighbors and training efforts are stymied by the nearby war exclusion zones and a constant alert status since 1980. The Kuwaiti armed forces suffer from manpower

---

[27]The United States has supplied over $1 billion in arms since the early 1970s, and several dozen U.S. military advisers are stationed in Kuwait. There are about 100 British military personnel in Kuwait, mostly attached to the army.

[28]For the first time, a few Soviet military advisers were admitted to Kuwait and some Kuwaiti missile personnel were sent to the Soviet Union for training. In addition, the Soviet deputy defense minister visited Kuwait in January 1986.

problems, both because of the country's small population and because in Kuwait, as in many countries, military service is not popular. As a consequence, expatriates are ubiquitous in the armed forces and a national draft is less than effective.[29]

Because of its proximity to Iraq and Iran, Kuwait is the GCC state most vulnerable to attack. It lived under the shadow of Iraqi claims to Kuwait in the 1960s and, despite its contributions to the Iraqi war effort, still must be on its guard against Iraqi efforts to seize the islands of Warba and Bubiyan, which dominate the approaches to the Iraqi naval base at Umm Qasr. Kuwait's hold on the islands was strengthened by the construction of a bridge from the mainland to Bubiyan in the early 1980s. Several Iranian airstrikes on Kuwaiti installations during the war, Iranian attacks on Kuwaiti shipping and Iranian support of the terrorist attacks inside its borders all contribute to Kuwaiti insecurity.

Although the prospect of an Iranian breakthrough on the Shatt al-Arab front seemed to subside after the stalled offensives of 1982, 1983, 1984 and February 1985, the Iranian capture of Iraq's al-Faw peninsula in February 1986 and Iraq's inability to dislodge the invaders meant that only the shallow Khawr Abdullah separated a hostile Iranian army from Kuwaiti territory. Both the Iranian air force and navy remain well within striking distance. In response, Kuwait strengthened its garrisons on Warba and Bubiyan and began constructing offshore naval installations to control access to its territorial waters. Still, immediate Kuwaiti defense needs include an advanced fighter, infantry fighting vehicles, a joint C^3 system and improved radar networks. The smaller GCC states have emphasized their determination to send ground forces to help Kuwait in case of attack, and the Kuwaitis may also call for Jordanian and British help.[30]

While national defense may be assured only under the GCC umbrella Kuwait does have a real need for effective internal security forces. In recent years, Kuwait has suffered through a number of acts of violence. In the late 1970s, there was a spate of bombings attributed to feuding among Palestinian factions. The underground *Dawa* movement, apparently with assistance from the Iranian government and radical Lebanese Shia, carried out bomb attacks on the U.S. embassy and Kuwaiti instal-

---

[29]The quality and professionalism of some soldiers is suspect. Kuwait has sought to ameliorate the potentially dangerous effects of this situation by reserving the occupation of pilot for native Kuwaitis and by reserving command positions for members of the al Sabah family.

[30]Nevertheless, there is no way around the stark conclusion that both the GCC and the United States may have to consider Kuwait expendable in the event of either an Iranian attack or a Soviet assault. Such an attack, however, is highly unlikely now or in the foreseeable future.

lations in December 1983. A Kuwait Airways plane was hijacked to Tehran in December 1984 and two passengers killed and several Kuwaitis wounded.

In May 1985 an assassination attempt barely missed killing Kuwait's ruler, and in July of that year 56 people were killed by bombs thrown at seaside cafes. In June 1986 explosions from planted bombs caused considerable damage in the country's oil installations near Mina Ahmadi. These attacks were also attributed to the radical international Shia underground taking credit under the *nom de guerre* of Islamic Jihad. If these attacks by outside forces were not enough, Kuwait has also experienced increased Islamic fundamentalist sentiment and some Sunni-Shia tensions. Kuwait's salvation from internal disruption may be the health and vitality of its elected National Assembly, the only one in the GCC. The Assembly, however, was suspended in July 1986, for the second time in its 24-year history.

United Arab Emirates

The UAE has generally ranked second in GCC defense spending in recent years, with about 40 percent of the federal budget allocated to defense. This can be attributed to the UAE's very late start in all aspects of development; the abundance of oil, particularly in Abu Dhabi and Dubai, which provides financial wherewithal; and the long competition and rivalry among the UAE's member states.[31]

The origins of armed forces in the UAE date back to 1951 and the formation of the Trucial Oman Levies, later Trucial Oman Scouts, under British supervision and with British officers and Jordanian noncommissioned officers. Upon independence in 1971, the Scouts were the logical choice for conversion into the armed forces of the new UAE state. But the Union Defense Force (UDF), as the Scouts were renamed, was not the only armed force in the new UAE, nor was it even the largest. Over the decade of the 1960s, the continuing competition between the seven emirates had embraced the development of competing military units. Thus in 1971, the Abu Dhabi Defense Force (ADDF) far eclipsed the UDF. In addition, there were also the Dubai Defense Force (DDF), the Ras al-Khaima Mobile Force, the Sharjah National Guard and the Ajman Defense Force (in the process of formation). Rather than serving as the armed forces for the entire state, the UDF existed as a somewhat neutral element among competing forces.

While logic dictated the merger of all these units, politics militated against it. Abu Dhabi and Dubai had fought a border war as recently as

---

[31]In addition to above sources, see Frauke Heard-Bey, *From Trucial States to United Arab Emirates: A Society in Transition* (London: Longman, 1982); and Ali Mohammed Khalifa, *The United Arab Emirates: Unity in Fragmentation* (Boulder, CO: Westview Press, 1979).

1948, and all the emirates envied Abu Dhabi's newfound wealth and muscle. The infusion of new wealth into traditional rivalries resulted in arms races within the UAE. By 1975, the ADDF had grown to 15,000 personnel equipped with 135 armored vehicles, two squadrons of Mirage IIIs and Vs, some Hawker Hunters and helicopters, Rapier amd Crotale SAMs, Vigilant ATGWs and Vosper Thornycroft and Fairey Marine Spear class patrol craft. The DDF had also expanded to rival the UDF in size, with 3,000 men, Ferret and Saladin armored cars, several kinds of helicopters and patrol craft. Only the UDF had tanks, however.

Despite the creation of a federal Ministry of Defense and the existence of the UDF, successful merger of the armed forces has lagged behind federal integration in other sectors. The UAE Armed Forces formally came into being only at the end of 1976. The ADDF became the Western Command, the DDF the Central Command and the Ras al-Khaima Mobile Force the Northern Command; the UDF was renamed the Yarmuk Brigade, and the Sharjah National Guard was merged with the federal police force. Nevertheless, the merger was still only on paper: the seven states continued separate arms-purchasing policies, and each force was commanded by the appropriate ruler's son.

Despite recent progress, some external security problems still remain. UAE naval capabilities are minimal, even though plans for expansion of the navy (essentially limited to Abu Dhabi) were announced before Iran began attacking tankers off the coast of Dubai. While the UAE has a modest air-defense capability, they lack the early warning or tactical air capability to defeat an air attack. UAE officials do not consider themselves covered by a GCC or Saudi defense umbrella and therefore argue within the GCC for a conciliatory, rather than a confrontational, attitude to Iran (Iran also remains Dubai's largest trading partner and a number of Iranians reside in the UAE). As in the other GCC states, the UAE armed forces are still heavily dependent on expatriate officers and trainers and require more time to digest the flood of new arms and equipment. Approximately 85 percent of the ranks, as well as some officers, are foreign (with a preponderance of Omanis); and all UAE nationals have been promoted to the officer corps.

Finally, the successful integration of the armed forces depends directly on the success of the federation experiment.[32] While a UAE lifespan of 15 years augurs well for the future, much depends on the personalities of Abu Dhabi's ruler Sheikh Zayed and Dubai's Sheikh Rashid. The newness of the UAE armed forces, their incomplete efforts toward

---

[32]On this topic, see J. E. Peterson, "The Future of Federalism in the United Arab Emirates," in H. Richard Sindelar, ed., *Swirling Currents: The Arabian Gulf in the 1980s* (Washington: Middle East Institute, forthcoming).

integration, and the political divisions inherent in a multistate system all work to its disadvantage as a factor in pan-GCC considerations.

Bahrain and Qatar

The other two GCC states, Bahrain and Qatar, have very modest armed forces. The Bahrain Defense Force grew out of the Bahrain Levy Corps, established after World War I, but it was utilized primarily as a police force until independence. Indeed, the few patrol craft and helicopters possessed by the nation belong to the police and are used to control immigration and smuggling. Bahrain recently received the first half of a dozen F-5 fighters from the United States. The 2,300-strong army is equipped with a few armored cars, TOW antitank missiles and the RBS-70 SAM system. Because of the British presence in Bahrain before 1971, the country boasts well-developed military facilities, however, including a large airfield and a naval base, where the U.S. Navy's small Mideastforce was formerly homeported and which it still uses on a regular basis.

Qatar is only slightly better armed. Since Britain was responsible for Qatar's defense before 1971, the Gulf state's armed forces have emerged out of the modest Public Security Department only since independence. In addition to the 5,000-strong army, which operates several dozen AMX-30 tanks and the usual mix of armored cars, Qatar boasts nine large patrol craft, several equipped with Exocets, and 17 combat aircraft, with more on order. Not surprisingly, both states suffer even more than their neighbors from manpower problems and rely heavily on expatriates (Qataris make up only 30 percent of the nation's army). Qatar's situation is enhanced, however, by its close relationship to Saudi Arabia. Bahrain and Qatar provide only a symbolic contribution to GCC military strength, and they are covered by Saudi combat air patrol and the AWACS against an Iranian air threat. The military capabilities of the UAE, Bahrain and Qatar together are essentially limited to policing functions and internal security. It falls to Saudi Arabia, and to a far lesser extent Oman and even less to Kuwait, to provide the backbone of GCC defense forces.

COLLECTIVE SECURITY UNDER THE GCC

Despite its short history, the GCC has undertaken significant economic, political and security initiatives. In the economic sphere the Unified Economic Agreement was drawn up in June 1981 and partly implemented in 1983. In political terms (and beyond the intangible benefit of regular meetings and consultation by the leaders and top officials of the member states), the principal effort has been directed toward mediation in the Iran-Iraq war. Beginning with the third GCC summit in November 1982, Kuwaiti and UAE representatives have visited both Tehran and Baghdad, as well as other capitals, in an effort to seek a peaceful solution to the end of the war. While this was not the first mediation effort, it has been the longest-serving one and, because of the vital interests of the mediators and their close ties to the combatants, probably stands the best chance of any to succeed. GCC efforts have been more successful in prompting the establishment of diplomatic relations between Oman and the PDRY. Efforts have also been made to settle the dispute between Bahrain and Qatar over the Hawar and other islands, which flared again in the summer of 1986.[33]

Not surprisingly, collective security efforts, with emphasis on internal security and military aspects, have figured high on the GCC's list of priorities. While Oman has urged attention to planning in this area since the GCC was formed, the fear of antagonizing Iran and Iraq prevented any serious discussion of security affairs until the November 1982 meeting of the Supreme Council. Redoubled concern over collective security was also prompted by fears of Iraq's collapse after the success of Iranian counteroffensives during that year. Bilateral security agreements, a collective air-defense system, joint military exercises, a joint strike force, a joint military command and an indigenous arms industry have all been considered. Furthermore, the wealthier GCC states have pledged several billion dollars to strengthen the defenses of Bahrain and Oman.

Not all of these self-defense schemes lend themselves to easy implementation, and some should be considered achievable only in the very long term. Nevertheless, the GCC's genuine security accomplishments should not be overlooked. Bilateral security arrangements were signed between Saudi Arabia and all the other states (with the exception of Kuwait) in early 1982, prompted by the abortive Bahrain coup attempt in December 1981 (as well as the earlier Mecca incident and Iran's bombing of Kuwait). These agreements called for joint action against security offenders, for the exchange of information, training and equipment and for the extradition of criminals.[34] Efforts to force a more

---

[33]In March 1986 Bahrain began to construct a coast-guard station on the tiny islet of Fasht al-Dibal. Qatar, disputing Bahrain's claim, seized the islet on April 26, installing artillery and antiaircraft guns, and also concentrated troops across from the disputed Hawar Islands. The confrontation was eased by GCC and especially Saudi mediation, and Qatari withdrawal from Fasht al-Dibal was supervised by military observers from the four noninvolved GCC states. In addition to these activities within the Gulf region, the GCC Supreme Council sent Kuwait's deputy prime minister and Qatar's minister of state for foreign affairs to Syria in late 1983 to try to end the infighting within the PLO at that time. Attempts were also made to mediate between Baghdad and Damascus and Rabat and Algiers.

[34]*An-Nahar Arab Report and MEMO*, March 1, 1981. Kuwait's desire to keep a healthy distance from more powerful Saudi Arabia appeared to be at the root of its reticence to sign the bilateral agreement. Similar concerns over Saudi hegemony have delayed, if not prevented, the signing of a GCC collective security agreement.

comprehensive internal security agreement failed to win approval at the November 1982 summit and have continued to languish. The escalation of Iraqi attacks against Kharg Island in mid-1985 and the attempt to assassinate Kuwait's head of state in that same year led to a renewed emphasis on security concerns and a reaffirmation of the GCC's readiness to mediate between Iran and Iraq at the November 1985 GCC summit in Muscat.[35]

Establishment of a collective air-defense system is more ambitious but seemingly within the range of GCC capabilities in the near future. Planning for an integrated system began in January 1982, and the go-ahead was received at the November 1982 summit. It is based on Saudi Arabia's AWACS radar and C^3I (command, control, communications and intelligence) capabilities, linked to antiaircraft missiles and interceptor aircraft. Ideally, the UAE's projected Lambda air-defense and electronic warfare system and Kuwait's Thomson radars and upgraded Hawk missiles eventually would be plugged into the GCC system.[36]

Another area in which cooperation has already been evident is joint military exercises, largely bilateral in nature. Saudi F-15s and F-5s were joined by Kuwaiti Skyhawks in 11-day maneuvers in November 1983, covering training in air bombardment, air interception operations, fast transfer and takeoff and other exercises. This followed a Saudi-Bahraini air exercise in land-and-sea search and rescue. Then in 1984 Oman and the UAE held joint air force exercises in February and April; Saudi, Qatari, Kuwaiti and Bahraini units participated in air mobilization exercises in Bahrain in April; Thamarit Air Base in Dhofar was the scene of Saudi-Omani exercises in August; Bahrain and Qatar conducted a naval exercise also in August; and additional maneuvers were held in Saudi Arabia in October.

During 1985 Qatar hosted a joint naval exercise with Kuwait in January; the Kuwaiti and Omani air forces carried out joint maneuvers near the Strait of Hormuz in March; Abu Dhabi was the site of a UAE-Kuwaiti exercise in March; the Kuwait navy participated in joint maneuvers with the Saudi navy in April; the Saudi, Qatari and Omani navies held a joint exercise off Oman in September; and Kuwait and Saudi Arabia conducted joint air exercises in December. Another potential

---

[35]*New York Times*, Nov. 7, 1985; *Washington Post*, Nov. 7, 1985. A flurry of activity in 1985, including the Saudi foreign minister's trip to Tehran in May and a Riyadh visit by his Iranian counterpart in December, raised expectations of a possible softening of the Iranian position. Iran's subsequent refusal to allow the Omani minister of state for foreign affairs, on behalf of the GCC, to visit Tehran doomed the initiative, however.

[36]*The Middle East*, No. 119 (Sept. 1984), pp. 15-18. Some information gathered by the Saudi-based AWACS on Iranian air movements has been shared with Kuwait since 1984. Gulf News Agency, June 22, 1984.

area of cooperation lies in joint naval patrols through the Strait of Hormuz (although only Oman and Saudi Arabia possess the necessary capability at present to contribute to this function).[37]

Ambitious plans for military coordination within the GCC framework go far beyond bilateral exercises. A Military Committee was established within the GCC Secretariat, the six chiefs of staff first met in September 1981 and their ministers in January 1982, and regular discussions between ranking military officials from all the member states on the ways and means of developing joint military coordination began in mid-1983. As a first step, the GCC has sought to create a joint strike force, and the "Peninsula Shield" joint exercises held in western Abu Dhabi in October 1983 were meant to demonstrate the feasibility of developing the GCC's own rapid-deployment force. Infantry, tank and artillery forces from all six states, along with Mirages and Ghazal helicopters from the UAE's air force, participated in a mock attack on an "enemy-held" hilltop position, with the final assault performed before an audience of the six GCC heads of state.[38] "Peninsula Shield II," held one year later at Hafr al-Batin in northeastern Saudi Arabia, was the second annual exercise of troops earmarked for the GCC RDF. The two weeks of maneuvers, involving 10,000 men from all six states, included parachute drops of men and equipment, air support and intercept missions, nighttime offensives and antiaircraft demonstrations.[39]

The Council, however, has a long way to go before realizing its RDF objective—not to mention the goal of a unified military command—despite the growing numbers of joint exercises. The difficulties encountered by the UAE in unifying its various armed forces stands as an example of the distance that the GCC has to go. There are more than enough obstacles with the proposed RDF alone:

---

[37]SPA (Riyadh) in Arabic, Nov. 30, 1983 (FBIS, Dec. 1, 1983); *MEED*, Apr. 20, 1984; WAKH (Manama) in Arabic, Apr. 2, 1984 (FBIS, Apr. 12, 1984); Muscat Domestic Service in Arabic, Aug. 16, 1984 (FBIS, Aug. 17, 1984); WAKH (Manama) in Arabic, Aug. 29, 1984 (FBIS, Aug. 30, 1984); *al-Qabas* (Kuwait), Sept. 3, 1984 (FBIS, Sept. 5, 1984); KUNA (Kuwait) in Arabic, Jan. 14, 1985 (FBIS, Jan. 15, 1985); WAKH (Manama) in English, Mar. 1, 1985 (FBIS, Mar. 5, 1985); QNA (Doha) in Arabic, Mar. 21, 1985 (FBIS, Mar. 21, 1985); and WAM (Abu Dhabi) in Arabic, Mar. 27, 1985 (FBIS, Mar. 28, 1985); Muscat Domestic Service in Arabic, Oct. 1, 1985 (FBIS, Oct. 2, 1985); *Arab Times*, Dec. 10, 1985.

[38]WAKH (Manama) in Arabic, Oct. 13, 1983 (FBIS, Oct. 14, 1983); *New York Times*, Oct. 16, 1983; and *The Middle East*, No. 109 (Nov. 1983), p. 17.

[39]WAKH (Manama) in Arabic, Oct. 10, 1984 (FBIS, Oct. 11, 1984); Riyadh Domestic Service in Arabic, Oct. 15, 1984 (FBIS, Oct. 15, 1984); *Washington Post*, Nov. 30, 1984. It was reported after the sabotage of Kuwait's oil installations in mid-1986 that Saudi forces were standing by for dispatch to Kuwait to secure the oil fields and confront Iranian threats. *Al-Ahram* International Edition (Cairo), Aug. 14, 1986 (FBIS, Aug. 15, 1986).

Formation of a Gulf strike force, for instance, is certain to face manpower problems and will have to rely mainly on the Saudi army and will most likely have a Saudi commander. Even then, the use of other Arab troops or Pakistani forces will probably have to be considered if the force is to be capable of handling anything other than the most minor local disturbances. There will also be logistical problems arising from the lack of roads suitable for the movement of troops across state borders.[40]

Nevertheless, an announcement was made at the Fifth Supreme Council meeting, held in Kuwait in November 1984, that it had been decided to create a joint GCC strike force under the command of a Saudi general, even though the GCC's secretary-general was candid enough to say that force would be largely "symbolic." Approval for the RDF appeared to be for a limited period, and it was not intended to be a permanent force but would be drawn from units of all six states in an emergency and then disbanded at the end of the crisis. The units participating in the "Peninsula Shield II" exercises in October 1984 were expected to be earmarked for the RDF.[41] By late 1985, all the GCC members had stationed small contingents at the King Khalid Military City (Hafr al-Batin), although the force was principally composed of Saudi and Kuwaiti units, presumably because of their particular concern over the Iran-Iraq war.

A final area of proposed cooperation lies in arms acquisition. At present, the GCC states are equipped with American, Brazilian, British, Chinese, French, German, Italian, Swiss and even Soviet arms (in Kuwait), which seriously hinders joint operations, prevents the transfer of spare parts and ammunition and hampers effective use of command, control and communications systems. Given the huge amounts of arms already delivered or on order, full coordination of military forces may be difficult to achieve. On the other hand, efforts to implement a unified procurement program, particularly where relevant to the collective air-defense system, cannot help but be beneficial if put into operation immediately. Despite the immense size of their previous purchases, the GCC states' defense spending, at about $40 billion annually, continues to account for approximately half of the total amount for the Third World.[42] Even Saudi Arabia, running budget deficits in 1984 and 1985, continued to spend over 25 percent of its budget on defense; the Omani figure has been over 40 percent. One effect of such a unified procurement policy may be a shift away from heavy reliance on purchases from the United States (particularly on the part of Saudi Arabia) because of

---

[40]*The Middle East*, No. 119 (Sept. 1984), pp. 15-18.

[41]*New York Times*, Nov. 30, 1984; *Washington Post*, Nov. 30, 1984; *The Middle East*, No. 123 (Jan. 1985), p. 6.

[42]*The Economist*, Jan. 21, 1984, p. 31.

the political difficulties in Arab purchases of sophisticated U.S. arms. The denial of sales of Stinger hand-held missiles to Kuwait in 1984 and of additional F-15 aircraft to Saudi Arabia in 1985, largely due to pro-Israel lobbying in the U.S. Congress, has caused many GCC and Arab countries to look elsewhere for more reliable suppliers.

An even more difficult task would be the establishment of an indigenous arms industry, given the level of economic development in these states. Although $1.4 billion has been allocated for this purpose, cooperation with one or more non-GCC states appears necessary along the lines of the earlier Arab Military Industrialization Organization based in Egypt. Jordan, Egypt, Turkey and Pakistan have all been mentioned as possible partners, although there are drawbacks to consideration of each of these countries.[43] Speculation has also centered on Iraq as potential partner. Toward this end, a tank prototype was apparently produced in Saudi Arabia in 1983, Saudi-Brazilian discussions in late 1985 reportedly included the possibility of a Saudi assembly plant for Brazilian tanks, and the Saudis soon after established a General Institution of Military Industries.[44]

The potential combined military capability of the six GCC states is not entirely negligible, representing 190,000 men, 900 main battle tanks, more than 3,500 other armored vehicles, over 425 interceptor and ground-attack aircraft, between 500 and 800 helicopters, 36 fast-attack naval vessels and, of course, the highly sophisticated air-defense and communications system.[45] GCC ground forces' capability to resist an overland attack rests principally on the Saudi armored brigades, supported by Kuwait's Chieftain tanks. There is greater variety in strike aircraft, although Saudi Arabia's 100 F-5s form the heart of GCC capabilities, to which the recently purchased Tornado ground-attack fighters can be added along with Kuwait's A-4 Skyhawks and Oman's Hunters and Jaguars. Most of the GCC states have invested heavily in air defense capabilities, and the Saudi E-3A AWACS will provide the basis for an integrated C^3I package, to which the Saudi F-15s, the Kuwaiti Mirage 1s, the UAE's Mirage 5s, Qatar's Mirage 1s and Omani Tornados (both on order) can be linked, along with a wide variety of surface-to-air missile systems.[46]

---

[43]*The Middle East*, No. 119 (Sept. 1984), pp. 15-18.

[44]*Arab Times*, Dec. 25, 1983 and Dec. 1, 1985, *Defense and Foreign Affairs Weekly*, Dec. 23, 1985.

[45]*The Economist*, Jan. 21, 1984, p. 31; *Middle East Economic Digest*, Oct. 28, 1983, p. 24. By way of comparison, Israel has 512,000 personnel, 3,600 tanks, over 8,000 other armored vehicles, 53 interceptor and ground-attack aircraft, over 200 helicopters, and a navy with three submarines and six corvettes, as well as 24 fast-attack craft. *The Military Balance, 1985-1986* (London: International Institute for Strategic Studies, 1985), pp. 77-78.

[46]McNaugher, "Arms and Allies," pp. 505-13.

But this is only the beginning of collective security. The absorption of large numbers of highly sophisticated weapons, the complex mix of various types of weapons from a wide variety of suppliers, the small base of indigenous manpower and serious training problems, the intensive competition for skilled manpower and the lack of combat experience, as well as differences in outlooks and policy goals among the defense institutions of the six member states, continue to hinder GCC attempts at self-defense. Just as in the political and economic fields, the most fundamental hurdle that GCC security efforts face is true coordination and integration. GCC defensive organization is not comparable to NATO, with its unified command structure and active American involvement in Western European defenses. It is therefore unrealistic at this early stage of their cooperation and development to expect a GCC security framework along the lines of NATO.

DOVETAILING GCC SECURITY NEEDS AND WESTERN ASSISTANCE

Obviously, the GCC states cannot be expected to cope adequately with the entire range of potential security threats. Thomas McNaugher of the Brookings Institution notes,

> . . . the GCC can be expected at best to police the Peninsula—to deal with various threats from the Yemens, and hopefully to settle disputes among themselves amicably. But they cannot hope to defend the Peninsula against external attack . . . [which] they can hope at best to deter by promising some damage to the attacker, to limit damage initially, and thus to buy time until reinforcements arrive.[47]

Gulf security clearly depends on a partnership between the states of the region and the West, principally the United States. But perhaps the most important thing to remember about this partnership is that the United States or Western role is that of "backup," to be invited in when the GCC states cannot handle a threat on their own. It is not up to the United States to take the initiative but to respond and provide assistance when asked. It is to be hoped that in such an event the United States will be able to live up to its commitment of guaranteeing Gulf security without this issue becoming entangled in the ongoing Arab-Israeli conflict.

In military terms, an "over-the-horizon" partnership is less than ideal, but it is workable. To a certain extent, the problem of distance can be offset by maintaining a naval presence in the Arabian Sea, prestocking equipment in Saudi Arabia and on ships in the Indian Ocean, improving and overbuilding Gulf (especially Saudi) military

---

[47]Ibid., p. 517.

installations, supplying AWACS and other equipment, and providing U.S. advisers to these states to assure a measure of standardization in arms and training. No matter how well prepared U.S. forces may be, their time of response to a Gulf contingency will be slowed. But those contingencies which unambiguously will require an American response, particularly a direct Soviet or Iranian attack on the GCC, will require lengthy and obvious preparation by the attackers and thus the greatest lead time for the defenders.

Fears of a Soviet threat, always more pronounced in the West than among the GCC countries, have abated. The rapid sequence of events at the beginning of the decade that seemed to mark decreased American influence and/or increased Soviet presence in a number of neighboring countries has ceased. Rather than acting to exacerbate the Iran-Iraq war, the Soviets have preferred a peaceful end to a war which poses considerable risks to their position in the Gulf. Instead of attacking the legitimacy of the Gulf Cooperation Council, the Soviet Union recently has moved toward rapprochement, approving the development of Omani-South Yemeni ties, establishing its own diplomatic relations with Oman and the UAE, providing additional arms to Kuwait (including SAM missiles after the American refusal), and continuing a fitful dialogue with Saudi Arabia.

Despite the attenuation of the war and Iran's inability to break Iraq's back, the Islamic republic has been careful not to expand the war to attacks on the GCC. To be sure, it has stressed its displeasure over moral, material and financial support for Iraq by promoting sabotage and "accidentally" bombing Kuwait and firing on Kuwaiti and Saudi oil tankers at various locations in the Gulf, including off Qatar, off Dubai and close to Saudi territorial waters. But GCC steadfastness and Western assurances of decisive action to counter a direct attack have appeared to convince Iranian policymakers of the dangers of "playing with fire." Even in the event of an Iraqi collapse and Iranian occupation of southern Iraq, it is debatable that Iran would push on militarily against the GCC. Certainly Kuwait's exposed position would require significant accommodation but the GCC and its protectors are likely to remain firm.

U.S. policy toward the Gulf has demonstrated a not-inconsiderable maturation in the last few years. The decline of overreactions to Western vulnerabilities and dependence on Gulf oil during the past decade provides a welcome breathing space in which to create the very necessary foundations of political cooperation and dialogue, perhaps even a constructive learning process for both Western and Gulf governments. It also means that the U.S. government probably has less opportunity to display its propensity for shooting itself in the foot as far as the Middle East is concerned, for undertaking rash actions and strident rhetoric under the pressure of crises and for disregarding the lessons of past experiences.

At the same time that American perceptions toward the Gulf have been changing, perceptions of the proper role of USCENTCOM have also been evolving. Within USCENTCOM, there is a widespread belief that it has grown more sophisticated in regard to its mission and requirements in just a few years. At the beginning, the Command was only an RDF, an interventionist force. By the middle of the 1980s, its principal mission came to be seen more as deterrence, with a strategy based on helping friendly nations defend themselves. Altered views were reflected in a 1984 Senate committee report which noted:

> Senior U.S. military commanders in the region don't envision any likely contingency in which this full array of U.S. forces might be needed. Whereas five years ago the Rapid Deployment Force was created with a Soviet invasion of Iran or other Gulf oil fields in mind, no one now expects this to happen. If the Gulf war should escalate to the point of U.S. military involvement, most military observers believe that a deployment might include several squadrons of U.S. fighter aircraft, additional AWACS and tankers, additional destroyers/frigates for convoy duty, and possibly a second carrier battle group. Senior U.S. military commanders in the region do not envision the need for U.S. ground troops except for security guard duty.[48]

Such responses as the dispatch of AWACS aircraft to Egypt in February 1983, to Sudan in July 1984 and the deployment of survey and countermeasures teams in the Red Sea during the mining threat of July 1984 (at the request of Egypt and Saudi Arabia) were cited in this regard. Rather than intervention, emphasis was placed on other functions, such as conducting joint maneuvers, administering security assistance training programs for the regions' armed forces, supervising arms transfers to the region and promoting military liaison.[49]

The United States has registered major accomplishments in a few short years. By 1984 it could be said that the U.S. military presence in the area was considerable but remarkably unobtrusive. There were 11,500 American sailors and soldiers in the Gulf and Arabian Sea area, and another 4,000 civilians were working under Defense Department contract in Saudi Arabia. The duties of these Americans included manning TPS-43 radar sites, flying AWACS in support of the Saudi combat air patrol and flying F-14 patrols in the Arabian Sea. Despite the size of

---

[48]U.S. Congress, Senate, *War in the Gulf*, p. 21.

[49]For a recent appraisal of USCENTCOM accomplishments and its role in the region by its commander, see Robert C. Kingston, "U.S. Central Command: Refocusing the Lens of Stability on a Region in Crisis," *Defense '84*, Nov.-Dec. 1984, pp. 29-34.

the U.S. presence, it was relatively unobtrusive, with all but about 1,000 military personnel serving at sea. The U.S. Navy presence in particular was considered to be "out of sight" since it was located outside the Gulf itself. In 1984, the United States deployed about 10 frigate/destroyer class ships in the area, one aircraft carrier with over 50 combat aircraft on board, four AWACS with four tanker aircraft flying out of Riyadh and four support ships, as well as various support aircraft with the carrier.[50]

From an American point of view, there are two related cornerstones of an effective policy that deserve as much or more consideration than unilateral military capabilities. The first involves the necessity of enhancing working security relationships with each of the GCC states. For the United States, "reassurance" of its friends in the GCC is just as important as deterrence of the Soviet Union.[51]

The United States has taken significant steps to improve its security ties to individual GCC states in the last few years. Several dozen U.S. military personnel and about 100 private contractors have been working in Kuwait in connection with the foreign military sales agreements totalling $1.3 billion. Their tasks include general training, flight training for about 150 Kuwaitis, advice on air defense, help in maintaining the I-Hawk missile system and A-4 Skyhawks and the institution of a computerized support system.

Bahrain received the first of the dozen F-5G Tigershark fighters (with Sidewinder missiles) it ordered from the United States in December 1985, some pilots and mechanics are undergoing training in the United States, the U.S. Army Corps of Engineers has assisted in planning for the new airbase in southern Bahrain and the United States intends to sell the emirate 54 M-60 tanks. An I-Hawk system is in the process of installation in the UAE, and the United States is wrapping up a $300 million military construction program in Oman, the only GCC state to allow regular access to its installations. While the activities of the pro-Israel lobby in the United States have forced Saudi Arabia to turn elsewhere for recent arms sales, and thereby set a precedent for future purchases, cooperation between the two countries in training and maintenance of existing Saudi equipment continues unabated.

Perhaps an even more important cornerstone of U.S. policy involves a serious commitment to repair and maintain what threatens to become

---

[50]U.S. Congress, Senate,"War in the Gulf," p. 18.

[51]"The object of deterrence is to persuade an adversary that the costs to him of seeking a military solution to his political problems will far outweigh the benefits. The object of reassurance is to persuade one's own people, and those of one's allies, that the benefits of military action, or preparation for it, will outweigh the costs." Michael Howard, "Reassurance and Deterrence: Western Defense in the 1980s," *Foreign Affairs*, Vol. 61, No. 2 (Winter 1982-1983), p. 317.

a crumbling political relationship. Official relations, economic ties and security cooperation with the GCC states continue to hold firm, but such U.S. actions as approval of Israel's raid on Tunisia; the freezing of Libyan assets in the United States; the American raid on Tripoli; and the U.S. arms-for-hostages agreement with Iran provoke increasing criticism, whether in official statements, in the press or among the general population. While the Gulf and the Arab-Israeli conflict are two separate issues, there is an unavoidable connection in the support that Arab Gulf states provide frontline Arab states and the Palestinians. The continuation of the Arab-Israeli conflict and unquestioned U.S. support of Israel have jeopardized and will continue to jeopardize the American position in the Middle East.

There are those skeptics who contend that the United States has heard this warning before and nothing has happened: the Gulf states remain politically tied to and security-dependent on the United States. This is a foolish argument. The ominous rise in vicious attacks perpetrated by Middle Eastern fanatics on American institutions and citizens is a direct product of American inattention. Popular opinion in the Arab world has long been favorable toward American society and people, even as it has been critical of U.S. government policy; but the criticism has risen to a crescendo in recent years. If the trend is not arrested, ties to the United States eventually will become a liability for Gulf governments, and they will be pressed to distance themselves from Washington. That lays the groundwork in a few years for a serious confrontation at a time when the West probably will be as dependent on Gulf oil, if not more so, than it was in 1973-1974.

In the final analysis, the GCC states have taken significant steps to acquire the ability to buy time until outside help arrives, and they have done very well in protecting themselves from more likely, if more limited, internal and regional threats. It is, of course, these states who bear the principal burden for their own security. As the secretary general of the GCC has put it, "The world may laugh at us when we say that the Gulf countries alone are authorized to defend the region, but whatever our capabilities may be, we insist that this is the basic principle for achieving security and peace for our peoples."[52]

---

[52]Abdulla Bishara quoted in the Kuwaiti newspaper *al-Qabas*, Aug. 26, 1983 (FBIS, Aug. 31, 1983).

Chapter 9

THE GULF COOPERATION COUNCIL: A COMPARATIVE NOTE

Ralph Braibanti

Ralph Braibanti is James B. Duke Professor of Political Science as well as the founder and director of Islamic and Arabian Development Studies at Duke University.

Two events in late 1986 call attention to the significance of the Gulf Cooperation Council. On November 26 the causeway connecting Saudi Arabia and Bahrain was officially opened by the rulers of the two states. On November 25 the Abul Bukoosh oil platform, about 100 miles northwest of Abu Dhabi and within UAE territory, was attacked by an unidentified aircraft. It was widely assumed that the aircraft was Iranian and that it was a repetition of an attack against the same oil field in October.

I

The first event dramatically points to the emerging physical and institutional structure of peaceful cooperation among six states of the Arabian peninsula. While it has positive consequences for the economies of GCC members, its psychological significance as a manifestation of the interior sense of Islamic and Arabian unity must not be underestimated. It is not insignificant that the *Arab News* of Jeddah described the causeway as a "bridge of love," and that the Emir of Bahrain, in a display of magnanimity in consonance with this ambience, officially named it the King Fahd causeway.

The Gulf Cooperation Council has a fortuitous base which few, if any, other comparable regional entities share. Geographic propinquity and commonality of interest are buttressed by the remarkable degree of cultural and religious homogeneity found in the six states. The depth of this homogeneity, shared by no other group of nations in the Islamic world of a billion adherents, justifies the use of the term "Arabians" as distinct from the term "Arabs." It was Peter Mansfield, the British author, who first made use of this important distinction by both the title and the substance of his book *The New Arabians,* first published in 1981. He used this term as a device for giving special identity to a small portion of the larger cultural group he had formerly characterized in his book *The Arabs,* published in 1976.

All six member states of the GCC embrace Sunni Islam and have constitutively Islamic polities. The modality of this Islam is consonant in varying degrees with that which is regnant in Saudi Arabia, though there are significant departures in social practices, especially in Kuwait and Bahrain. Where a significant Shiite minority exists, as in Bahrain, the successful evolution of political and social accommodations has thus far forestalled rents in the fabric. The presence of large numbers of expatriates is a problem shared by all, and the gradual fulfillment of manpower needs by GCC nationals is proceeding in much the same way, though not necessarily at the same pace, in each of the countries. This cultural unity is graphically expressed by the fact that these are the only states in the Arab world where national dress is proudly worn in daily life by people of every status, including rulers and bedouin. This manifestation of pride in one's culture, unique in the Arab world and uncommon in the Muslim world (Iran and Pakistan excepted), must not be minimized. It is a powerful external symbol of an inner sense of distinctive identity.

The GCC states also share the heritage of a relative absence of colonial rule as compared to the experience of other Islamic states, such as those of the Maghrib, Pakistan or Indonesia. That is not to say, however, that colonial influence was totally absent in the Gulf. Certainly the emirates, as trucial states, were subject to a series of treaties with the British as early as 1820. Bahrain's treaty dependency with Britain dates from 1861 and that of Qatar from 1867. While these treaty relations lasted until independence in 1971, the British were concerned more with preventing territory from being ceded to other powers and preserving their dominance in the surrounding waters. In contrast to the case of India, for example, the penetration of British culture was not deep, and Arabian culture was certainly not displaced.

The political forms found in the six member states share common characteristics. Their polities defy conventional Western, social-science classificatory schemes. They are moving along a spectrum from patrimonial to rationalized bureaucratic systems. These two spheres of validity contract and expand at different rhythms in the six systems. There is not necessarily a consistent unilinear movement toward contraction of the patrimonial and expansion of the bureaucratic sphere. But viewed over a period of half a century, the move in that direction is perceptible.

Clearly none of these systems is a theocracy, nor an absolute monarchy nor a medieval skeikhdom. Neither are they constitutional monarchies in the British sense, nor presidential or parliamentary systems. They are Islamic polities undergoing rapid transformation economically and somewhat more deliberate change politically. They are intriguing blends of familial, tribal, religious and technocratic rule, which have been able to maintain both a social and psychological connection between rulers and ruled. In so doing a consensus is achieved within the context of tribal traditions and in the shadow of a pervasive and unbroken continuum of Arabianism and Islam.

II

The remarkable degree of cultural, political and experiential homogeneity characterizing the GCC is startlingly evident by a brief excursus into comparable entities. The most recent regional grouping organized primarily for mutual security is the South Asian Association for Regional Cooperation (SAARC), comprising India, Pakistan, Sri Lanka, Bangladesh and Nepal. Two of the members are Islamic states; two are predominantly Hindu. Sri Lanka is Buddhist-Sinhalese with a fractious minority of Hindu Tamils. Traditions of enmity undergird the new cooperative structure. Pakistan, created from India in 1947 in a partition marked by massacres of enormous proportions, fought three wars with India. Bangladesh seceded from Pakistan in 1971 in a bloody civil war substantially helped by India. Sri Lanka's relationship with India is marred by the Sri Lankan perception that India aids and abets the Tamil insurgency.

The SAARC members have divergent foreign alliances. Pakistan has strong relations with the United States, Saudi Arabia and China and remains wary of the Soviet Union. India, having fought border wars with China in 1959 and 1962, has cool relations with the Chinese but has treaty relations with the Soviets. Bangladesh remains within an Islamic orbit, and made peace with Pakistan at the Lahore summit of the Organization of the Islamic Conference in 1974. Its earlier friendly relations with India, an ally in the Bengali secession of 1971, have changed to bitterness and animosity.

Thus, in SAARC we have neither a national architectonics, religion, language, foreign policy or similarity of polities to unite the association. It is in a sense a cooperative framework of desperation designed for security purposes and to discourage external intervention in regional affairs. Finally, it is inevitably dominated by India. The richness and solidity of the institutional base of the GCC is tellingly revealed by this comparison.

The short-lived entity rather awkwardly called Regional Cooperation for Development (RCD), established by Pakistan, Iran and Turkey in 1964, had many of the same defects in institutional cohesion as the SAARC. The League of Arab States, established in 1945 and with a current membership of 22 states, also lacks cohesion. To some extent it has been eclipsed by the reality that Arab problems now transcend the Arab world and must be dealt with in the larger Islamic and global spheres. The pan-Arabism of Nasser and later of Gadhafi have given way to a pan-Islam which may be a more authentic expression of the *ummah,* the commonwealth of predominantly Muslim nations. This has been accentuated by the imminent threat of the exportability of the non-Arab Iranian revolution of Khomeini. Moreover, the Arab League was weakened by the suspension of Egypt after the Camp David accords and the consequent shifting of its headquarters to Tunis.

The Organization of the Islamic Conference, established under the aegis of King Faisal of Saudi Arabia in 1971, holds great promise for the realization of the *ummah.* Its 45-nation membership gives it a base too broad to make for any cohesion except that generated by a common adherence to Islam. Yet it has been uncommonly successful in promoting a mutuality of interest and bringing a degree of coherence not only to foreign policy but to such Islamic matters as the interpretation of *fiqh* (Islamic law). Additionally, the viability and influence of the Organization of the Islamic Conference can conceivably be enhanced by smaller groups operating within its framework.

There are four other potential territorial groupings of Islamic states in addition to the GCC for which a case for homogeneity may be advanced. But their conditions for successful integrative efforts are not nearly as strong as those of the GCC states. Their contrasts with the peninsular Arabians are startling. The Maghrib consists of four contiguous states sharing a Mediterranean littoral. Their colonial experiences with France, Italy and Spain were marred by bloody liberation struggles, especially in Algeria. Their polities differ markedly, ranging from quasi-constitutional monarchies to the "people's congresses" of Libya. Their intraregional relations are contorted by the dispute over the Western Sahara and by abortive efforts at federation with Egypt and other states. Their Islamicity lacks the cohesion of peninsular Arabian Islam, influenced to some degree by the Saudi modality of Islam.

Another possible group are the pre-Balfour Levant states, now divided into a seemingly anti-Islamic Alawite Syria and a devastated Lebanon with subnational enclaves dominated by foreign powers such as Iran, Syria and Israel. There is the remote possibility of a reunited Levant under domination of a Greater Syria. But there is also a less remote probability of an expansionist Eretz Israel, controlling much of Lebanon and eventually even Jordan as well as the Occupied Territories. The fractured, troubled polities as they now exist and the possibility of some sort of hegemony under conditions of force hardly make for a positive comparison with the Gulf Cooperation Council.

The third potential regional grouping is found in Southeast Asia. The southern Philippines (Mindanao, Sulu and Palawan) have an ethnic, linguistic and religious affinity with the Indonesian islands of the Celebes and Moluccas to the south and with the Malaysian states of Sabah and Sarawak and the Sultanate of Brunei Darussalam to the southwest. In 1963 the heads of state of Malaysia, Indonesia and the Philippines agreed to a loose cooperative federation to be called "Maphilindo." This association was never more than a name and was soon forgotten. The impetus for "Maphilindo" was based almost exclusively on territorial claims rather than on religious commonality. It does, however, suggest the web of ethnicity, colonial legacies and geographic proximity which linked the three nations.

These bonds, however, are ephemeral compared with those of the Gulf Cooperation Council. The Philippines is overwhelmingly Roman Catholic and the Muslim area in the south has long sustained political and cultural dissonance with the dominant ethos. Indonesia, while avowedly Muslim, has strong non-Muslim, particularly Hindu, elements, and the polity is unsympathetic to vigorous political manifestations of Islam. The plight of Muslims has become worse in recent years under the leadership of Suharto and the imposition of an official secular ideology, *Pancasila,* which severely restricts the rights of Muslims. Malaysia, under the recent leadership of its Prime Minister Dr. Mahathir bin Mohammed, is aggressively Islamic, but its Muslim population is only a slim majority and its Islamicity has a Southeast Asian casualness contrasting with the relatively stricter attitudes of Pakistan, Afghanistan and Saudi Arabia.

The fourth area of Muslim states in which there could be some semblance of cooperation, if not federation, is Southwest Asia—Pakistan, Afghanistan, Iran and Iraq. Although some regional entity would be ideal, it is even less likely than the other three possibilities explored above. Only Iraq is Arab; the Soviets occupy Afghanistan; some five million Afghan refugees are in Pakistan and Iran; Iraq and Iran wage a bitter war; and Sunni-Shiite differences reach their epitome in this area. This fragmentation makes the regional grouping of Gulf states seem like a textbook ideal.

Neither Arabism nor Islam has been a strong enough bond to hold a polity together. Cultural insensitivity and a perception of economic distress fragmented Pakistan, created in 1947 in the name of Islam. Nor has Arabism succeeded in uniting Egypt with Syria or Libya. The forces of nationalism and the allegiances of Muslim states with one of the superpowers or with allegedly nonaligned structures seem more powerful than either pan-Arabism or pan-Islam. Herein lies the strength of the Gulf Cooperation Council: it is almost totally Islamic, completely Arabian, and is unencumbered by other external alliances which exert centrifugal forces.

III

The second event of late 1986 alluded to at the beginning of this chapter—the attack on Abu Dhabi territory by aircraft presumed to be Iranian—directs our attention to the mutual security aspects of the Gulf Cooperation Council. The technical military aspects of security have been treated fully elsewhere in this volume, particularly in the chapter by J.E. Peterson. It is clear from his analysis that the total military strength of the six peninsular states is no match for neighboring powers. Their forces consist of no more than 145,000 men, possibly 260,000 if paramilitary and contract personnel are included. Saudi Arabia's contribution alone to this latter figure is 53 percent, while it contributes 68 percent of the total air force personnel. Saudi technical equipment is also the dominant element in the total GCC security force. The United States Central Command (USCENTCOM), designed to lend support to the area if called upon, can, at full deployment, make available 291,000 troops from all three services. This is obviously a condition of abject dependence which must offend the Arabian *karamah* (self respect).

The relationship between internal security and dependence on outside powers is especially critical in the Gulf states. They, like most of the Third World, must struggle to maintain an endogenous culture resistant to the enormous radiating power of American transnational commercial and cultural dynamism. This relationship has been analyzed in quasi-Marxian terms by Latin American economists as *dependencia* theory. It is based on the assumption that the world economy, formed by colonial capitalism, exploits raw materials of the Third World and limits the evolution of Third World economies. Nothing less than a wholesale restructuring of the world economy will, this theory asserts, remedy this condition.

It is of particular interest to note that this idiom of dependence, couched in global economic terms, has not characterized the relationship of the Gulf states with the industrialized West. Even the Iranian revolution, repudiating the close ties which the Pahlavi regime had with the West and denouncing particularly the United States as an agent of Satan, was, and continues to be, obsessed with cultural rather than economic intervention.

Several reasons for this may be ventured. The economic relationship of the Gulf states with the West has, in recent times, been based primarily on the single commodity of petroleum. The bonds of an imperial dependency economy were relatively easily cut either by nationalization of petroleum or, as in the case of Saudi Arabia, by an amicable indigenization, as with Aramco and Petromin. Whatever dependency existed was the obverse of the Latin American relationship, i.e., the industrialized West was dependent. This relationship and its consequent accumulation of capital required an economic context amenable to investment opportunities, venture capital and entrepreneurship of world-class sophistication. Bahrain and, to a lesser extent Kuwait, quickly became major centers of international finance. Lebanon, before its dismemberment, was a similar international center, linked somewhat more with France than with the United States.

The management of large cash income and reserves in such states as Saudi Arabia, Kuwait, Abu Dhabi and Bahrain required both a technologically advanced banking infrastructure and world-class managerial competence. These were developed within a decade. Hence the top-level financial apparatus, both public and private, of these states can be compared favorably with that of older industrial nations.

Finally, the Gulf states have been concerned with maintaining the integrity of their Islamic culture and the purity of their religious faith. To them it is Western mores which threaten their civilization, not Western economic behavior. It is made more acute by the presence of expatriate manpower, in some cases equalling or exceeding the indigenous population. A symposium held in Muscat in June 1985 deplored this invasion of an alien "techniculture" which was perceived as threatening Islamic-Arabian civilization. This is the danger, the evil, the *haram* which commands their energies and nurtures their fears.

It is useful at this juncture to restore to political dialogue the term "irredentist," first used in the 1880s in Italy to refer to the recovery of Italian-speaking areas under the control of other countries. The term has considerable explanatory power for contemporary events if it is endowed with a somewhat new dimension. In the contemporary world, efforts toward the recovery of land are accompanied also by actions designed to protect the identity of peoples within the countries of their adopted domicile. There are several manifestations of both forms of irredentism which affect the security of the Gulf states. The Palestinian diaspora and the failure to find a just solution to what amounts to Palestinian genocide is a lingering tragedy which gnaws at the soul of the whole Arab nation and, at the least, pricks the conscience of the non-Arab Islamic *ummah* of some eight hundred million believers.

Security in the Gulf is affected also by disparate levels of economic and industrial development, changing concentrations and skill levels of

211

sources of manpower, and—most critically—by the everwidening differences in the technological competence of nations. While one system barely accustoms itself to the internal combustion engine or the germ theory of disease, other systems explore outer space, transplant human parts and artificially reproduce the species almost as routine behaviors.

Such disparity is of significance to issues of internal security. One of its consequences is fluctuation in the perceptions of the value of different labor skills. This results in extensive labor migration—a phenomenon found in the United States and Europe as well as in the Gulf states. In the Gulf it is a more acute problem. It has implications for the ethical issue of a sense of the dignity and value of all human effort, whether based on somatic or intellectual skills. Immigrant laborers may function as an agent of destabilization under the control or ideological influence of hostile foreign regimes or bodies of thought. Or they may agitate against a regime, demanding political rights, citizenship or other improvements in status. When labor migrants have extended domicile in the host country, or when they constitute a significant portion or a majority of the total population, a threat to security exists. When the migrant labor is stateless, the problem is aggravated. These conditions exist in all the Gulf states.

A second consequence of this disparity is the increase in military technology dependence. However much a state may struggle to maintain military independence, each notch in technological disparity locks the weaker systems ever more tightly in the escalating ratchet of dependence. It is to escape this spiral that weaker systems desperately seek to develop domestic capacity in weapons manufacture or a nuclear capability.

Most Islamic states, including those of the Gulf, are entangled in a new web of cultural, economic and strategic dependence. Escape from this web is more difficult than ever. Its weave is tighter and its strands stickier. Before independence the means of escape was revolution, insurrection, mutiny, passive resistance, insurgency, attrition and nationalization. In whatever form it took it was successful. It was a relatively clean-cut action. Physical resistance, whether active or passive, was its means; sovereignty its end.

There is no such simple means of extrication now. Internal security depends on too many variables whose values fluctuate in unpredictable ways: changing worth of raw materials, whimsy of consumer tastes and demands, natural catastrophe, superpower rivalries, technological invention, labor resources, industrial capacity and agricultural yield, to name but a few. Save for a few cases such as Albania and Burma, whose policies have been based on almost total withdrawal from the international system, there is no national self-sufficiency, no autarky. The greater the integration in the world system and the greater the need for security and material prosperity, the greater the dependence on technologically advanced polities and the greater the threat to distinctive indigenous values.

The enmeshing of Arab Islamic and, to a lesser extent, Gulf polities in the web of the new imperialism and their frenzied search for an authentic endogenous body politic is complex. It has a special poignancy because it is governed to a large extent by the irrepressible effervescence of Islam. The end of empire released powerful forces partially suppressed or at least sedated by colonialism. By its very existence, that superordinate-subordinate relationship eroded confidence in Arab culture. Imperial hubris elevated values of the metropolitan powers. In some realms, particularly the French and to a lesser degree British and Dutch, the consequent dialectic came perilously close to the substitution of one culture for another.

A variety of strategies have been tried to extricate Muslim states from the web of dependence. Each has made an effort to establish some sort of Islamic state. The variations are baffling. Pakistan has its *Nizam-i-Mustafa;* Libya Gadhafi's *Green Book;* Saudi Arabia the Holy *Quran;* Morocco and Jordan, variations of constitutional monarchy. Syria and Iraq live in the somewhat distorted shadow of Michel Aflaq, though his legacy of Baathism has taken different turns in each. Some Muslim states apostatize others. In consequence, we cannot say what constitutes a modern Islamic state.

With respect to the Islamic Gulf states, this antimonarchic feeling is acerbated even by Islamic sources when Khomeini and radical Muslims apostatize the institution of monarchy as being un-Islamic. This antimonarchism is echoed by other Muslim sources as well, particularly Libya and the two Yemens, and in more muted rhetoric even by Kuwait and Lebanon. In truth, the "proper" or "authorized" constitutive nature of an Islamic state is ambiguous at best. Only partisanship, rather than historical objectivity or Islamic piety, can denounce regimes as being Islamic or non-Islamic. This ambiguity has its origin in perceptions of leadership. In the Islamic world the leader was, after the death of the Prophet, originally determined by consensus—a condition which lasted through the four "Pious" or "Orthodox" Caliphs (Abu Bakr, Omar, Osman, Ali) from 632 A.D. to 661 A.D. Upon the death of Ali, there occurred the split between Sunni and Shiites over the issue of succession—whether by consensual election (the Sunni view) or by genealogical heritage (the Shiite view).

The contemporary Khomeini regime in Iran is, of course, based categorically on the Shiite view of succession interrupted by the disappearance of the imam and a kind of surrogate imam ruling until the ultimate reappearance of a hidden imam. As the Islamic empires of the Umayyads, Abbasids and Ottomans evolved and as nation-states or colonies (such as India) were formed, the question of leadership became more ambiguous with various sultans and caliphs in authority in different systems. Finally, a fragile unity was dissolved with Kemal Ataturk's abolition of the Ottoman caliphate (which was only nominal, devoid of spiritual or temporal power) in the new republican Turkey in 1924.

Hence, contemporary uncertainty about the primary element—leadership—in the structure of an Islamic state is rooted in ambiguities 1,400 years old. The classic condition for rulership is piety. Constitutive variations on this theme of rulership are those rooted in a long history of sectarian cleavage, the division of the Muslim world into colonies, empires or nations, and the rise of the postcolonial nation-state with nationalism eclipsing Muslim global unity. Few subjects in Islam have been argued more vigorously and with so little consensus. The Gulf state polities do not fit comfortably into Western schema, nor should they. They must be classified and assessed in terms of their own internally generated criteria.

Threats to the stability of the Gulf regimes come from four possible sources. The first is the global militancy of Shiite Islam as manifest in Khomeini's Iran. This is closely related to the ability of Khomeini to brand these regimes as un-Islamic by virtue of their monarchism and to "purify" their Islamicity. It is not without significance that King Fahd in October 1986 ordered the elimination of the title "His Majesty" in favor of *Khadam Al-Haramain Al Sharifain*. The first press announcement of this order on October 28 translated this as "Servant of the Two Holy Harams." Subsequent use of the title in the Saudi press translates it "Custodian of the Two Holy Mosques." Perhaps this is a symbolic counter to the antimonarchism of Khomeini and a reminder of the globally Islamic and distinctive nature of the Saudi polity. The Khomeini Shiite perception of divine will motivates the war against Iraq, which seeks to topple the Sunni regime and implicitly to replace it with Shiite dominion. The linkage of this ideology with the Palestinian cause and the manipulation of Palestinian refugees whose entire lives have been spent in camps has serious potential for further destabilization in the region. Hence, without question, the root concern is both the containment of Iran and the alleviation of Palestinian desperation. Ever more baffled by and distrustful of American policy vis-a-vis Iran, the Gulf is slowly evolving a new perception of the role of the Soviet Union. Diplomatic recognition of the USSR by Oman, Kuwait and the United Arab Emirates must have been done with Saudi approval, if the Gulf Cooperation Council has any meaning at all. These could very well be trial balloons leading to similar actions by other states in the region. The plight of Muslims in the Soviet Union is followed carefully by the Gulf regimes. There is a perception, whether true or not, that the atheistic stance of the Soviets has either mellowed or was never as fervently applied to Muslims as to Christians and Jews.

The second perceived threat is the military power of Israel and its growing militancy towards Arabs. The most alarming expansion of Israeli interventionism is the strategy of the preemptive strike which sanctions attack against enemies thought to be contemplating military action against the preemptor. To some degree, resort to this strategy is understandable when a nation is constantly subject to guerrilla incursions from adjacent states. It appears less justifiable when it takes the form of air strikes over long distances as, for example, the Israeli bombing of the nuclear plant in Baghdad. The Baghdad of yesterday may be the Islamabad of tomorrow or the Tabuk or Muscat of the day after. Since the assessment of threat is made exclusively by the preemptor, it is difficult to judge whether it is real or contrived. This perception of Israel by Gulf Arabians is compounded by a strand of Israeli ideology—"Eretz Israel." This is a kind of irredentism sanctioned by divine authority and confirmed by sacred scripture. Here it is not a people who are to be reincorporated; rather it is a territory allegedly inhabited by antecedent coreligionists far removed in time. This ideology undergirding great military power is comparable to the globalism of Khomeini Shiism. Indeed, it is the possible collaboration of Khomeini Shiism with the notion of "Eretz Israel" that is most disturbing to the Gulf regimes. The revelations of December 1986 relating to covert arms transfers to Iran via Israel do little to relieve this anxiety.

The third threat is that of insurgency. This arises from the capacity of the regimes to meet the increasing demands entering the policy process and the capacity of that process to convert these demands into meaningful outputs. At some point an escalation of appetites, both material and political, may overwhelm the polity. If this combines with the disaffection of minority groups and expatriate labor agitated by external forces such as Khomeini Shiism, by depressed economies and by disenchantment with the United States, the regimes will be sorely tested. That point has not yet been reached and there is no evidence to suggest that it is imminent. But it must not be kept out of any analytical prognosis.

The fourth source of threat to the Gulf regimes is the imperial expansion of the Soviet Union moving inexorably to control the Gulf's petroleum wealth or at least to deny it to the West. Few would forecast an invasion; this is no longer a tactic in modern imperialism. What is feared is a kaleidoscopic array of forces falling unpredictably in place: Soviet influence in Iran; manipulation of Baluch, Kurd and Arab minorities in Iran, Iraq and Pakistan so as to form real or fictitious independent republics; destabilization of Pakistan; the use of the Peoples Democratic Republic of Yemen as an expansionist base. These possibilities are significant only when linked to a dominant Iran antagonistic to the Gulf regimes. It is the perception of these connections and the seeming incapacity or unwillingness of the United States to comprehend them that worries the Gulf regimes.

IV

The true significance of the Gulf Cooperation Council lies in its potential as a building block in the construction of a global Islamic political society—the realization of *ummah*. The political solidarity of the billion Muslims dispersed from Saudi Arabia to Brunei in a variety of territorial and political configurations is essential for its achievement. A global structure of Islamic nations united in an institutional form embracing both the Islamic states and the minorities is the greatest hope for the preservation of the faith and the stability of polities committed to that preservation. It is doubtful that such a union will supersede nation states, yet is clear that beneath the shifting cleavages that emerge in both the Arab and the larger Islamic domains, the rudiments of a global structure are emerging. The League of Arab States, the Organization of the Islamic Conference, the Rabitat Al-Alam al-Islami, the Academy of Sharia, the Islamic banking movement, various economic entities such as the Arab Fund for Economic and Social Development and the Kuwait Fund for Arab Economic Development, philanthropies such as the King Faisal Foundation, the Agha Khan Foundation and the Hamdard Foundation are merely suggestive of a longer list of such entities. The Gulf Cooperation Council stands out among these as a textbook model. The brief comparative analysis made earlier in this chapter reveals its distinctive qualities: geographic contiguity, cultural and religious homogeneity, similarity of polities, comparable economic base in petroleum and its derivatives, relative freedom from colonial domination, pride in the Arabianness of its history and current behavior, sense of responsibility for the use of the wealth of some of its members and for the custodianship of the holy places of one of the world's great religions and civilizations.

DOCUMENTATION

I. CHARTER OF THE COOPERATION COUNCIL FOR THE ARAB STATES OF THE GULF

The States of
United Arab Emirates
State of Bahrain
Kingdom of Saudi Arabia
Sultanate of Oman
State of Qatar
State of Kuwait

Being fully aware of their mutual bonds of special relations, common characteristics and similar systems founded on the Creed of Islam; and Based on their faith in the common destiny and destination that link their peoples; and

In view of their desire to effect coordination, integration and interconnection between them in all fields; and

Based on their conviction that coordination, cooperation and integration between them serve the higher goals of the Arab Nation; and, In order to strengthen their cooperation and reinforce their common links; and

In an endeavor to complement efforts already begun in all vital scopes that concern their peoples and realize their hopes for a better future on the path to unity of their States; and

In conformity with the Charter of the League of Arab States which calls for the realization of closer relations and stronger bonds; and

In order to channel their efforts to reinforce and serve Arab and Islamic causes, have agreed as follows:

ARTICLE ONE, Establishment of Council

A council shall be established hereby to be named The Cooperation Council for the Arab States of the Gulf, hereinafter referred to as Cooperation Council.

ARTICLE TWO, Headquarters

The Cooperation Council shall have its headquarters in Riyadh, Saudi Arabia.

ARTICLE THREE, Cooperation Council Meetings

The Council shall hold its meetings in the state where it has its headquarters, and may convene in any member state.

ARTICLE FOUR, Objectives
The basic objectives of the Cooperation Council are:

1. To effect coordination, integration and interconnection between member states in all fields in order to achieve unity between them.

2. Deepen and strengthen relations, links and scopes of cooperation now prevailing between their peoples in various fields.

3. Formulate similar regulations in various fields including the following:
   a. Economic and financial affairs
   b. Commerce, customs and communications
   c. Education and culture
   d. Social and health affairs
   e. Information and tourism
   f. Legislation and administrative affairs.

4. Stimulate scientific and technological progress in the fields of industry, mineralogy, agriculture, water and animal resources; the establishment of scientific research centers, implementation of common projects, and encourage cooperation by the private sector for the good of their peoples.

ARTICLE FIVE, Council Membership
The Cooperation Council shall be formed of the six states that participated in the Foreign Ministers' meeting held at Riyadh on 4 February 1981.

ARTICLE SIX, Organizations of the Cooperation Council
The Cooperation Council shall have the following main organizations:

1. Supreme Council to which shall be attached the Commission for Settlement of Disputes

2. Ministerial Council

3. Secretariat General

Each of these organizations may establish branch organizations as necessary.

ARTICLE SEVEN, Supreme Council
1. The Supreme Council is the highest authority of the Cooperation Council and shall be formed of heads of member states. Its presidency shall be rotatory based on the alphabetical order of the names of the member states.

2. The Supreme Council shall hold one regular session every year. Extraordinary sessions may be convened at the request of any member seconded by another member.

3. The Supreme Council shall hold its sessions in the territories of member states.

4. A Supreme Council shall be considered valid if attended by two thirds of the member states.

ARTICLE EIGHT, Supreme Council's Functions

The Supreme Council shall endeavor to achieve the objectives of the Cooperation Council, particularly as concerns the following:

1. Review matters of interest to the member states.

2. Lay down the higher policy for the Cooperation Council and the basic line it should follow.

3. Review the recommendations, reports, studies and common projects submitted by the Ministerial Council for approval.

4. Review reports and studies which the Secretary-General is charged to prepare.

5. Approve the bases for dealing with other states and international organizations.

6. Approve the rules of procedures of the Commission for Settlement of Disputes and nominate its members.

7. Appoint the Secretary-General.

8. Amend the Charter of the Cooperation Council.

9. Approve the Council's Internal Rules.

10. Approve the budget of the Secretariat General.

ARTICLE NINE, Voting in Supreme Council

1. Each member of the Supreme Council shall have one vote.

2. Resolutions of the Supreme Council in substantive matters shall be carried by unanimous approval of the member states participating in the voting, while resolutions on procedural matters shall be carried by majority vote.

ARTICLE TEN, Commission for Settlement of Disputes

1. The Cooperation Council shall have a commission called "Commission for Settlement of Disputes" and shall be attached to the Supreme Council.

2. The Supreme Council shall form the Commission for every case separately based on the nature of the dispute.

3. If a dispute arises over interpretation or implementation of the Charter and such dispute is not resolved within the Ministerial Council or the Supreme Council, the Supreme Council may refer such dispute to the Commission for Settlement of Disputes.

4. The Commission shall submit its recommendations or opinion, as applicable, to the Supreme Council for appropriate action.

ARTICLE ELEVEN, Ministerial Council

1. The Ministerial Council shall be formed of the Foreign Ministers of the member states or other delegated Ministers. The Council's presi-

dency shall rotate among members every three months by alphabetical order of the states.

2. The Ministerial Council shall convene every three months and may hold extraordinary sessions at the invitation of any member seconded by another member.

3. The Ministerial Council shall decide the venue of its next session.

4. A Council's meeting shall be deemed valid if attended by two thirds of the member states.

ARTICLE TWELVE, Functions of the Ministerial Council
The Ministerial Council's functions shall include the following:

1. Propose policies, prepare recommendations, studies and projects aimed at developing cooperation and coordination between member states in the various fields and adopt required resolutions or recommendations concerning thereof.

2. Endeavor to encourage, develop and coordinate activities existing between member states in all fields. Resolutions adopted in such matters shall be referred to the Ministerial Council for further submission, with recommendations, to the Supreme Council for appropriate action.

3. Submit recommendations to the Ministers concerned to formulate policies whereby the Cooperation Council's resolutions may be put into action.

4. Encourage means of cooperation and coordination between the various private sector activities, develop existing cooperation between the member states' chambers of commerce and industry, and encourage the flow of working citizens of the member states among them.

5. Refer any of the various facets of cooperation to one or more technical or specialized committees for study and presentation of relevant proposals.

6. Review proposals related to amendments to this Charter and submit appropriate recommendations to the Supreme Council.

7. Approve the Ministerial Council's Rules of Procedures as well as the Rules of Procedures of the Secretariat General.

8. Appoint the Assistant Secretaries-General, as nominated by the Secretary-General, for a renewable period of three years.

9. Approve periodic reports as well as internal rules and regulations related to administrative and financial affairs proposed by the Secretary-General, and submit recommendations to the Supreme Council for approval of the budget of the Secretariat General.

10. Make arrangements for the Supreme Council's meetings and prepare its agenda.

11. Review matters referred to it by the Supreme Council.

ARTICLE THIRTEEN, Voting at Ministerial Council
1. Every member of the Ministerial Council shall have one vote.
2. Resolutions of the Ministerial Council in substantive matters shall be carried by unanimous vote of the member states present and participating in the vote, and in procedural matters by majority vote.

ARTICLE FOURTEEN, Secretariat General
1. The Secretariat General shall be composed of a Secretary-General who shall be assisted by assistants and a number of staff as required.
2. The Supreme Council shall appoint the Secretary-General, who shall be a citizen of one of the Cooperation Council states, for a period of three years which may be renewed for one time only.
3. The Secretary-General shall nominate the Assistant Secretaries-General.
4. The Secretary-General shall appoint the Secretariat General's staff from among the citizens of member states, and may not make exceptions without the approval of the Ministerial Council.
5. The Secretary-General shall be directly responsible for the work of the Secretariat General and the smooth flow of work in its various organizations. He shall represent the Cooperation Council with other parties within the powers vested in him.

ARTICLE FIFTEEN, Functions of the Secretariat General
The Secretariat General shall undertake the following functions:
1. Prepare studies related to cooperation and coordination, and to integrated plans and programmes for member states' common action.
2. Prepare periodic reports on the Cooperation Council's work.
3. Follow up the execution by the member states of the resolutions and recommendations of the Supreme Council and Ministerial Council.
4. Prepare reports and studies ordered by the Supreme Council for Ministerial Council.
5. Prepare the draft of administrative and financial regulations commensurate with the growth of the Cooperation Council and its expanding responsibilities.
6. Prepare the Cooperation Council's budget and closing accounts.
7. Make preparations for meetings and prepare agenda and draft resolutions for the Ministerial Council.
8. Recommend to the Chairman of the Ministerial Council the convocation of an extraordinary session of the Council whenever necessary.
9. Any other tasks entrusted to it by the Supreme Council or Ministerial Council.

ARTICLE SIXTEEN
The Secretary-General and the Assistant Secretaries-General and all the Secretariat General's staff shall carry out their duties in complete

independence and for the common interest of the member states. They shall refrain from any action or behavior that is incompatible with their duties and from divulging the secrets of their jobs either during or after their tenure of office.

ARTICLE SEVENTEEN, Privileges and Immunities

1. The Cooperation Council and its organizations shall enjoy on the territories of all member states such legal competence, privileges and immunities as required to realize their objectives and carry out their functions.

2. Representatives of the member states of the Council, and the Council's employees, shall enjoy such privileges and immunities as are specified in agreements to be concluded for this purpose between the member states. A special agreement shall organize the relation between the Council and the state in which it has its headquarters.

3. Until such time as the two agreements mentioned in item 2 above are prepared and put into effect, the representatives of the member states in the Cooperation Council and its staff shall enjoy the diplomatic privileges and immunities established for similar organizations.

ARTICLE EIGHTEEN, Budget of the Secretariat General

The Secretariat General shall have a budget to which the member states shall contribute equal amounts.

ARTICLE NINETEEN, Charter Implementation

1. This Charter shall go into effect as of the date it is signed by the heads of state of the six member states named in this Charter's preamble.

2. The original copy of this Charter shall be deposited with Saudi Arabia's Ministry of Foreign Affairs which shall act as custodian and shall deliver a true copy thereof to every member state, pending the establishment of the Secretariat General at which time the latter shall become depository.

ARTICLE TWENTY, Amendments to Charter

1. Any member state may request an amendment of this Charter.

2. Requests for Charter amendments shall be submitted to the Secretary-General who shall refer them to the member states at least four months prior to submission to the Ministerial Council.

ARTICLE TWENTY-ONE, Closing Provisions

No reservations may be voiced in respect of the provisions of this Charter.

ARTICLE TWENTY-TWO
The Secretariat General shall arrange to deposit and register copies of this Charter with the League of Arab States and the United Nations, by resolution of the Ministerial Council.
This Charter is signed on one copy in Arabic language at Abu Dhabi City, United Arab Emirates, on 21 Rajab 1401 corresponding to 25 May 1981.

United Arab Emirates
State of Bahrain
Kingdom of Saudi Arabia
Sultanate of Oman
State of Qatar
State of Kuwait

II. RULES OF PROCEDURES OF THE SUPREME COUNCIL

ARTICLE ONE, Definitions
These regulations shall be called Rules of Procedures of the Supreme Council of the Gulf Arab States Cooperation Council and shall encompass the rules that govern procedures for convening the Council and the exercise of its functions.

ARTICLE TWO, Membership
1. The Supreme Council shall be composed of the heads of state of the Cooperation Council member states. The Presidency shall be rotatory based on the alphabetical order of the states' names.
2. Each member state shall notify the Secretary-General of the names of the members of its delegations to the Council meeting, at least seven days prior to the date set for opening the meeting.

ARTICLE THREE
With due regard to the objectives of the Cooperation Council and the jurisdiction of the Supreme Council as specified in Articles 4 and 8 of the Charter, the Supreme Council may perform the following:
1. Form technical committees and select their members from member states' nominees who specialize in the committees' respective fields.
2. Call one or more of its members to a specific subject and submit a report thereon to be distributed to the members sufficiently in advance of the meeting set for discussing that subject.

ARTICLE FOUR, Convening the Supreme Council
1. a. The Supreme Council shall hold one regular session every year, and may hold extraordinary sessions at the request of any one member seconded by another member.

b. The Supreme Council shall hold its sessions at the heads of state level.

c. The Supreme Council shall hold its sessions in the member states' territories.

d. Prior to convening the Supreme Council, the Secretary-General shall hold a meeting to be attended by delegates of the member states for consultation on matters related to the session's agenda.

2. a. The Secretary-General shall set the opening date of the Council's session and suggest a closing date.

b. The Secretary-General shall issue the invitations for convening a regular session no less than thirty days in advance, and for convening an extraordinary session, within no more than five days.

ARTICLE FIVE

1. The Supreme Council shall at the start of every session decide whether the meetings shall be secret or public.

2. A meeting shall be considered valid if attended by heads of state of two thirds of the member states. Its resolutions in substantive matters shall be carried by unanimous agreement of the member states present and participating in the vote, while resolutions in procedural matters shall be carried by majority vote. Any member abstaining shall document his being not bound by the resolution.

ARTICLE SIX

1. The Council shall hold an extraordinary session based on:

a. Resolution issued in a previous session.

b. Request of a member state seconded by another state. In this case, the Council shall convene within no more than five days from the date of issue of the invitation for holding the extraordinary session.

2. No matters may be placed on the extraordinary session's agenda other than those for which the session was convened to discuss.

ARTICLE SEVEN

1. Presidency of the Supreme Council shall, at the opening of each regular session, go to a head of state by rotation based on the alphabetical order of the member states' names. The President shall continue to exercise the functions of the Presidency until such functions are entrusted to his successor at the beginning of the next regular session.

2. The head of a state that is party to an outstanding dispute may not preside over a session or meeting called to discuss the subject of the dispute. In such case, the Council shall designate a temporary president.

3. The President shall declare the opening and closing of sessions and meetings, the suspension of meetings, and clotures, and shall see that the Cooperation Council Charter and these Rules of Procedures are duly complied with. He shall give the floor to speakers based on the

order of their requests, submit suggestions for acceptance by the membership, direct voting procedures, give final decisions on points of order, announce resolutions, follow up on works of committees, and inform the Council of all incoming correspondence.

4. The President may take part in deliberations and submit suggestions in the name of the state which he represents and may, for this purpose, assign a member of his state's delegation to act on his behalf in such instances.

ARTICLE EIGHT, Supreme Council Agenda

1. The Ministerial Council shall prepare a draft agenda for the Supreme Council, and such draft agenda shall be conveyed by the Secretary-General, together with explanatory notes and documentation, to the member states under cover of the letter of convocation at least thirty days before the date set for the meeting.

2. The draft agenda shall include the following:

a. A report by the Secretary-General on the Supreme Council's activities between the two sessions, and actions taken to carry out its resolutions.

b. Reports and matters received from the Ministerial Council and the Secretariat General.

c. Matters which the Supreme Council had previously decided to include on the agenda.

d. Matters suggested by a member state for necessary review by the Supreme Council.

3. Every member state may request inclusion of additional items on the draft agenda provided such request is tabled at least fifteen days prior to the date set for opening the session. Such matters shall be listed in an additional agenda which shall be sent, along with relevant documentation, to the member state, at least five days before the date set for the session.

4. Any member state may request inclusion of extra items on the draft agenda as late as the date set for opening a session, if such matters are considered both important and urgent.

5. The Council shall approve its agenda at the start of every session.

6. The Council may, during the session, add new items that are considered urgent.

7. The ordinary session shall be adjourned after completion of discussions of the items placed on the agenda. The Supreme Council may decide to suspend the session's meeting before completion of discussions on agenda items, and resume such meetings at a later date.

ARTICLE NINE, Office and Committees of Supreme Council

1. The Supreme Council Office shall be formed, in every session, of the Council President, the Chairman of the Ministerial Council and the

Secretary-General. The Office shall be headed by the Supreme Council President.

2. The Office shall carry out the following functions:

a. Review the text of resolutions passed by the Supreme Council without affecting their contents.

b. Assist the President of the Supreme Council in directing the activities of the session in a general way.

c. Other tasks indicated in these Rules of Procedures or other matters entrusted to it by the Supreme Council.

ARTICLE TEN

1. The Council may, at the start of every session, create any committees that it deems necessary to allow adequate study of matters listed on the agenda. Delegates of member states shall take part in the activities of such committees.

2. Meetings of committees shall continue until they complete their task, with due regard for the date set for closing the session. The resolutions shall be carried by majority vote.

3. Every committee shall start its work by selecting a chairman from among its members. The rapporteur of the committee shall act for the chairman in directing the meeting in the absence of the chairman. The chairman, or other rapporteur in the chairman's absence, shall submit to the Council all the explanations that it requests on the committee's reports. The chairman may, with the approval of the session's President, take part in the discussions, without voting if he is not a member

of the Supreme Council.

4. The Council may refer any of the matters included in the agenda to the committees, based on their specialization for study and reporting. Any one item may be referred to more than one committee.

5. Committees may neither discuss any matter not referred to them by the Council, nor adopt any recommendation which, if approved by the Council, may produce a financial obligation, before the committee receives a report from the Secretary-General regarding the financial and administrative results that may ensue from adopting the resolution.

ARTICLE ELEVEN, Progress of Deliberations and Suggestions

1. Every member state may participate in the deliberations and committees of the Supreme Council as stipulated in these Rules of Procedures.

2. The President shall direct discussion of the items as presented in order on the meeting's agenda and may, when necessary, call the Secretary-General or his representative to the meeting to explain any point as necessary.

3. The President shall give the floor to speakers in the order of their requests. He may give priority to the chairman or rapporteur of a committee to submit a report or explain specific points.

4. Every member may, during deliberations, raise points of order which the President shall resolve immediately and his decisions shall be valid unless contradicted by a majority of the Supreme Council member states.

ARTICLE TWELVE

1. Every member may, during the discussion of any subject, request suspension or adjournment of the meeting or discussion of the subject, or cloture. Such requests may not be discussed, but the President shall put them to the vote, if duly seconded, and decision shall be by majority of the member states.

2. With due regard to provisions of item 4 of the preceding Article, suggestions indicated in item 1 of the Article, shall be given priority over all others based on the following order:

    a. Suspend the meeting
    b. Adjourn the meeting
    c. Postpone discussion of the matter on hand
    d. Cloture of discussion of the matter on hand

3. Apart from suggestions concerning language or procedural matters, draft resolutions and substantive amendments shall be submitted in writing to the Secretary-General or his representative who shall distribute them as soon as possible to the delegations. No draft resolution may be submitted for discussion or voting before the text thereof is distributed to all the delegations.

4. A proposal that has already been decided upon in the same session may not be reconsidered unless the Council decides otherwise.

ARTICLE THIRTEEN

The President shall follow the activities of the committees, inform the Supreme Council of correspondence received, and formally announce before members all the resolutions and recommendations arrived at.

ARTICLE FOURTEEN, Voting

Every member state shall have one vote and no state may represent another state or vote for it.

ARTICLE FIFTEEN

1. Voting shall be by calling the names in the alphabetical order of the states' names, or by raising hands. Voting shall be secret if so requested by a member by decision of the President. The Supreme Council may decide otherwise. The vote of every member shall be documented in the minutes of the meeting if voting is effected by calling the names.

The minutes shall indicate the result of voting, if the vote is secret or by show of hands.

2. A member may abstain from a vote or express reservations over a procedural matter or part thereof, in which case the reservation shall be read at the time the resolution is announced and shall be duly documented in writing. Members may present explanations about their stand in the voting after voting is completed.

3. Once the President announces that voting has started, no interruption may be made unless the matter relates to a point of order relevant to the vote.

ARTICLE SIXTEEN

1. If a member requests amendment of a proposal, voting on the amendment shall be carried out first. If there are more than one amendment, voting shall first be made on the amendment which in the President's opinion is farthest from the original proposal, then on the next farthest, and so on until voting is completed on all proposed amendments. If one or more such amendments is passed, then voting shall be made on the original proposal as amended.

2. Any new proposal shall be deemed as an amendment to the original proposal if it merely entails an addition to, omission from or change to a part of the original proposal.

ARTICLE SEVENTEEN

1. The Supreme Council may create technical committees charged with giving advice on the design and execution of Supreme Council programmes in specific fields.

2. The Supreme Council shall appoint the members of the technical committees from specialists who are citizens of the member states.

3. The technical committees shall meet at the invitation of the Secretary-General and shall lay down their work plans in consultation with him.

4. The Secretary-General shall prepare the committees' agendas after consultation with the chairman of the committee concerned.

ARTICLE EIGHTEEN, Amendment of Rules of Procedures

1. Any member state may propose amendments to the Rules of Procedures.

2. No proposed amendments may be considered unless the relevant proposal is circulated to the member states by the Secretariat General prior to tabling with the Ministerial Council by at least thirty days.

3. No basic changes may be introduced to the proposed amendment mentioned in the preceding item unless the text of such proposed changes have been circulated to the member states by the Secretariat General before tabling with the Ministerial Council by at least fifteen days.

4. Except for items based on the provisions of the Charter, and with due regard to preceding items, these Rules of Procedures shall be amended by a resolution of the Supreme Council approved by majority of the members.

ARTICLE NINETEEN, Effective Date

These Rules of Procedures shall go into effect as of the date of approval by the Supreme Council and may not be amended except in accordance with procedures set forth in the preceding Article.

These Rules of Procedures are signed at Abu Dhabi City, United Arab Emirates on 21 Rajab 1401 AH corresponding to 25 May 1981 AD.

United Arab Emirates
State of Bahrain
Kingdom of Saudi Arabia
Sultanate of Oman
State of Qatar
State of Kuwait

III. RULES OF PROCEDURES OF THE MINISTERIAL COUNCIL

ARTICLE ONE

1. These regulations shall be called Rules of Procedures of the Ministerial Council of the Gulf Arab States Cooperation Council and shall encompass rules governing Council meetings and exercise of its functions.

2. The following terms as used in these shall have the meanings indicated:

Cooperation Council—The Gulf Arab States Cooperation Council

Charter—Statute establishing the Gulf Arab States Cooperation Council

Supreme Council—The highest body of the Gulf Arab States Cooperation Council

Council—Ministerial Council of the Gulf Arab States Cooperation Council

Secretary-General—The Secretary-General of the Gulf Arab States Cooperation Council

Chairman—The Chairman of the Ministerial Council of the Gulf Arab States Cooperation Council

ARTICLE TWO, State Representation

1. The Ministerial Council shall be composed of the member states' Foreign Ministers or other delegated Ministers.

2. Every member state shall, at least one week prior to the convening of every Ministerial Council's ordinary session, convey to the Secretary-General a list of the names of the members of its delegation. For

extraordinary sessions, the list shall be submitted three days before the date set for the session.

ARTICLE THREE, Convening the Sessions
1. The Ministerial Council shall decide in every meeting the venue of its next regular session.
2. The Secretary-General shall decide, in consultation with the member states, the venues of extraordinary sessions.
3. If circumstances should arise that preclude the convening of an ordinary or extraordinary session at the place set for it, the Secretary-General shall so inform the member states and shall set another place for the meeting after consultation with them.

ARTICLE FOUR, Ordinary Sessions
1. The Council shall convene in ordinary session once every three months.
2. The Secretary-General shall set the date for opening the session and suggest the date of its closing.
3. The Secretary-General shall address the invitation to attend a Council ordinary session at least fifteen days in advance, and shall indicate therein the date and place set for the meeting, as well as attach thereto the session's agenda, explanatory notes and other documentation.

ARTICLE FIVE, Extraordinary Sessions
1. The Council shall hold an extraordinary session at the request of any member state seconded by another member.
2. The Secretary-General shall address the invitation to the Council's extraordinary session and attach a memorandum containing the request of the member which asked for the meeting.
3. The Secretary-General shall specify in the invitation the place, date and agenda of the session.

ARTICLE SIX
1. The Council may itself decide to hold extraordinary sessions, in which case it shall specify the agenda, time and place of the session.
2. The Secretary-General shall send out to the member states the invitation to attend the Council's extraordinary meeting, along with a memorandum containing the Council's decision to this effect, and specifying the date and agenda of the session.
3. The extraordinary session shall be convened within a maximum of five days from the date of issue of the invitation.

ARTICLE SEVEN
No matters, other than those for which the extraordinary session was called, may be included on its agenda.

ARTICLE EIGHT, Agenda
The Secretary-General shall prepare a draft agenda for a Council's ordinary session and such draft shall include the following:
1. The Secretary-General's Report on the Cooperation Council's work.
2. Matters referred to him by the Supreme Council.
3. Matters which the Council had previously decided to include on the agenda.
4. Matters which the Secretary-General believes should be reviewed by the Council.
5. Matters suggested by a member state.

ARTICLE NINE
Member states shall convey to the Secretary-General their suggestions on matters they wish to include on the Council's agenda at least thirty days prior to the date of the Council's ordinary session.

ARTICLE TEN
Member states or the Secretary-General may request the inclusion of additional items on the Council's draft agenda at least ten days prior to the date set for opening an ordinary session. Such items shall be listed on an additional schedule which shall be conveyed along with relevant documentation to the member states at least five days prior to the date of the session.

ARTICLE ELEVEN
Member states or the Secretary-General may request inclusion of additional items on the Council's ordinary session's agenda up to the date set for opening the session if such matters are both important and urgent.

ARTICLE TWELVE
The Council shall approve its agenda at the beginning of every session.

ARTICLE THIRTEEN
A Council's ordinary session shall end upon completion of discussion of matters listed on the agenda. The Council may, when necessary, decide to suspend its meetings temporarily before discussion of agenda items is completed and resume its meetings at a later date.

ARTICLE FOURTEEN
The Council may defer discussion of certain items on its agenda and decide to include them with the others, when necessary, on the agenda of a subsequent session.

ARTICLE FIFTEEN, Council's Chairmanship
1. Chairmanship of the Council shall be entrusted every six months to a head of delegation on rotation based on the alphabetical order of the member states' names, and if necessary, to the next in order.

231

2. The Chairman shall exercise his functions until he passes his post on to his successor.

3. The Chairman shall, as well, preside over the extraordinary sessions.

4. The representative of a state that is party to an outstanding dispute may not chair the session or meeting assigned for discussing such dispute, in which case the Council shall name a temporary Chairman.

ARTICLE SIXTEEN

1. The Chairman shall announce the opening and closing of sessions and meetings, the suspension of meetings and cloture of discussions, and shall see that the provisions of the Charter and these Rules of Procedures are duly respected.

2. The Chairman may participate in the Council's deliberations and vote in the name of the state he represents. He may, for such purpose, delegate another member of his delegation to act on his behalf.

ARTICLE SEVENTEEN, Council's Office

1. The Council Office shall include the Chairman, Secretary-General, and heads of working subcommittees which the Council decides to form.

2. The Council Chairman shall preside over the Office.

ARTICLE EIGHTEEN

The Office shall carry out the following tasks:

1. Help the Chairman direct the sessions proceedings;

2. Coordinate the work of the Council and the subcommittees;

3. Supervise the drafting of the resolutions passed by the Council;

4. Other tasks indicated in these Rules of Procedures or entrusted to it by the Council.

ARTICLE NINETEEN, Subcommittees

1. The Council shall utilize preparatory and working committees to accomplish its tasks.

2. The Secretariat General shall participate in the work of the committees.

ARTICLE TWENTY

1. The Secretary-General may, in consultation with the Chairman of the session, form preparatory committees charged with the study of matters listed on the agenda.

2. Preparatory committees shall be composed of delegates of member states and may, when necessary, seek the help of such experts as they may deem fit.

3. Each preparatory committee shall meet at least three days prior to the opening of the session by invitation of the Secretary-General. The work of the committee shall end at the close of the session.

ARTICLE TWENTY-ONE

1. The Council may, at the start of each session, form working committees and charge them with specific tasks.

2. The work of the working committees shall continue until the date set for closing the session.

ARTICLE TWENTY-TWO

1. Each subcommittee shall start its work by electing a chairman and a rapporteur from among its members. When the chairman is absent, the rapporteur shall act for him in directing the meetings.

2. The chairman or rapporteur of each subcommittee shall submit a report on its work to the Council.

3. The chairman or rapporteur of a subcommittee shall present to the Council all explanations required about the contents of the subcommittee's report.

ARTICLE TWENTY-THREE

1. The Secretariat General shall organize the technical secretariat and subcommittees of the Council.

2. The Secretariat General shall prepare minutes of meetings documenting discussions, resolutions and recommendations. Such minutes shall be prepared for all meetings of the Council and its subcommittees.

3. The Secretary-General shall supervise the organization of the Council's relations with the information media.

4. The Secretary-General shall convey the Council's resolutions and recommendations and relevant documentation to the member states within fifteen days after the end of the session.

ARTICLE TWENTY-FOUR

The Council's Secretariat and subcommittees shall receive and distribute documents, reports, resolutions and recommendations of the Council and its subcommittees and shall draw up and distribute minutes and daily bulletins, as well as safeguard the documents and carry out any other tasks required by the Council's work.

ARTICLE TWENTY-FIVE

Texts of resolutions or recommendations made by the Council may not be announced or published except by decision of the Council.

ARTICLE TWENTY-SIX, Deliberations

Every member state may take part in the deliberations of the Council and its subcommittees in the manner prescribed in these Rules of Procedures.

ARTICLE TWENTY-SEVEN

1. The Chairman shall direct deliberations on matters in hand in the order they are listed on the Council's agenda.

2. The chairman shall give the floor to speakers in the order of their requests. Priority may be given to the chairman or rapporteur of a certain committee to present its report or explain certain points therein. The floor shall be given to the Secretary-General or his representative whenever it is necessary.

3. The Council Chairman may, during deliberations, read the list of the names of members who requested the floor, and with the approval of the Council, close the list. The only exception is exercise of the right of reply.

ARTICLE TWENTY-EIGHT

The Council shall decide whether the meetings shall be open or secret.

ARTICLE TWENTY-NINE

1. Every member may raise a point of order which the chairman shall resolve immediately and his decision shall be final unless opposed by majority of the member states.

2. A member who raises a point of order may not go beyond the point he raised.

ARTICLE THIRTY

1. Every member may, during discussion of any matter, suggest the suspension or adjournment of the meeting, or discussion of the matter on hand or cloture. The Chairman shall in such cases submit the suggestion to the vote directly, if the suggestion is seconded by another member, and it requires the approval of the majority of the member states to pass.

2. With due regard to the provisions of the preceding item, suggestions indicated therein shall be submitted to the vote in the following order:

   a. Suspension of meeting
   b. Adjournment of meeting
   c. Postponement of discussion of the matter in hand.
   d. Cloture of discussion of the matter in hand.

ARTICLE THIRTY-ONE

1. Member states may suggest draft resolutions or recommendations, or amendments thereto, and may withdraw such suggestions unless they are voted upon.

2. Drafts indicated in the preceding item shall be submitted in writing to the Secretariat General for distribution to delegations as soon as possible.

3. Except for suggestions concerning language or procedures, drafts indicated in this Article may not be discussed or voted upon before their texts are distributed to all delegations.

4. A suggestion already decided upon in the same session may not be reconsidered unless the Council decides otherwise.

ARTICLE THIRTY-TWO

The Chairman shall follow the work of the committees, inform the Council of incoming correspondence, and formally announce before members the resolutions and recommendations that have been arrived at.

ARTICLE THIRTY-THREE, Voting

1. The Council shall pass its resolutions with the unanimous approval of the member states present and participating in the vote, while decisions in procedural matters shall be passed by a majority vote. The member abstaining from the vote shall document his nonsubscription to the decision.

2. If members of the Council should disagree on the definition of the matter being put to the vote, the matter shall be settled by majority vote of the member states present.

ARTICLE THIRTY-FOUR

1. Every member state shall have one vote.

2. No member state may represent another state or vote for it.

ARTICLE THIRTY-FIVE

1. Voting shall be by calling the names in the alphabetical order of the states' names, or by raising hands.

2. Voting shall be by secret ballot if so requested by a member or by decision of the Chairman. The Council, however, may decide otherwise.

3. The vote of every member shall be documented in the minutes of the meeting if voting is effected by calling the names. The minutes shall indicate the result of voting if the vote is secret or by show of hands.

4. Member states may explain their positions after the vote and such explanations shall be written down in the minutes of the meeting.

5. Once the Chairman announces that voting has started, no interruption may be made except for a point of order relating to the vote or its postponement in accordance with the provisions of this Article and the next Article.

ARTICLE THIRTY-SIX

1. The Council Chairman with the help of the Secretary-General shall endeavor to reconcile the stands of member states on disputed matters and obtain their agreement to a draft resolution before submitting it to the vote.

2. The Council Chairman, the Secretary-General or any member state may request postponement of a vote for a specific period during which further negotiations may be made concerning the item submitted to the vote.

235

ARTICLE THIRTY-SEVEN

1. If a member requests amendment of a proposal, voting on the amendment shall be carried out first. If there is more than one amendment, voting shall first be made on the amendment which the Chairman considers to be farthest from the original proposal, then on the next farthest, and so on until all proposed amendments have been voted upon. If one or more amendments are passed, then voting shall be made on the original proposal as amended.

2. A new proposal shall be deemed as an amendment to the original proposal if it merely entails an addition to, omission from, or change to a part of the original proposal.

ARTICLE THIRTY-EIGHT

1. Any member state or the Secretary-General may propose amending these Rules of Procedures.

2. No proposed amendment to these Rules of Procedures may be considered unless the relevant proposal is circulated to the member states by the Secretariat General at least thirty days before submission to the Council.

3. No basic changes may be introduced to the proposed amendment mentioned in the preceding item unless the texts of such proposed change have been circulated to the member states at least fifteen days prior to submission to the Council.

4. Except for items based on provisions of the Charter, and with due regard to preceding items, these Rules of Procedures shall be amended by a resolution of the Council approved by majority of its members.

ARTICLE THIRTY-NINE, Effective Date

These Rules of Procedures shall go into effect as of the date of approval by the Council and may not be amended except in accordance with procedures set forth in the preceding article.

Thus, these Rules of Procedures are signed at Abu Dhabi City, United Arab Emirates, on 21 Rajab 1401 AH corresponding to 25 May 1981 AD.

United Arab Emirates
State of Bahrain
Kingdom of Saudi Arabia
Sultanate of Oman
State of Qatar
State of Kuwait

IV. RULES OF PROCEDURES OF THE COMMISSION FOR SETTLEMENT OF DISPUTES

Preamble

In accordance with the provisions of Article Six of the Charter of the Gulf Arab States Cooperation Council; and in execution of the provision of Article Ten of the Cooperation Council Charter a Commission for Settlement of Disputes, hereinafter referred to as The Commission shall be set up and its jurisdiction and rules for its proceedings shall be as follows:

ARTICLE ONE, Terminology
Terms used in these Rules of Procedures shall have the same meanings established in the Charter of the Gulf Arab States Cooperation Council.

ARTICLE TWO, Commission's Seat and Meetings
The Commission shall have its headquarters at Riyadh, Saudi Arabia, and shall hold its meetings on the territory of the state where its headquarters is located, but may hold its meetings elsewhere, when necessary.

ARTICLE THREE, Jurisdiction
The Commission shall, once installed, have jurisdiction to consider the following matters referred to it by the Supreme Council:
1. Disputes between member states.
2. Differences of opinion as to the interpretation or execution of the Cooperation Council Charter.

ARTICLE FOUR, Commission's Membership
1. The Commission shall be formed of an appropriate number of citizens of member states not involved in the dispute as the Council selects in every case separately depending on the nature of the dispute, provided that the number shall not be less than three members.
2. The Commission may seek the advice of any such experts as it may deem necessary.
3. Unless the Supreme Council decides otherwise, the Commission's task shall end with the submission of its recommendations or opinion to the Supreme Council which, after the conclusion of the Commission's task, may summon it at any time to explain or elaborate on its recommendations or opinions.

ARTICLE FIVE, Meetings and Internal Procedures
1. The Commission's meeting shall be valid if attended by all members.
2. The Secretariat General of the Cooperation Council shall prepare procedures required to conduct the Commission's affairs, and such procedures shall go into effect as of the date of approval by the Ministerial Council.
3. Each party to the dispute shall send representatives to the Commission who shall be entitled to follow proceedings and present their defense.

ARTICLE SIX, Chairmanship
The Commission shall select a chairman from among its members.

ARTICLE SEVEN, Voting
Every member of the Commission shall have one vote, and shall issue its recommendations or opinions on matters referred to it by majority of the members. In case of a tie, the party with the Chairman's vote shall prevail.

ARTICLE EIGHT, Commission's Secretariat
1. The Secretary-General shall appoint a recorder for the Commission, and a sufficient number of employees to carry out secretarial work.
2. The Supreme Council may create an independent organization to carry out the Commission's secretarial work when the need arises.

ARTICLE NINE, Recommendations and Opinions
1. The Commission shall issue its recommendations or opinions in accordance with the Cooperation Council's Charter, international laws and practices, and the principles of Islamic Shariah. The Commission shall submit its findings on the case in hand to the Supreme Council for appropriate action.
2. The Commission may, while considering any dispute referred to it and pending the issue of its final recommendations thereon, ask the Supreme Council to take interim action called for by necessity or circumstances.
3. The Commission's recommendations or opinions shall spell out the reasons on which they were based and shall be signed by the chairman and recorder.
4. If an opinion is passed wholly or partially by unanimous vote of the members, the dissenting members shall be entitled to document their dissenting opinion.

ARTICLE TEN, Immunities and Privileges
The Commission and its members shall enjoy such immunities and privileges in the territories of the member states as are required to realize its objectives and in accordance with Article Seventeen of the Cooperation Council Charter.

ARTICLE ELEVEN, Commission's Budget
The Commission's budget shall be considered part of the Secretariat General's budget. Remunerations of the Commission's members shall be established by the Supreme Council.

ARTICLE TWELVE, Amendments
1. Any member state may request for amendments of these Rules of Procedures.
2. Requests for amendments shall be submitted to the Secretary-General who shall relay them to the member states by at least four months before submission to the Ministerial Council.

3. An amendment shall be effective if approved unanimously by the Supreme Council.

ARTICLE THIRTEEN, Effective Date
These Rules of Procedures shall go into effect as of the date of approval by the Supreme Council.
These Rules of Procedures were signed at Abu Dhabi City, United Arab Emirates on 21 Rajab 1401 AH corresponding to 25 May 1983 AD.

United Arab Emirates
State of Bahrain
Kingdom of Saudi Arabia
Sultanate of Oman
State of Qatar
State of Kuwait

V. THE UNIFIED ECONOMIC AGREEMENT OF THE COOPERATION COUNCIL FOR THE ARAB STATES OF THE GULF

With the help of God Almighty;
The Governments of the member states of the Gulf Cooperation Council;
In accordance with the Charter thereof, which calls for closer relations and stronger links; and,
Desiring to promote, expand and enhance their economic ties on solid foundations, in the best interest of their peoples; and,
Intending to coordinate and unify their economic, financial and monetary policies, as well as their commercial and industrial legislation, and customs regulations; have agreed as follows:

CHAPTER ONE
TRADE EXCHANGE

ARTICLE 1
a. The member states shall permit the importation and exportation of agricultural, animal, industrial and natural resource products that are of national origin. Also, they shall permit exportation thereof to other member states.
b. All agricultural, animal, industrial and natural resource products that are from member states shall receive the same treatment as national products.

ARTICLE 2
1. All agricultural, animal, industrial and natural resource products that are of national origin shall be exempted from customs duties and other charges having equivalent effect.

2. Fees charged for specific services such as demurrage, storage, transportation, haulage or unloading, shall not be considered as customs duties when they are levied on domestic products.

ARTICLE 3

1. For products of national origin to qualify as national manufactured products, the value added ensuing from their production in member states shall not be less than 40 percent of their final value. In addition, the share of the member states citizens in the ownership of the producing plant shall not be less than 51 percent.

2. Every item to be exempted hereby shall be accompanied by a certificate of origin duly authenticated by the government agency concerned.

ARTICLE 4

1. Member states shall establish a uniform minimum customs tariff applicable to the products of countries other than GCC member states.

2. One of the objectives of the uniform customs tariff shall be the protection of national products from foreign competition.

3. The uniform customs tariff shall be applied gradually within five years from the date on which this agreement becomes effective. Arrangements for its gradual implementation shall be agreed upon within one year from the said date.

ARTICLE 5

Member states shall grant all facilities for the transit of any member state's goods to other member states, exempting them from any duties and taxes whatsoever, without prejudice to the provisions of Paragraph 2 of Article 2.

ARTICLE 6

Transit shall be denied to any goods that are barred from entry into the territory of a member state by its local regulations. Lists of such goods shall be exchanged between the customs authorities of the member states.

ARTICLE 7

Member states shall coordinate their commercial policies and relations with other states and regional economic groupings and blocs with a view to creating balanced trade relations and favorable circumstances and terms of trade therewith.

To achieve this goal, the member states shall make the following arrangements:

1. Coordination of import/export policies and regulations.

2. Coordination of policies for building up strategic food stocks.

3. Conclusion of collective economic agreements in cases where joint benefits to member states would be realized.

4. Taking of action for the creation of collective negotiating power to strengthen their negotiating position vis-à-vis foreign parties in the field of importation of basic needs and exportation of major products.

CHAPTER TWO
MOVEMENT OF CAPITAL, CITIZENS AND EXERCISE OF ECONOMIC ACTIVITIES

ARTICLE 8
The member states shall agree on the executive rules which would insure that each member state shall grant the citizens of all other member states the same treatment granted to its own citizens without any discrimination or differentiation in the following fields:
1. Freedom of movement, work and residence.
2. Right of ownership, inheritance and bequest.
3. Freedom to exercise economic activity.
4. Free movement of capital.

ARTICLE 9
The member states shall encourage their respective private sectors to establish joint ventures in order to link their citizens' economic interest in the various spheres of activity.

CHAPTER THREE
COORDINATION OF DEVELOPMENT

ARTICLE 10
The member states shall endeavor to achieve coordination and harmony among their respective development plans with a view to achieving integration in economic affairs.

ARTICLE 11
1. The member states shall endeavor to coordinate their policies with regard to all aspects of the oil industry including extraction, refining, marketing, processing, pricing, exploitation of natural gas and development of energy sources.
2. The member states shall endeavor to formulate unified oil policies and adopt common positions vis-à-vis the outside world, and in the international and specialized organizations.

ARTICLE 12
To achieve the objectives specified in this Agreement, the member states shall perform the following:
1. Coordinate industrial activities, formulate policies and mechanisms aimed at the industrial development and the diversification of their productive bases on an integrated basis.

241

2. Standardize their industrial legislation and regulations and guide their local production units to meet their needs.

3. Allocate industries between member states according to relative advantages and economic feasibility, and encourage the establishment of basic as well as ancillary industries.

ARTICLE 13

Within the framework of their coordinating activities, the member states shall pay special attention to the establishment of joint ventures in the fields of industry, agriculture and services, and shall support them with public, private or mixed capital in order to achieve economic integration, productive interface and common development on sound economic bases.

CHAPTER FOUR
TECHNICAL COOPERATION

ARTICLE 14

The member states shall collaborate in finding spheres for common technical cooperation aimed at building a genuine local base founded on encouragement and support of research and applied sciences and technology as well as adapting imported technology to meet the needs of the region and to achieve the objectives of progress and development.

ARTICLE 15

The member states shall establish procedures, make arrangements and lay down terms for the transfer of technology, selecting the most suitable or introducing such changes thereto as would serve their various needs. Member states shall also, whenever feasible, conclude uniform agreements with foreign governments and scientific or commercial firms to achieve these objectives.

ARTICLE 16

The member states shall formulate policies and implement coordinated programs for technical, vocational and professional training and qualification at all levels and stages. They shall also upgrade educational curricula at all levels to link education and technology with the development needs of the member states.

ARTICLE 17

The member states shall coordinate their manpower policies and shall formulate uniform and standardized criteria and classifications for the various categories of occupations and crafts in different sectors in order to avoid harmful competition among themselves and to optimize the utilization of available human resources.

CHAPTER FIVE
TRANSPORT AND COMMUNICATION

ARTICLE 18
The member states shall accord means of passenger and cargo transportation belonging to citizens of the other member states, when transiting or entering their territory, the same treatment they accord to the means of passenger and cargo transportation belonging to their own citizens, including exemptions from all duties and taxes whatsoever. However, local means of transportation are excluded.

ARTICLE 19
1. The member states shall cooperate in the fields of land and sea transportation and communication. They shall also coordinate and establish infrastructure projects such as seaports, airports, water and power stations and roads, with a view to realizing common economic development and linking their economic activities with each other.
2. The contracting states shall coordinate aviation and air transport policies among them and promote all spheres of joint activities at various levels.

ARTICLE 20
The member states shall allow steamers, ships and boats and their cargoes, belonging to any member state freely to use the various port facilities and grant them the same treatment and privileges granted to their own in docking or calling at the ports as concerns fees, pilotage, and docking services, haulage, loading and unloading, maintenance, repair, storage of goods and other similar services.

CHAPTER SIX
FINANCIAL AND MONETARY COOPERATION

ARTICLE 21
The member states shall seek to unify investment in order to achieve a common investment policy aimed at directing their internal and external investments towards serving their interest, and realizing their peoples' aspirations in development and progress.

ARTICLE 22
The member states shall seek to coordinate their financial, monetary and banking policies and enhance cooperation between monetary agencies and central banks, including an endeavor to establish a common currency in order to further their desired economic integration.

ARTICLE 23
Member states shall seek to coordinate their external policies in the sphere of international and regional development aid.

243

CHAPTER SEVEN
CLOSING PROVISIONS

ARTICLE 24

In the execution of the Agreement and determination of the procedures resulting therefrom, consideration shall be given to differences in the levels of development between the member states and the local development priorities of each. Any member state may be temporarily exempted from applying such provisions of this Agreement as may be necessitated by temporary local situations in that state or specific circumstances faced by it. Such exemption shall be for a specified period and shall be decided by the Supreme Council of the Gulf Arab States Cooperation Council.

ARTICLE 25

No member state shall give to any nonmember state any preferential privilege exceeding that given herein.

ARTICLE 26

a. This Agreement shall enter into force four months after its approval by the Supreme Council.

b. This Agreement may be amended by consent from the Supreme Council.

ARTICLE 27

In case of conflict with local laws and regulations of member states, execution of the provisions of this Agreement shall prevail.

ARTICLE 28

Provisions herein shall supersede any similar provisions contained in bilateral agreements.

Drawn up at Riyadh on 15 Muharram 1402, corresponding to 11 November 1982.

VI. TRANSIT SYSTEM
Regulations governing Transit Goods in the Cooperation Council for the Arab States of the Gulf

(These regulations have been approved by the Financial and Economical Cooperation Committee in its second meeting on June 19-20th 1982, for implementing the Fifth Article of the Unified Economic Agreement.

These regulations were effective from the First of March 1983 and were applied to commodities coming through land, sea and air).

FIRST:

Permitting the shipment of commodities in means of Transportation through the lands of all the countries signatory to the Unified Economic

Agreement, without delay, restriction or discrimination on the type of the containers.

Transit containers have to meet the following conditions:
1. They have to be designed for shipping commodities according to the Customs' Seals System.
2. Possibility of the Customs' Seals to be stamped easily and effectively.
3. Impossibility of taking out any commodities from the stamped part, or putting any thing in it, without leaving a clear spot or breaking the Customs' Seals.
4. They should not contain unseen cavities that would make it easy to hide any commodity in them.
5. The uncovered means of Transportation must be packed with tight covers, tied with ropes and wrapped with a wire from outside, leaving it possible to stamp with the Customs' Seals ensuring the safety of the load.

SECOND:
Wrapping Requirements:
1. The cover must consist of a single untorn piece that would make it impossible to reach the load.
2. The whole truck box must be covered completely on both sides.
3. The cover must have certain rings fixed inside and around the cloth.
The rope must consist of one piece, in a length that would allow gathering the two sides after passing through the cover's rings, and the box to be stamped by lead.

THIRD:
Customs' Seals:
Customs' Seals must be clear and carry the word (CUSTOMS) and the country's name in Arabic.

FOURTH:
Transit Manifest:
Means of Transportation must be accompanied with a Transit manifest according to the Layout approved by the GCC countries.

FIFTH:
Exceptional shipments such as the commodities which can't be wrapped but can be examined and counted are excluded from the condition provided for in paragraphs 1st, 2nd and 3rd shown above.

245

SIXTH:

Exchanging the Signatures of the Custom's officials who are authorized to sign on clearing documents, and the official Customs' Seals for this purpose.

VII. TEXT OF MEMORANDUMS FROM THE GCC ON FOOD SECURITY

Activities Undertaken by the Cooperation Council of the Arab States of the Gulf to Strengthen Food Security (n.d.)

1. Unified Agricultural Policy:

Kings and amirs of the Cooperation Council of the Arab States of the Gulf, in their sixth summit held in Muscat, Sultanate of Oman, November 1985, have endorsed the Unified Agricultural Policy of the six member states. The policy, approved previously by the GCC agriculture ministers, includes four main programs, i.e.:

    a. Agriculture and food production.

    b. Agriculture policies of the member states.

    c. Studies and research.

    d. Technology transfer and mechanizations.

2. GCC Water Resources Conservation Act. This act was endorsed by the GCC agriculture ministers, published and has been in effect since 1985.

3. Veterinary Medicine Registration Act and the Veterinery Medicine Use Act were also endorsed by the GCC agriculture ministers, published and have been in effect since June 1985.

4. Fertilizers' Act and Pesticides Act of the GCC members states were endorsed by the agriculture ministers, published and have been in effect since June 1985.

5. Unified Act for fishing and conservation of the live water wealth, was also endorsed by the agriculture ministers, published and has been in effect since June 1985.

6. Two veterinary feasibility studies for the establishment of a viral disease diagnostic lab and for a vaccine production laboratory were finished recently and will be submitted to the ministers of agriculture for endorsement. The two studies' aim is the protection and conservation of the animal wealth for better food security.

7. Strategic Food Reserve:

GCC ministers of trade have endorsed the establishment of local strategic food reserves for the six member states for a minimum of six months. Coordination in this regard is being done among the GCC member states.

AGRICULTURE (n.d.)

Three ministerial meetings by the agriculture ministers of the six member states have been held since January 1983, and the fourth will be held in September 1986 in the Sultanate of Oman. The joint agricultural policy approved by the ministers was endorsed by the Supreme Council last November in Muscat. The Secretariat General is now undertaking the execution of the four main programs of the policy. Legislation and laws were also approved by the ministers related to water conservation, veterinary vaccines, insecticides, fertilizers and fisheries.

A number of joint agriculture companies were introduced to the private sector in poultry, seed production and marketing, and poultry and dairy equipment, while others are under study.

In addition, studies were conducted to establish two veterinary laboratories, one for the production of vaccines and the other for virus disease diagnosis.

VIII. GENERAL DESCRIPTION OF THE GULF INVESTMENT CORPORATION[1]

In May 1981, the Gulf Cooperation Council, an association of six Arabian Gulf States of Bahrain, Kuwait, Oman, Qatar, Saudi Arabia and the United Arab Emirates, was established to promote closer political, cultural, economic and defence ties amongst its members. Recognising the important role that investment should play in developing their national resources, one of the early decisions of the GCC was to establish Gulf Investment Corporation (GIC), the first such institution set up under the auspices of and jointly owned by the governments of the six member states.

By virtue of the size of its available resources, the nature and scale of its objectives, and the style and scope of its projected activities, Gulf Investment Corporation is ready to make a major contribution to the economic and industrial development of GCC countries.

Organization and capital structure

The authorized capital of Gulf Investment Corporation is US$2.1bn, subscribed equally by the six shareholding governments. To date the paid up capital is US$540m and total shareholders' equity as of September 30, 1985, was US$637m.

The Board of Directors is composed of twelve members, of whom six are the Ministers of Finance of their respective countries. The position of Chairman of the Board rotates every two years in alphabetical order of the shareholder countries. The current chairman is H. E.

---

[1]Source: "Document" in *Arab Banker*, London Vol. VI, No. 4 (July/August 1986) pp. 21, 30.

Ahmed Humaid Al Tayer, Minister of State for Finance and Industry in the UAE. The Deputy Chairman, who also chairs the seven-man executive committee, is H. E. Ibrahim Abdul-Karim, Minister of Finance and National Economy in Bahrain. Dr. Khaled Mohammad Al-Fayez was appointed by the Board as the Chief Executive Officer.

Aims and objectives

The principal aims and objectives of Gulf Investment Corporation, as specified in its Memorandum and Articles of Association, are as follows:

— To contribute to the economic development and integration of the shareholding states.
— To promote the development of the shareholders' financial resources.
— To assist the shareholding countries to diversify their sources of income.
— To provide a commercially acceptable return on the shareholders' investment.

Whilst this gives GIC a broad mandate, the Corporation intends initially to concentrate on those activities which it believes the Gulf region primarily needs. In this context, two key areas have been identified for priority action.

The first is the promotion of new ventures in the various economic sectors within the GCC countries. Gulf Investment Corporation plans to play a leading role in identifying feasible projects, evaluating and structuring these projects and participating in their equity, as well as providing supplementary financing. These will be undertaken jointly with the private and/or public sectors as well as foreign companies in joint-venture partnerships. GIC will also be active in investing outside the GCC countries in companies and projects which have a direct bearing on the economic prosperity of the shareholder states.

The second area is the promotion and development in the Gulf of a capital market, which to date has been eclipsed by the substantial expansion, witnessed over the last decade, of the money market. Gulf Investment Corporation plans to encourage local companies to finance their operations by the issuance of various forms of capital-market instruments, and stands ready to make a market in these instruments, thus providing improved liquidity, which will enhance their acceptance. GIC will encourage other financial institutions in the area to cooperate and participate in this endeavour, thereby strengthening the development of a capital market.

In order to maximise the achievement of its aims and objectives, Gulf Investment Corporation will, in the fullness of time, expand its activities both within the GCC countries and internationally to include the following:

- Promotion and establishment of, and investment in, potentially profitable projects in the industrial, agricultural, commercial, mining, and service sectors, particularly those serving the aims of the shareholding countries in developing their economies and achieving integration amongst them.
- Acquisition of, investment in, or participation with companies and organisations which can assist the Corporation in attaining its objectives.
- Management, underwriting and investment in a wide range of marketable securities such as fixed- and floating-rate notes, certificates of deposit, equity and equity-related instruments, shares, stocks and similar negotiable paper.
- Extension of, participation in and management of loans, and issuance of guarantees.
- Management of customers' investment portfolios and acting as agent or trustee.
- Investment of various currencies, precious metals, commodities, and other moveable and immovable assets.
- Real estate investments of all kinds.
- Execution of studies and surveys relating to capital investments, evaluation of investment projects in line with the Corporation's objectives, and the provision of consultant and investment services to third parties.

Progress to date

Gulf Investment Corporation opened its doors for business in May 1984 with a staff of three. Since then it has expanded rapidly and by the end of 1985 a staff count of 110 is anticipated. Located on the 8th–13th floors of the Kuwait Real Estate Bank building in the Joint Banking Centre in Kuwait City, the Corporation is already beginning to make its presence felt. The Treasury is active in the money markets and foreign exchange. The Marketable Securities Division has started trading in fixed income and floating rate notes. GIC is already committed in principle to a number of projects with a total estimated cost of US$750m. At the same time, the Direct Investment Group is undertaking the evaluation of a dozen or so other projects. In addition GIC has been awarded a mandate to act as financial adviser to Aluminium Bahrain BSC, which is planning a two-phase modernisation programme at an estimated total cost of US$150m. Internally, strong emphasis is being placed on the establishment of efficient control systems and procedures.

IX. GULF COOPERATION COUNCIL: ECONOMIC INDICATORS

BAHRAIN

Official name. State of Bahrain

Head of state. HH Shaikh Isa Bin Sulman Al-Khalifa

Area. The State of Bahrain consists of a group of small islands with a total area of about 660 square kilometers. The largest islands in the group are Bahrain (560 square kilometers), Muharraq, Nabih Saleh, Umm Nasan and Sitra.

Date of Independence. September 1, 1971.

Capital and main cities. Manama, on the Bahrain Island (capital), Awali, Isa Town, Muharraq, Rifaa.

Population. 358,857 (1981 Official Census)

Population growth rate. 5.1 percent (1970-80 annual average estimate by World Bank).

Gross national product. (at market prices) $3,240 million (1981 World Bank estimate).

Per capita GNP. $8,960 (1981 World Bank estimate).

State budget 1984-85. Two-year budget revenue and expenditure balance at BD 1,120 million (BD 545 million in 1984 and BD 575 million in 1985).

Gross domestic product 1982. (at current prices) BD 1,740 million.

GDP growth rate 1982. 8.2 percent.

Total exports 1982. BD 1,425 million ($3,789 million). Refined oil exports BD 1,182 million.

Total imports cif 1982. BD 1,402 million ($ 3,729 million). Crude oil imports BD 694 million.

Main suppliers 1982. Saudi Arabia (BD 700 million - $1,862 million); U.S. (BD 142 million - $378 million); Japan (BD 106 million -$282 million); U.K. (BD 98 million - $261 million); Australia (BD 74 million - $197 million); West Germany (BD 46 million - $122 million).

Oil production 1982. 16 million barrels.

Crude oil imports 1982. (for refinery) 54.8 million barrels, all from Saudi Arabia.

Refined oil exports 1982. 86.8 million barrels.

Monetary agency. Bahrain Monetary Agency.

Commercial banks. At the end of 1982, there were 18 commercial banks in Bahrain.

Offshore Banking Units (OBUs). At the end of 1983, there were over 75 offshore banking units in Bahrain with assets totalling $58,030 million at the end of October.

Change in consumer prices 1982. 6.4 percent.

Main port. Mina Sulman.

Main airport. Bahrain International Airport on Muharraq Island is about six kilometers north-east of Manama.

KUWAIT
Official name. State of Kuwait.
Head of state. HH Shaikh Jaber al Ahmad al Sabah

Area. 17,818 square kilometers.

Date of independence. June 19, 1961.

Capital and main cities. Kuwait City (capital), Hawalli, Salmiya.

Population. 1,562,000 (mid-1982 government estimate).

Population growth rate. 6.3 percent (1970-80 annual average estimate by World Bank).

Workforce to population ratio 1981. 52 percent (World Bank estimate).

Gross national product. (at market prices) $30,600 million (1981 World Bank estimate).

Per capita GNP. $20,900 (1981 World Bank estimate).

State budget 1983/84. Planned expenditure KD 3,376 million (excluding allocations to Reserve Fund for Future Generations and Kuwait Fund for Arab Economic Development), estimated revenue KD 3,037 million.

Gross domestic product 1982. (at current prices) KD 5,776 million (provisional estimate).

GDP change 1982. -14.7 percent.

Main origins of GDP 1982. (provisional figures) Oil sector (48.2 percent); domestic trade (9 percent); manufacturing (7.3 percent); construction (4.8 percent); financial institutions (4.6 percent).

Total exports 1982. (IMF figures) KD 2,833 million ($9,841 million). Oil exports KD 2,183 million ($7,583 million).

251

Total imports cif 1982. $8,453 million (IMF estimate); 1981 KD 1,945 million ($6,978 million - government figure).

Main suppliers 1982. (IMF figures) Japan ($1,965 million); U.S. ($1,035 million); West Germany ($894 million); Italy ($690 million); U.K. ($640 million).

Main customers 1982. (IMF figures) Japan ($1,287 million); South Korea ($938 million - estimate); Iraq ($826 million); Italy ($543 million); Pakistan ($427 million).

Estimated oil reserves. 69,000 million barrels.

Crude oil production 1982. 300 million barrels (825,000 barrels a day).

Crude oil exports 1982. 135 million barrels.

Refined oil production 1982. 153 million barrels.

Refined oil exports 1982. 129 million barrels.

Main crude oil customers 1982. Taiwan (37 million barrels); Japan (30 million barrels); South Korea (18 million barrels); Netherlands (9 million barrels).

Main refined oil customers 1982. Japan (20 million barrels); Italy (19 million barrels); Pakistan (13 million barrels); Malaysia and Singapore (11 million barrels).

Central bank. Central Bank of Kuwait.

Commercial banks. There are seven commercial banks: National Bank of Kuwait, Gulf Bank, Alahli Bank, Burgan Bank, the Bank of Kuwait & the Middle East, Commercial Bank of Kuwait and the Bank of Bahrain & Kuwait.

Other financial institutions. Kuwait has about 27 finance and investment companies of which some of the most well known are: Kuwait Investment Company; Kuwait International Investment Company and Kuwait Foreign Trading Contracting & Investment Company.

Change in consumer prices 1982. 7.8 percent.

Main ports. Shuwaikh, Shuaiba, Mina Al-Ahmadi.

Main airport. Kuwait International Airport, 16 kilometers south of city center

OMAN

Official name. Sultanate of Oman.

Head of state. HM Sultan Qaboos Bin Said.

Area. Oman has a total land area of 300,000 square kilometers, making it the second largest country in the Arabian peninsula.

Date of independence. November 18, 1970.

Capital and main cities. Muscat (capital), Sur, Nizwa, Sohar, Salalah.

Population. 919,000 (mid-1981 World Bank preliminary estimate).

Population growth rate. 3.2 percent (1970-80 annual average estimate by World Bank).

Expatriate workforce 1981. 181,208 (government estimate).

Gross national product. (at market prices) RO 2,239 million ($6,482 million - 1982 government estimate); $5,440 million (1981 World Bank estimate).

Per capita GNP. $5,920 (1981 World Bank estimate).

State budget 1984. Planned expenditure RO 1,765 million, estimated revenue RO 1,561 million (of which, oil exports RO 1,100 million).

Second five-year plan (1981-85). Expenditure RO 7,365 million.

Gross domestic product. (at market prices) 1982 RO 2,488 million.

GDP growth rate 1982. 4.9 percent.

Main origins of GDP 1982. Oil and gas (56.8 percent; domestic trade and hotels (12 percent); public administration and defense (10.6 percent); construction (6.2 percent).

Total exports 1982. RO 1,528 million (oil exports, RO 1,410 million).

Total imports cif 1982. RO 1,087 million ($3,147 million).

Main suppliers 1982. Japan ($555 million); U.K. ($386 million); UAE ($375 million); West Germany ($224 million).

Main customers 1982. Japan ($1,589 million); Singapore ($887 million); Netherlands ($339 million); West Germany ($182 million); France ($172 million).

Estimated oil reserves. 2,982 million barrels (January 1983).

Oil production 1982. (by Petroleum Development Oman and Elf Aquitaine Oman) 123 million barrels (335,000 barrels a day).

Crude oil exports 1982. (by same companies) 119 million barrels.

Main oil customers 1982. Japan (46.3 million barrels); Singapore (25.8 million barrels).

Central bank. Central Bank of Oman.

Commercial banks. Twenty-two commercial banks were licensed to operate in Oman at the end of 1983. Of these, eight are locally incorporated: National Bank of Oman; Bank of Oman, Bahrain & Kuwait; Oman International Bank; Al-Bank Al-Ahli Al-Omani; Commercial Bank of Oman; Union Bank of Oman; Bank of Oman & the Gulf; Oman Overseas Trust Bank.

Specialized banks. Oman Bank for Agriculture & Fisheries, Oman Development Bank, Oman Housing Bank.

Change in consumer prices. (capital area only, 1982) 1.1 percent.

Main port. Mina Qaboos (1.3 million tons of cargo unloaded in 1982).

Main airport. Seeb International Airport, about 40 kilometers from Muscat.

QATAR

Official name. State of Qatar.

Head of State. HH Shaikh Khalifa Bin Hamad Al-Thani.

Area. Qatar covers a peninsula of about 11,400 square kilometers which projects northwards from the Arabian mainland.

Date of independence. September 1, 1971.

Capital and main cities. Doha (capital), Umm Said, Dukhan, Umm Bab, Al-Khor, Al-Ruwais and Al-Wakrah.

Population. 260,000 (1982 government estimate).

Population growth rate. 6.9 percent (1970-80 annual average estimate by World Bank).

Gross national product. (at market prices) $6,540 million (1981 World Bank estimate).

Per capita GNP. $27,720.

State budget 1983. (preliminary estimates) Expenditure QR 14,261 million; revenue QR 8,911 million (of which, oil exports QR 6,654 million).

Gross domestic product. (at current prices) 1982 QR 28,839 million.

GDP change 1982. -9.4 percent.

Main origins of GDP 1982. Oil and gas (52.8 percent); domestic trade, restaurants and hotels (8.6 percent); finance, insurance and real estate

254

services (7.7 percent); construction (7.4 percent); manufacturing (5.5 percent).

Total exports 1982. QR 16,405 million (oil exports QR 15,339 million).

Total imports cif 1982. QR 7,088 million ($1,947 million).

Main suppliers 1982. Japan ($428 million); U.K. ($315 million); France ($190 million); U.S. ($176 million).

Main customers 1982. Japan ($1,6l8 million); France ($534 million); Italy ($329 million); Thailand ($197 million).

Estimated oil reserves. 3,434 million barrels (January 1982).

Estimated natural gas reserves. 100 million million cubic feet in the huge offshore North Field.

Oil production 1982. 119.7 million barrels (328,000 barrels a day).

Crude oil exports 1982. 117.8 million barrels (323,000 barrels a day).

Main oil customers 1982. Japan (48 million barrels); France (15.6 million barrels); Italy (10.3 million barrels).

Monetary agency. Qatar Monetary Agency.

Commercial banks. Qatar National Bank, Doha Bank, Commercial Bank of Qatar, Arab Bank, Bank Al-Mashrek, Bank of Oman, Grindlays Bank, Chartered Bank, British Bank of the Middle East, Banque de Paris & des Pays-Bas, Citibank, Bank Saderat Iran, United Bank.

Change in consumer prices 1982. 4.4 percent.

Main ports. Doha (commercial - 1 million tons of imports unloaded in 1982); Umm Said (commercial and industrial - 1.2 million tons of cargo unloaded in 1982).

Main airport. Doha International Airport is about six kilometers from central Doha.

SAUDI ARABIA

Official name. Kingdom of Saudi Arabia.

Head of State. HM King Fahd Bin Abdul-Aziz.

Area. 2,240,000 square kilometers.

Date of independence. September 23, 1932.

Capital and main cities. Riyadh (capital), Jeddah, Al Khobar, Dhahran, Makkah, Medina, Taif.

Population. 9,305,000 (mid-1981 World Bank estimate).

Population growth rate. 4.6 percent (1970-80 annual average estimate by World Bank).

Workforce to population ratio 1981. 52 percent (World Bank estimate).

Gross national product. (at market prices) $117,240 million (1981 World Bank estimate).

Per capita GNP. $12,600 (1981 World Bank estimate).

State budget 1983/84. Planned expenditure SR 260,000 million, estimated revenue SR 225,000 million.

Third five-year development plan 1980-85). Expenditure SR 783,000 million.

Gross domestic product. (at current prices) 1981/82 SR 524,733 million (preliminary)

Non-oil GDP growth 1982/83. 7.5 percent, 1981/82 10.5 percent.

Main origins of GDP 1981/82. (preliminary) Oil and gas, including refining (64.1 percent); construction (11 percent); domestic trade, restaurants and hotels (4.8 percent); transport, storage and communications (3.8 percent).

Total exports 1982. SR 271,090 million ($79,095 million).

Total imports cif 1982. SR 139,335 million ($40,653 million).

Main suppliers 1982. U.S. (SR 29,193 million - $8,517 million); Japan (SR 26,658 million - $7,778 million); West Germany (SR 15,310 million - $4,467 million), U.K. (SR 9,166 million - $2,674 million).

Main customers 1982. Japan (SR 64,434 million - $18,799 million); France (SR 24,321 million - $7,096 million); U.S. (SR 21,127 million - $6,164 million); Singapore (SR 14,412 million - $4,205 million); Italy (SR 13,412 million - $3,913 million).

Proven oil reserves. (Aramco only) 116,747 million barrels (end 1981).

Crude oil production 1983. (first half) 4.3 million barrels a day, 1982 (full year) 6.5 million barrels a day, 2,367 million barrels.

Crude and refined oil exports 1983. (first half) 659 million barrels; 1982 (full year) 2,255 million barrels.

Crude oil exports by main region 1982. Asia and Far East (913.4 million barrels); West Europe (727.7 million barrels); North America (171 million barrels).

Monetary authority. Saudi Arabian Monetary Agency.

Commercial banks. There are now 10 commercial banks in Saudi Arabia, including eight Saudiized banks. The ten are: National Commercial Bank; Riyad Bank; United Saudi Commercial Bank; Al-Bank Al-Saudi Al-Fransi; Al-Bank Al-Saudi Al-Hollandi; Al-Bank Al-Saudi Al-Britani; Bank Al-Jazira; Arab National Bank; Saudi Cairo Bank; Saudi American Bank.

Other financial institutions. Saudi Arabia also has several specialized banks and credit funds (such as Saudi Arabian Agricultural bank, Saudi Credit Bank, Saudi Industrial Development Fund, Real Estate Development Fund and Public Investment Fund) as well as several investment institutions (including Saudi Investment Banking Corporation) and is the home of several regionally owned institutions, such as the Islamic Development Bank, The Arab Investment Company and the OAPEC-owned Arab Petroleum Investments Corporation.

Change in consumer prices 1982/83. (all consumers) 0.5 percent.

Main ports. Jeddah, Dammam, Yanbu, Jizan, Jubail.

Main airports. Jeddah, Riyadh, Dhahran.

UNITED ARAB EMIRATES

Official name. United Arab Emirates (comprising the seven emirates of Abu Dhabi, Dubai, Sharjah, Ras Al-Khaimah, Fujairah, Ajman and Umm Al-Qawain).

Head of state. HH Shaikh Zayed Bin Sultan Al-Nahyan.

Area. 85,000 square kilometers.

Date of independence. December 2, 1971.

Capital and main cities. Abu Dhabi is the administrative center of the federation and Dubai is the main commercial center. Al-Ain, Sharjah, Ajman, Umm Al-Qawain, Ras Al-Khaimah and Fujairah.

Population. 1,091,000 (mid-1981 World Bank estimate).

Population growth rate. 17.7 percent (1970-80 annual average estimate by World Bank).

Gross national product. (at market prices) $26,910 million (1981 World Bank estimate).

Per capita GNP. $24,660 (1981 World Bank estimate).

Federal spending 1982. (includes planned federal budget expenditure of Dh 22,559 million as well as individual expenditure allocations by Abu Dhabi, Dubai, Ras Al-Khaimah and Sharjah) Dh 41,778 million.

Federal revenue 1982. (includes estimated federal budget revenue of Dh 20,276 million as well as individual revenues of Abu Dhabi, Dubai, Ras Al-Khaimah and Sharjah) Dh 39,477 million.

Gross domestic product 1982. Dh 108,900 million.

GDP change 1982. -7.3 percent.

Total exports 1982. Dh 61,808 million ($16,836 million), oil exports Dh 56,768 million ($15,463 million).

Total imports cif 1982. Dh 34,577 million ($9,419 million). Abu Dhabi, Dh 12,708 million. Dubai, Dh 18,789 million. Sharjah, Dh 3,080 million.

Main suppliers 1982. Japan ($1,638 million); U.S. ($1,211 million); U.K. ($1,076 million); West Germany ($795 million); Bahrain ($724 million); France ($596 million).

Main customers 1982. Japan ($7,253 million); U.S. ($1,945 million); France ($1,480 million); Spain ($810 million); Netherlands Antilles ($698 million).

Estimated oil reserves. Over 32,000 million barrels.

Crude oil production 1982. 462 million barrels, 1.2 million barrels a day.

Crude oil exports 1982. 422 million barrels.

Main oil customers 1981. Japan (192 million barrels); France (56 million barrels); U.S. (37 million barrels); Netherlands (33 million barrels).

Central Bank. United Arab Emirates Central Bank.

Commercial banks. Fifty-two commercial banks, including 29 foreign banks, have branches in the UAE. In addition, about 14 international banks have representative offices there. There are also three merchant banks and two specialized banks (Emirates Industrial Bank and the UAE Development Bank), as well as several other investment and financial institutions.

Main ports. Mina Zayed (Abu Dhabi), Mina Rashid (Dubai), Mina Jebel Ali (Dubai) and Mina Khaled (Sharjah).

International airports. Abu Dhabi International Airport, 19 kilometers from the city; Dubai International Airport, 4 kilometers from the city; Sharjah International Airport, 10 kilometers from the city.

Compiled by the Arab-British Chamber of Commerce

BIBLIOGRAPHY

ECONOMICS AND OIL

Abdul Razzak, Sufyan. *The Impact of Oil Revenues on Arab Gulf Development*. Dover, NH: Croom Helm, 1984.

Aburdene, Odeh. "U.S. Economic and Financial Relations with Saudi Arabia, Kuwait and the United Arab Emirates." *American-Arab Affairs*, No. 7 (Winter 1983-84), pp. 76-84.

Allen, Robin. "Economic Integration Means Toeing the Line." *Middle East Economic Digest*, Vol. 27, No. 43 (Oct. 28, 1983), pp. 22-23.

———. "Gulf Co-operation—Theory or Practice?" *Middle East Economic Digest*, Vol. 27, No. 43 (Oct. 28, 1983), pp. 14-15.

Anckonie, Alex, III. "The Banking Sector as an Agent of Economic Diversification in the Arab Gulf Countries." *American-Arab Affairs*, No. 11 (Winter 1984-85), pp. 92-100.

Askari, Hossein. "Management of External Surpluses in the Gulf Countries." *American-Arab Affairs*, No. 7 (Winter 1983-84), pp. 100-05.

Al-Azhary, M.S., ed. *The Impact of Oil Revenues on Arab Gulf Development*. London: Croom Helm; Boulder, CO: Westview Press, 1984.

"Bahrain Seeks Closer Gulf Monetary Links but Saudis Are Wary." *An-Nahar Arab Report and Memo*, Vol. 7, No. 51 (Dec. 19, 1983), pp. 5-6.

Beblawi, Hazem. *The Arab Gulf Economy in a Turbulent Age*. London: Croom Helm; New York: St. Martin's Press, 1984.

———. "The Arab Oil Era (1973-1983): A Story of Lost Opportunity." *Journal of Arab Affairs*, Vol. 5, No. 1 (Spring 1986), pp. 15-34.

———. "Gulf Foreign Investment Co-ordination: Needs and Modalities." *Arab Gulf Journal*, Vol. 3, No. 1 (Apr. 1983), pp. 41-59.

Beseisu, Fouad Hamdi. "Sub-Regional Economic Cooperation in the Arab Gulf." *Arab Gulf Journal*, Vol. 1, No. 1 (Oct. 1981), pp. 45-54.

Dickman, Francois M. "Economic Realities in the Gulf." *American-Arab Affairs*, No. 7 (Winter 1983-84), pp. 50-54.

Erb, Richard D., ed. *The Arab Oil Producing States of the Gulf: Political and Economic Development*. Washington: American Enterprise Institute, 1980.

Fargues, Philippe. *Réserves de main-d'oeuvre et rente pétrolière: étude démographique des migrations de travail vers les pays arabes de golfe*. Beirut: Centre d'Etudes et de Recherches sur le Moyen-Orient Contemporain; Lyon: Presses universitaires de Lyon, 1980.

Al-Fayez, Khaled. "The Gulf Investment Corporation." *American-Arab Affairs*, No. 11 (Winter 1984-85), pp. 34-37.

Feer, Frederick S. "Problems of Oil Supply Disruptions in the Persian Gulf." In George Horwich and Edward Mitchell, eds., *Policies for*

Coping with Oil Supply Disruptions. Washington, DC: American Enterprise Institute, 1982, pp. 11-30.

Fesharaki, Fereidun, and David T. Isaak. *OPEC, the Gulf and the World Petroleum Market*. Boulder, CO: Westview Press, 1983.

"GCC Introduces Unified Import and Export Regulations." *An-Nahar Arab Report and Memo*, Vol. 6, No. 30 (Aug. 13, 1982), p. 6.

"GCC Investments Total 338 BN Dollars." *Saudi Economic Survey*, No. 887 (Oct. 24, 1984), p. 5.

"The GCC Is Making Progress Towards Economic and Political Unity." *An-Nahar Arab Report and Memo*, Vol. 6, No. 3 (Jan. 18, 1982), pp. 2-3.

"GCC Move on Labour." *Arabia*, No. 13 (Sept. 1982), pp. 56-57.

"GCC Moves Forward on Gulf Investment Corporation." *An-Nahar Arab Report and Memo*, Vol. 7, No. 43 (Oct. 24, 1983), p. 4.

"GCC Port Services Rates Unified." *Saudi Economic Survey*, Vol. 18, No. 890 (Nov. 14, 1984), p. 8.

"GCC States to Record Massive Deficits." *Middle East Economic Digest*, Vol. 28, No. 1 (Jan. 6, 1984), p. 4.

"GCC States Undertake Collective Purchasing Policy." *Middle East Economic Survey*, Vol. 26, No. 12 (Jan. 3, 1983), p. 7.

"General Secretariat of the Gulf Chambers of Commerce and Industry Urges Establishment of Joint Marketing Companies." *Saudi Arabia Newsletter*, No. 151 (July 22, 1985), p. 5.

"The Gulf Cooperation Council Economic Agreement." *Arab Economist*, Vol. 14, No. 150 (Mar. 1982), pp. 36-37.

"Gulf Cooperation: New Measures Mark First Effective Steps to a Gulf Common Market." *An-Nahar Arab Report and Memo*, Vol. 7, No. 10 (Mar. 7, 1983), p. 2.

"Gulf Council Discusses Import Controls." *Middle East Economic Digest*, Vol. 25, No. 43 (Oct. 23, 1981), p. 13.

"Gulf Industrial Cooperation." *Saudi Economic Survey*, Vol. 15, No. 737 (Oct. 28, 1981), p. 4.

"Gulf Ministers Lay Foundations for United Oil Front Among Gulf Producers." *Middle East Economic Survey*, Vol. 25, No. 17 (Feb. 8, 1982), pp. 2-3.

"Gulf Plans for an Industrial Future." *Eight Days*, Vol. 4, No. 6 (Feb. 13, 1982), p. 38.

"Gulf States Cut Payments Deficit." *Middle East Economic Digest*, Vol. 29, No. 3 (Jan. 18, 1985), p. 5.

Hayman, Andrew. *Business Opportunities in the Gulf States*. London: Metra Consulting, 1981.

Hitris, Theodore, and Michael H. Hoyle. "Monetary Integration in the Arab Gulf." *Arab Gulf Journal*, Vol. 6, No. 1 (Apr. 1986), pp. 33-42.

"Integrating the Gulf Economies." *Euromoney* (Oct. 1982), pp. 14-15.

Johany, Ali D., et al. *The Saudi Arabian Economy*. Baltimore: The Johns Hopkins University Press, 1986.

Khayata, Abdul Wahab. "The Future of Investments in the Gulf." *American-Arab Affairs*, No. 11 (Winter 1984-85), pp. 6-18.

Kohut, John. "Gulf States Grooming Private Sector for Role in Industry." *Middle East Times*, Vol. 2, No. 15 (Apr. 7, 1984), p. 1.

Kubursi, Atif A. *Oil, Industrialization & Development in the Arab Gulf States*. Dover, NH: Croom Helm, 1984.

————. *The Economies of the Arabian Gulf: A Statistical Source Book*. Dover, NH: Croom Helm, 1984.

Kuwari, Ali Khalifa. *Oil Revenues in the Gulf Emirates: Patterns of Allocation and Impact on Economic Development*. Boulder, CO: Westview Press, 1978.

Iskander, Marwan. "The Outlook for Gulf Oil Exporters in the 1980s." *An-Nahar Arab Report and Memo*, Vol. 8, No. 1 (Jan. 2, 1984), pp. 12-21.

McLachan, Keith Stanley, and George Joffee. *The Gulf War: A Survey of Political Issues and Economic Consequences*. London, 1984.

McMaster, A. K. *The Economies of the Arabian Gulf: A Statistical Source Book*. Dover, NH: Croom Helm, 1983.

Al-Mazrui, Ghanim Faris. "U.S.-Gulf Economic Relations." *American-Arab Affairs*, No. 4 (Spring 1983), pp. 77-80.

Middle East Economic Consultants. *Gulf Economic Integration, Progress and Problems*. Beirut: Middle East Economic Consultants, 1984.

Mohyuddin, Badr I. "An Economic Strategy for Arab Gulf Co-operation in Industrialisation." *Arab Gulf Journal*, Vol. 4, No. 1 (Apr. 1984), pp. 37-49.

————. "Industrialization of the Arab Gulf." *Journal of Arab Affairs*, Vol. 4, No. 1 (Spring 1985), pp. 47-64.

Nimatallah, Yusuf A. "Economic Trends in the Gulf Countries and Their Implications for Relations with the West." *American-Arab Affairs*, No. 7 (Winter 1983-84), pp. 69-75.

Nye, Roger P. "Political and Economic Integration in the Arab States of the Gulf." *Journal of South Asian and Middle Eastern Studies*, Vol. 2, No. 1 (Fall 1978), pp. 3-21.

O'Sullivan, Edmund. "Gulf States (2): Joint Projects Bring Diversity to an Oil-Dependent Economy." *Strategic Digest*, Vol. 11, No. 9 (Sept. 1981), pp. 787-89.

Rumaihi, Muhammad. *Beyond Oil: Unity & Development in the Gulf*. London: Al Saqi Books, 1986.

Sharif, Walid I. *Oil and Development in the Arab Gulf States: A Selected Annotated Bibliography*. Dover, NH: Croom Helm, 1985.

Shreeve, Gavin. "Central Banks Try to Be Tough." *Euromoney*, May 1985.

————. "Learning to Live with Recession." *Euromoney*, May 1985, pp. 223-33.

"The Ties That Bind." *The Economist* (Special Survey: Oil and the Gulf), Vol. 292, No. 7352 (July 28, 1984), pp. 45-50.

"U.A.E. and GCC Trade." *Middle East Newsletter*, No. 268 (Aug. 12, 1985), p. 10.

Al-Yousuf, Ala'a. "Industrialisation and Economic Integration in the Arab Gulf." *Arab Gulf Journal*, Vol. 6, No. 1 (Apr. 1986), pp. 25-32.

SECURITY

Akins, James E., et al., *Oil and Security in the Arabian Gulf*. New York: St. Martin's Press, 1981.

Ali, S. "A Sense of Security." *Far Eastern Economic Review*, Vol. 126 (Nov. 15, 1984), pp. 34-36.

Allen, Robert C. "Regional Security in the Persian Gulf." *Military Review*, Vol. 63, No. 12 (Dec. 1983).

Allen, Robin. "Defence—Towards a Common Strategy." *Middle East Economic Digest*, Vol. 27, No. 43 (Oct. 28, 1983), pp. 23-24.

Alvi, Salim. "Gulf Security—Not by Arms Alone." *Pakistan and Gulf Economist*, Vol. 1, No. 5 (Apr. 24-30, 1982), pp. 8-10.

American Foreign Policy Institute. *The Impact of the Iranian Events Upon Persian Gulf and United States Security*. Washington, DC: American Foreign Policy Institute, 1979.

Amirsadeghi, Hossein, ed. *The Security of the Persian Gulf*. New York: St. Martin's Press, 1981.

Axelgard, Frederick W. " 'The Tanker War' in the Gulf: Background and Repercussions." *Middle East Insight*, Vol. 3, No. 6 (Nov.-Dec. 1984), pp. 26-33.

Al-Azhary, M. S. *The Gulf Cooperation Council and Regional Defense in the 1980s*, Center for Arab Gulf Studies, University of Exeter, Paper No. 1. Exeter, England: University of Exeter, 1982.

Bell, Raymond E., Jr. "The Rapid Deployment Force: How Much, How Soon?" *Army*, Vol. 30 (July 1980), pp. 18-24.

Bloomfield, Lincoln P., Jr. "Saudi Arabia Faces the 1980s: Saudi Security Problems and American Interest." *The Fletcher Forum*, Vol. 5, No. 2 (Summer 1981), pp. 243-77.

Bowie, Christopher. *Concepts of Operations and USAF Planning for Southwest Asia*. Santa Monica, CA: Rand, 1984.

Brown, William R. "Middle East Policy and Gulf Defense." *Middle East Insight*, Vol. 2, No. 5 (Jan.-Feb. 1983), pp. 39-44.

The Changing Balance of Power in the Persian Gulf: Report of an International Seminar at the Center for Mediterranean Studies, Rome, June 26 to July 1st, 1972. New York: American Universities Field Staff, 1972.

Chaoul, Melhem. *La sécurité dans le golfe arabo-persique*. Paris: Fondation pour les études de defense nationale, 1978.

Cordesman, Anthony H. "The Gulf Crisis and Strategic Interests: A Military Analysis." *American-Arab Affairs*, No. 9 (Summer 1984), pp. 8-15.

————. *The Gulf and the Search for Strategic Stability: Saudi Arabia, the Military Balance in the Gulf, and Trends in the Arab-Israeli Military Balance*. Boulder, CO: Westview Press, 1984.

————. "U.S. Military Assistance to the Middle East: National Security or Election-Year Politics?" *Armed Forces Journal International*, Vol. 71, No. 6 (Jan. 1984), pp. 26-33.

————. "U.S. Search for Strategic Stability in the Persian Gulf: The Impact of U.S. Arms Sales to Saudi Arabia on the Arab-Israeli Balance." *Armed Forces Journal*, Vol. 119, No. 1 (Sept. 1981), pp. 61-68, 84-85.

Cottrell, Alvin J. "The Political-Military Balance in the Persian Gulf Region." In Joseph S. Szyliowicz and Bard E. O'Neill, eds., *The Energy Crisis and U.S. Foreign Policy*. New York: Praeger, 1975, pp. 125-38.

Cottrell, Alvin J., and Frank Bray. *Military Forces in the Persian Gulf*. Beverly Hills, CA: Sage Publications, 1978.

Cummings, J. H., et al. "Military Expenditures and Manpower Requirements in the Arabian Peninsula." *Arab Studies Quarterly*, Vol. 2 (1980).

Darius, Robert G., et al., eds. *Gulf Security into the 1980s: Perceptual and Strategic Dimensions*. Stanford, CA: Hoover Institution Press, 1984.

Dawisha, Adeed I. *Saudi Arabia's Search for Security*, Adelphi Paper No. 158. London: International Institute for Strategic Studies, Winter 1979-80.

Dawisha, Karen. "Moscow's Moves in the Direction of the Gulf—So Near and Yet So Far." *Journal of International Affairs*, Vol. 34, No. 2 (1980-1981), pp. 219-34.

"Defending the Gulf: A Survey." *The Economist*, Vol. 279, No. 7188 (June 6-12, 1981), pp. 1-38+.

Dergham, Raghida. "We Don't Need Volunteers to Protect Our House," interview with Secretary-General Abdulla Bishara. *Middle East*, No. 109 (Nov. 1983), pp. 13-14.

Dixon, Michael. "Soviet Policy in the Persian Gulf." *Journal of Defense and Diplomacy*, Vol. 3, No. 2 (Feb. 1985), pp. 23-27.

Dunn, Keith A. "Constraints on the USSR in Southwest Asia: A Military Analysis." *Orbis*, Vol. 25, No. 3 (Fall 1981).

————. "Soviet Strategy, Opportunities and Constraints in Southwestern Asia," *Soviet Union/Union Sovietique*, Vol. 11, Part 2 (1984).

263

Dunn, Michael Collins. "Can the Gulf Secure Itself?" *Defence & Foreign Affairs*, June 1985, p. 9+.

———. "Gulf Security: The States Look After Themselves." *Defence & Foreign Affairs*, Vol. 10 (June 1982), pp. 6-9+.

———. "Soviet Interests in the Arabian Peninsula: The Aden Pact and Other Paper Tigers." *American-Arab Affairs*, No. 8 (Spring 1984), pp. 92-98.

Eilts, H. F. "Security Considerations in the Persian Gulf." *International Security*, Vol. 5, No. 2 (1980), pp. 79-113.

Farid, Abdel Majid, ed. *Oil and Security in the Arabian Gulf*. London: Croom Helm; New York: St. Martin's Press, 1981.

Fukuyama, Francis. *The Soviet Threat to the Persian Gulf*, Rand Paper No. P-6596. Santa Monica, CA: Rand Corporation, March 1981.

"GCC Joint Military Force." *Saudi Arabia Newsletter*, No. 156 (Sept. 30, 1985), p. 3.

"GCC States to Form Joint Defense Force." *Monday Morning*, Vol. 13, No. 645 (Dec. 3, 1984), pp. 26-27.

"GCC Summit Homes in on Defense." *Middle East Economic Digest*, Vol. 28, No. 49 (Dec. 7, 1984), p. 63.

Gordon, Michael R. "The Rapid Deployment Force—Too Large, Too Small or Just Right for Its Task?" *National Journal*, Mar. 13, 1982, pp. 451-55.

Gordon, Murray, ed. *Conflict in the Persian Gulf*. New York: Facts on File, 1981.

"Gulf Cooperation Council States to Develop Rapid Deployment Force." *An-Nahar Arab Report and Memo*, Vol. 7, No. 20 (Oct. 3, 1983), p. 4.

"Gulf Co-operation Council to Discuss Security." *Eight Days* (May 23, 1981), pp. 6-13.

"Gulf States to Establish Their Own Rapid Deployment Force." *An-Nahar Arab Report and Memo*, Vol. 7, No. 25 (June 20, 1983), p. 4.

Halliday, Fred. *Soviet Policy in the Arc of Crisis*. Washington, DC: Institute for Policy Studies, 1981.

———. *Threat from the East? Soviet Policy from Afghanistan and Iran to the Horn of Africa*, rev. ed. Harmondsworth, Middlesex, England: Penguin, 1982.

Halloran, Richard. "Poised for the Persian Gulf." *New York Times Magazine*, Apr. 1, 1984, pp. 38-40, 61.

Hart, Jo-Anne. "Joint Task Force Operations and U.S. Gulf Policy." *Journal of Arab Affairs*, Vol. 5, No. 1 (Spring 1986), pp. 35-57.

Hameed, Mazher A. *An American Imperative: The Defense of Saudi Arabia*. Washington, DC: Middle East Assessments Group, 1981.

———. *Arabia Imperilled: The Security Imperatives of the Arab Gulf States*. Washington, DC: Middle East Assessments Group, 1986.

Hottinger, Arnold. "Notes from the Gulf: Security Problems." *Swiss Review of World Affairs*, Vol. 33, No. 12 (Mar. 1984), pp. 14-21.

Ispahani, Mahnaz Zehra. "Alone Together: Regional Security Arrangements in Southern Africa and the Gulf." *International Security*, Vol. 8, No. 4 (Spring 1984), pp. 152-75.

Jabber, Paul. "U.S. Interests and Regional Security in the Middle East." *Daedalus*, Vol. 59, No. 4 (Fall 1980), pp. 67-80.

Johnson, Maxwell Orme. *The Military As an Instrument of U.S. Policy in Southwest Asia: The Rapid Deployment Joint Task Force, 1979-1982*. Boulder, CO: Westview Press, 1983.

————. "U.S. Strategic Operations in the Persian Gulf." *Proceedings of the Naval Institute*, Feb. 1981.

Johnson, Thomas M., and Raymond T. Barrett. "The Rapid Deployment Joint Task Force." *U.S. Naval Institute Proceedings*, Vol. 106, No. 11 (Nov. 1980), pp. 95-98.

"Joint Military Strike Force Established by the GCC to Deal with Threats of External Aggression." *Saudi Arabia Newsletter*, Vol. 7, No. 138 (Jan. 21, 1985), p. 4.

Katz, Mark N. "Soviet Policy on the Gulf States." *Current History*, Vol. 84, No. 498 (Jan. 1985), pp. 25-28, 41.

————. *Russia and Arabia: Soviet Foreign Policy toward the Arabian Peninsula*. Baltimore, MD: Johns Hopkins University Press, 1986.

Kechichian, Joseph A. "The Gulf Cooperation Council: Search for Security," *Third World Quarterly*, Vol. 7, No. 4 (Oct. 1985), pp. 853-81.

Kemp, Geoffrey. "Strategic Problems in the Persian Gulf Region." In George S. Wise and Charles Issawi, eds., *Middle East Perspectives: The Next Twenty Years*. Princeton, NJ: Darwin Press, 1981, pp. 71-79.

Kodmans, Bassma, ed. *Quelle securite pour le Golfe?* Paris: Institut francaise des relations internationelles, 1984.

Koury, Enver M., and Emile A. Nakhleh, eds., with Thomas W. Mullen. *The Arabian Peninsula, Red Sea and Gulf: Strategic Considerations*. Hyattsville, MD: Institute of Middle Eastern and North African Studies, 1979.

"Kuwait Denies Participation in GCC Security Pact." *Gulf States Newsletter*, Vol. 10, No. 271 (Sept. 23, 1985), pp. 5-6.

Lawrence, Robert G. "Arab Perceptions of U.S. Security Policy in Southwest Asia." *American-Arab Affairs*, No. 5 (Summer 1983), pp. 27-38.

Lenczowski, George. "The Soviet Union and the Persian Gulf: An Encircling Strategy." *International Journal*, Vol. 37, No. 2 (1982), pp. 307-327.

Litwak, Robert. *Security in the Persian Gulf: Sources of Inter-State Conflict*. London: International Institute for Strategic Studies, 1982.
————. *Sources of Inter-State Conflict*. Montclair, NJ: Published for the International Institute for Strategic Studies by Allanheld, Osmun, 1981.
MacDonald, Charles G. "The United States and Gulf Conflict Scenarios." *Middle East Insight*, Vol. 3, No. 1 (May-July 1983), pp. 23-27.
McNaugher, Thomas L. "Arms and Allies on the Arabian Peninsula." *Orbis*, Vol. 28, No. 3 (Fall 1984), pp. 489-526.
————. *Arms and Oil: U.S. Military Strategy and the Persian Gulf*. Washington, DC: Brookings Institution, 1985.
————. "Balancing Soviet Power in the Persian Gulf." *Brookings Review*, Vol. 1, No. 4 (1983), pp. 20-25.
————. "Deterring Soviet Forces in Southwest Asia." In Stephen J. Cimbala, ed., *National Security Strategy: Choices and Limits*. New York: Praeger, 1984; Foreign Policy Research Institute Series, pp. 125-54.
————. *Gulf Security: The Military Dimension*. Washington, DC: The Brookings Institution, 1984.
————. "Southwest Asia: The Crises that Never Came." In B. M. Blechman and E. N. Luttwak, eds. *International Security Yearbook 1984/85*. Washington, DC: Center for Strategic and International Studies, 1985.
Al-Maaghi, Mahmoud. "Of Stingers and Sams: Gulf's Arms Bazaar." *Arabia*, Vol. 4, No. 37 (Sept. 1984), pp. 6-9.
Malik, Hafeez, ed. *International Security in Southwest Asia*. New York: Praeger, 1984.
Mansur, Abdul Kasim (pseud.). "The Military Balance in the Persian Gulf: Who Will Guard the Gulf States from Their Guardians?" *Armed Forces Journal International*, Nov. 1980.
Martin, Lenore G. *The Unstable Gulf: Threats from Within*. Lexington, MA: Lexington Books, 1984.
Meo, Leila. *U.S. Strategy in the Gulf: Intervention Against Liberation*. Belmont, MA: Association of Arab-American University Graduates, 1981.
"Middle East Military Survey 1984—the Persian Gulf." *Defense Update International*, No. 44 (1984), pp. 30-1.
Monroe, Elizabeth (rapporteuse). *The Changing Balance of Power in the Persian Gulf: The Report of an International Seminar at the International Center for Mediterranean Studies; Rome*, Sir Denis Wright, Chairman. New York: American Universities Field Staff, 1972.
Muraka, Dev. "Soviet Perceptions of the Gulf." *Middle East International*, No. 187 (Nov. 12, 1982), pp. 12-13.

Naff, Thomas, ed. *Gulf Security and the Iran-Iraq War.* Washington, DC: National Defense University Press, 1985.

Neumann, Robert G., and Shireen T. Hunter. "Crisis in the Gulf: Reasons for Concern But not Panic." *American-Arab Affairs*, No. 9 (Summer 1984), pp. 16-21.

Newsom, David D. "American EnGulfed." *Foreign Policy*, No. 43 (Summer 1981), pp. 17-32.

Noyes, James H. *The Clouded Lens: Persian Gulf Security and U.S. Policy*, 2nd ed. Stanford, CA: Hoover Institution Press, 1982.

O'Neill, Bard E. *Petroleum and Security: The Limitations of Military Power in the Persian Gulf*, Research Directorate Monograph 77-4. Washington: National Defense University, Oct. 1977.

Page, Stephen. "Moscow and the Arabian Peninsula." *American-Arab Affairs*, No. 8 (Spring 1984), pp. 83-91.

———. "Patterns of Soviet Activity in Southwest Asia." *International Journal*, Spring 1986.

Patton, Kieran. "Gulf States to Meet to Discuss Security Cooperation." *An-Nahar Arab Report and Memo*, Vol. 9, No. 16 (June 14, 1985), pp. 5-7.

Perera, Judith. "Gulf Security: Is Self-Defence a Myth?" *Middle East*, No. 119 (Sept. 1984), pp. 15-18.

Peterson, J. E. "American Policy in the Gulf and the Sultanate of Oman," *American-Arab Affairs*, No. 8 (Spring 1984), pp. 117-30.

———. *Defending Arabia*. New York: St. Martin's Press, 1986.

———. "Defending Arabia: Evolution of Responsibility." *Orbis*, Vol. 28, No. 3 (Fall 1984), pp. 465-88.

"The Policemen of Hormuz." *Gulf States Newsletter*, No. 184 (Apr. 5, 1982), pp. 2-4.

Popatia, Mahboob A. "Gulf's Security Perspectives." *Pakistan Horizon*, Vol. 34, No. 2 (1981), pp. 66-77.

Price, David Lynn. "Moscow and the Persian Gulf." *Problems of Communism*, Vol. 28, No. 2 (Mar.-Apr. 1979), pp. 1-13.

Pryer, Melvyn. *A View from the Rimland: An Appraisal of Soviet Interest and Involvement in the Gulf*. Durham City: Centre for Middle Eastern and Islamic Studies, University of Durham, England, 1981.

Raj, Christopher S. "U.S. Gulf Strike Force." *Strategic Analysis*, Vol. 4, No. 12 (Mar. 1981), pp. 575-80.

Ramazani, Rouhollah K. "Security Issues in the Gulf Region." *Defence Journal*, Vol. 7, No. 3 (1981), pp. 6-8.

———. "Security in the Persian Gulf." *Foreign Affairs*, Vol. 57, No. 4 (1979), pp. 821-35.

Record, Jeffrey. *The Rapid Deployment Force and U.S. Military Intervention in the Persian Gulf*. Cambridge, MA: Institute for Foreign Policy Analysis, 1981.

Ross, Dennis. *Considering Threats to the Persian Gulf*, International Studies Program, No. 29. Washington, DC: The Wilson Center, 1981.

Ross, Dennis. "Considering Soviet Threats to the Persian Gulf." *International Security*, Vol. 6, No. 2 (1982), pp. 159-80.

———. "The Soviet Union and the Persian Gulf." *Political Science Quarterly*, Vol. 99, No. 4 (Winter 1984-85), pp. 615-35.

Rowe, Donald S. "Collective Security and the Rapid Deployment Joint Task Force." *Joint Perspectives*, Vol. 1, No. 3 (Winter 1981), pp. 3-17.

Rubinstein, Alvin Z., ed. *The Great Game: Rivalry in the Persian Gulf and South Asia*. New York: Praeger, 1983.

Samore, Gary. "The Persian Gulf." In David A. Deese and Joseph S. Nye, eds., *Energy and Security*. Cambridge, MA: Ballinger, for the Harvard Energy and Security Research Project, 1981.

"Shaikh Khalifa: The Security of the Gulf Is Our Responsibility," (interview). *The Emirates*, No. 60 (Apr. 1982), pp. 6-7.

Singh, Kunwar Rajendra. *The Persian Gulf: Arms and Arms Control*. Canberra; Miami, FL: Strategic and Defense Studies Centre, Research School of Pacific Studies, Australian National University, 1981.

Sreedhar. *The Gulf, Scramble for Security*. New Delhi: ABC Publishing House, 1983.

Stookey, Robert W., ed. *The Arabian Peninsula: Zone of Ferment*. Stanford, CA: Hoover Institution Press, 1984.

Tahtinen, Dale R. *Arms in the Persian Gulf*. Foreign Affairs Studies, No. 10. Washington, DC: American Enterprise Institute for Public Policy Research, 1974.

Thompson, W. Scott. "The Persian Gulf and the Correlation of Forces." *International Security*, Vol. 7, No. 1 (Summer 1982), pp. 157-80.

U.S. Congress. House. Committee on Foreign Affairs. *U.S. Security Interests in the Persian Gulf: Report of a Staff Study Mission to the Persian Gulf, Middle East, and Horn of Africa, Oct. 21-Nov. 13, 1980*. Washington, DC: GPO, 1981.

———. Senate. Committee on Foreign Relations. Staff Report. *War in the Gulf*. August 1984. Washington, DC: GPO, 1984.

"U.S. Military in Saudi Arabia: Investing in Stability or Disaster?" *Strategic Digest*, Vol. 11, No. 10 (Oct. 1981), pp. 813-30.

Waltz, Kenneth N. "A Strategy for the Rapid Deployment Force." *International Security*, Vol. 5, No. 4 (1981), pp. 49-73.

"We May Create an Arms Industry," interview with Abdulla Bishara by James Pingle. *Newsweek*, Vol. 101, No. 15 (Apr. 11, 1983), p. 56.

Witton, Peter. "GCC Security Issues Remain Unsolved." *Middle East Economic Digest*, Vol. 26, No. 46 (Nov. 12, 1982), pp. 18-20.

Wohlstetter, Albert. "Les Etats-Unis et la sécurité du Golfe." *Politique Etrangère*, Vol. 46, No. 1 (Mar. 1981), pp. 75-88.

————. "Meeting the Threat in the Persian Gulf." *Survey*, Vol. 25, No. 2 (Spring 1980), pp. 128-88.

Yorke, Valerie. "Security in the Gulf: A Strategy of Pre-emption." *World Today*, Vol. 37, No. 7 (July 1980), pp. 239-50.

GENERAL

Abdul Razzak, Sufyan. *Die Interessen- und Konfliktkonstellationen in der arabischen Golf-Region: eine Studie zu den Abhängigkeitsstrukturen der Peripherien.* Hamburg: Borg, 1982.

Ali, S. "All for One, One for All." *Far East Economic Review*, Vol. 126 (Nov. 15, 1984), pp. 32-35.

Al-Ameri, Abdul Kader B. "Interview on the GCC." *American-Arab Affairs*, No. 15 (Winter 1985-86), pp. 71-74.

Amin, Sayed Hassan. *International and Legal Problems of the Gulf.* London: Middle East and North African Studies Press; Boulder, CO: Westview Press, 1981.

————. *Political and Strategic Issues in the Gulf.* Glasgow: Royston, 1984.

Amirie, Abbas, ed. *The Persian Gulf and Indian Ocean in International Politics.* Tehran: Institute for International Political and Economic Studies, 1975.

Anthony, John Duke. *Arab States of the Lower Gulf: People, Politics, Petroleum.* Washington, DC: Middle East Institute, 1975.

————. "The Gulf Cooperation Council." *Orbis*, Vol. 28, No. 3 (Fall 1984), pp. 447-450.

————. *Historical and Cultural Dictionary of the Sultanate of Oman and the Emirates of Eastern Arabia, with contributions from John Peterson and Donald Sean Abelson.* Metuchen, NJ: Scarecrow Press, 1976.

Al-Baharna, Husain M. *The Legal Status of the Arabian Gulf States,* 2nd ed. Beirut: Librarie du Liban, 1975.

————. *The Modern Gulf States: Their International Relations and the Development of Their Political, Legal and Constitutional Positions.* Beirut, 1973.

Arabian American Oil Co., Government Relations Department, Research Division. *Oman and the Southern Shore of the Persian Gulf.* Aramco, 1952.

Ballantyne, W. M. "The Constitutions of the Gulf States: A Comparative Study." *Archer Law Quarterly*, Feb. 1980.

————. *Legal Development in Arabia.* London: Graham & Trotman, 1980.

Barger, Thomas C. *Arab States of the Persian Gulf.* Newark, DE: Center for the Study of Marine Policy, University of Delaware, 1975.

Bayati, Ahmed B. *Der arabisch-persische Golf: eine Studie zur histor., polit. u. ökonom. Entwicklung d. Golf-Region*. Munich: Olschläger, 1978.

Bishara, Abdulla Yacoub. "The Gulf Cooperation Council: Achievements and Challenges." *American-Arab Affairs*, No. 7 (Winter 1983-84), pp. 40-44.

———. "Interview on the GCC." *American-Arab Affairs*, No. 17 (Summer 1986), pp. 26–29.

———. "We Don't Need Volunteers to Protect Our House." *The Middle East* (London), Nov. 1983, pp. 13-17.

Blake, Gerald. "The Red Sea and the Arabian Gulf: Strategic and Economic Links." In Abdel Majid Farid, ed., *The Red Sea: Prospects for Stability*. London: Croom Helm, 1984, pp. 84-94.

Bradley, C. Paul. *Recent United States Policy in the Persian Gulf (1971-82)*. Grantham, NH: Tompson & Rutter; Hamden, CT: Distributed by the Shoe String Press, 1982.

Brown, Harold. "Protecting U.S. Interests in the Persian Gulf Region." *Department of State Bulletin*, Vol. 80, No. 2038 (May 1980), pp. 63-67.

Bulliet, Richard W. *The Gulf Scenario*. New York: St. Martin's Press, 1984.

Bullock, John. *The Gulf: A Portrait of Kuwait, Qatar, Bahrain, and the UAE*. London: Century Publications, 1984.

———. *The Persian Gulf Unveiled*. New York: Congdon and Weed, 1985.

Burrell, R. M. *The Persian Gulf*, Washington Papers, No. 1. New York: New York Library Press, for the Georgetown University Center for Strategic and International Studies, 1972.

Christie, John. "Self-Reliance." *Middle East*, No. 123 (Jan. 1985), p. 6.

Cordesman, Anthony H. "The Oil Glut and the Strategic Importance of the Gulf States." *Armed Forces Journal International*, Vol. 121, No. 3 (Oct. 1983).

Cottrell, Alvin J., ed. *The Persian Gulf States: A General Survey*. Baltimore: The Johns Hopkins University Press, 1980.

Cottrell, Alvin J., and Michael L. Moodie. *The United States and the Persian Gulf: Past Mistakes, Present Needs*. New Brunswick, NJ: Transaction Books (for the National Strategy Information Center), 1981.

Djalili, Mohammad Reza. *Le golfe persique: problèmes et perspectives*. Paris: Dalloz, 1978.

"Don't Drag Us In." *The Economist*, Vol. 291, No. 7344 (June 2, 1984), p. 32.

Duncan, Andrew. *Money Rush*. London: Hutchinson, 1979.

Dunn, Michael Collins. "The Gulf Cooperation Council (GCC)) Organizes for Strength." *Defence & Foreign Affairs*, Vol. 9 (June 1981), p. 32.

Al-Ebraheem, Hassan Ali. *Kuwait and the Gulf: Small States and the International System*. Washington, DC: Croom Helm, 1984.

Ehrenberg, Eckehart. *Rüstung und Wirtschaft am Golf: Iran und seine Nachbarn (1965-1978)*. Hamburg: Deutsches Orient-Institut, 1978.

Eilts, Hermann F. "A Conversation with Ambassador Hermann F. Eilts: The Dilemma in the Persian Gulf"; Held on May 7, 1980 at the American Enterprise Institute for Public Policy Research, Washington, D.C., 1980.

Farley, Jonathan. "The Gulf War and the Littoral States." *World Today*, Vol. 40, No. 7 (July 1984), pp. 269-276.

"Food Security Is a Priority for GCC." *An-Nahar Arab Report and Memo*, Vol. 7, No. 46 (Nov. 1983), pp. 6-7.

Freedman, Robert O. "Moscow, Washington and the Gulf." *American-Arab Affairs*, No. 1 (Summer 1982), pp. 127-39.

"GCC: First Steps Towards Integration." *Arab Economist*, Vol. 14, No. 153 (June 1982), p. 6.

"The GCC Is Now a Reality." *Middle East*, No. 109 (Nov. 1983), pp. 15-16.

"GCC States Lay Basis for Joint Military and Economic Systems." *An-Nahar Arab Report and Memo*, Vol. 6, No. 5 (Feb. 1, 1982), pp. 3-4.

"Gulf Cooperation Needs More Thought If Inequality Is to Be Avoided." *An-Nahar Arab Report and Memo*, Vol. 9, No. 1 (Jan. 7, 1985), pp. 5-7.

The Gulf Directory 1984/85. Manama, Bahrain: Falcon Publishing, 1984.

The Gulf Emirates: Kuwait, Bahrein, Qatar, United Arab Emirates, prepared by M. Philippe Lannois. Geneva: Nagel, 1976.

Hameed, Mazher A. *The Middle East in Review, 1984-1985*. Washington, DC: Middle East Assessments Group, 1986.

Heard-Bey,Frauke. *Die arabischen Golfstatten im Zeichen der islamischen Revolution: innen-, aussen- und sicherheitspolitische Zusammenarbeit im Golf-Rat*. Bonn: Forschungsinstitut der Deutschen Gesellschaft für Auswärtige Politik: Vertrieb; Europa Union Verlag, 1983.

———. *From Trucial States to United Arab Emirates*. New York: Longman, Inc., 1983.

Hendawi, Hamza. "Gulf Arab States Moving to Implement Islamic Law." *Middle East Times*, Vol. 2, No. 11 (Mar. 10, 1984), p. 20.

Hijab, Nadia. "Gulf Council Shifts into Second Gear." *Middle East*, No. 84 (Oct. 1981), pp. 25-26.

Hunter, Shireen T. "Arab-Iranian Relations and Stability in the Persian Gulf." *The Washington Quarterly*, Vol. 7, No. 3 (Summer 1984), pp. 67-76.

Hunter, Shireen, ed. *The Gulf Cooperation Council: Problems and Prospects*. Washington, DC: CSIS, 1984

———. *OPEC and the Third World: The Politics of Oil*. Bloomington, IN: Indiana University Press, 1984.

Hurewitz, Jacob Coleman. *The Persian Gulf: After Iran's Revolution*. New York: Foreign Policy Association, 1979.

"Industry Ministers on GCC, Saudi Plans." *Khaleej Times* (Nov. 15, 1982), p. 4.

Il Golfo della crisi: tensioni e politica dell'Italia nel Golfo Persico-Arabo. Ipalma, Istituto per le relazioni tra L'Italia e i paesi dell'Africa, America Latina e Medio Oriente. Milan: F. Angeli, 1983.

Iskandar, Marwan. "Gulf States Are Taking Cooperation Seriously." *An-Nahar Arab Report and Memo*, Vol. 5, No. 38 (Sept. 21, 1981), p. 1.

Izzard, Molly. *The Gulf: Arabia's Western Approaches*. London: J. Murray, 1979.

Katz, Mark N. "North Yemen Between East and West." *American-Arab Affairs*, No. 8 (Spring 1984), pp. 99-107.

Kelly, John Barrett. *Arabia, the Gulf and the West: A Critical View of the Arabs and Their Oil Policy*. New York: Basic Books, 1980.

Khalidi, Rashid, and Camille Mansour, eds. *Palestine and the Gulf: Proceedings of an International Seminar, IPS, Beirut, November 2-5, 1981*. Beirut: Institute for Palestine Studies, 1982.

Khalifa, Ali Mohammed. *The United Arab Emirates: Unity in Fragmentation*. Boulder, CO: Westview Press, 1979.

Kilner, Peter. *The Gulf Handbook: A Guide to the Eight Persian Gulf Countries*. Garrett Park, MD: Garrett Press, 1980.

Koury, Enver M. "The Impact of the Geopolitical Situation of Iraq upon the Gulf Cooperation Council." *Middle East Insight*, Vol. 2, No. 5 (Jan. 1983), pp. 28-35.

Kuniholm, Bruce Robellet. *The Persian Gulf and United States Policy: A Guide to Issues and References*. Claremont, CA: Regina Books, 1984.

Kuwait. Ministry of Information. *Gulf Cooperation Council: Towards New Horizons*. Kuwait: Ministry of Information, n.d.

"Kuwait Moves on GCC Agreement." *An-Nahar Arab Report and Memo*, Vol. 6, No. 45 (Dec. 27, 1982), p. 6.

El-Kuwaiz, Abdullah. "The Gulf Cooperation Council and the Concept of Economic Integration." *American-Arab Affairs*, No. 7 (Winter 1983-84), pp. 45-49.

"Leaving It to the Saudis, with Awacs and a Prayer." *The Economist*, Vol. 291, No. 7343 (May 25, 1984), pp. 47-48.

Long, David F. *The Persian Gulf: An Introduction to Its Peoples, Politics, and Economics*, 2nd ed. Boulder, CO: Westview Press, 1978.

Lorimer, John Gordon. *Gazeteer of the Persian Gulf, 'Oman, and Central Arabia*. Amersham, England: Demand Editions, 1984.

MacDonald, Charles G. *Iran, Saudi Arabia, and the Law of the Sea: Political Interaction and Legal Development in the Persian Gulf*. Westport, CT: Greenwood Press, 1980.

McDermott, Anthony. "Saudi Arabia: The Arab Helping Hand." *Middle East International*, No. 243 (Feb. 8, 1985), p. 12.

Maull, Hanns W. "Strength from Weakness? Development and Prospect of the Gulf Co-operation Council." *Vierteljahresberichte Probleme der internationalen Zusammenarbeit* (Problems of International Co-operation), Vol. 97 (Sept. 1984), pp. 253-62.

Maurizi, Romano. "Il Consiglio de cooperazione del Golfo." *Affari esteri*, Vol. 58 (Spring 1983), pp. 177-10.

The Middle East Institute. *The Gulf and the Peninsula: American Interests and Policies in the Eighties*, 34th Annual Conference, September 1980. Washington, DC: The Middle East Institute, 1980.

Mughisuddin, Mohammad, ed. *Conflict and Cooperation in the Persian Gulf*. New York: Praeger, 1977.

Al-Nafeesi, Abdullah Fahad. "Gulf Cooperation Council: The Political and Strategic Framework." *Al-Khalij al-Arabi*, Vol. 15, No. 1 (1983), pp. 13-48.

Nakhleh, Emile A. *Arab-American Relations in the Persian Gulf*. Washington, DC: American Enterprise Institute for Public Policy Research, 1975.

————. *The Gulf Cooperation Council: Policies, Problems and Prospects*. New York, Westport, CT; London: Praeger, 1986.

————. *The Persian Gulf and American Policy*. New York: Praeger, 1982.

Niblock, Tim, ed. *Social and Economic Development in the Arab Gulf*. Dover, NH: Croom Helm; Exeter: Centre for Arab Gulf Studies, 1980.

Novati, Giampaolo Calchi. "The EEC and the Gulf Cooperation Council." *Politique Internationale*, Vol. 4, No. 1 (Spring 1985), pp. 110-18.

Nyrop, Richard F., ed. *Persian Gulf States*, 2nd ed. Washington, DC: Foreign Area Studies, The American University, 1985.

Osbourne, Christine. *The Gulf States and Oman;* Text and Photos by Christine Osbourne. Dover, NH: Croom Helm, 1977.

O'Sullivan, Edmund. "GCC Summit: Securing the Future." *Middle East Economic Digest*, Vol. 28, No. 46 (Nov. 16, 1984), pp. 20-21.

Page, Stephen. *The Soviet Union and the Yemens: Influence in Asymmetrical Relationships*. New York: Praeger, 1985.

Papers Presented to the Historical Studies Conference on Eastern Arabia, Doha, Qatar, 21st to 28th March 1976. Doha: Association of Arab Historians, 1977.

Persian Gulf States. (Collection of statistics: 12 titles on microfiche). Zug, Switzerland: Inter Documentation Company AG, (1984?).

Peterson, J. E. *The Politics of Middle Eastern Oil*. Washington, DC: The Middle East Institute, 1983.

————. *Yemen—The Search for a Modern State*. Washington, DC: The Johns Hopkins University Press, 1982.

Pranger, Robert J., and Dale R. Tahtinen. *American Policy Options in Iran and the Persian Gulf*. Washington, DC: American Enterprise Institute, 1979.

Price, David Lynn. *Stability in the Gulf: The Oil Revolution*. London: Institute for the Study of Conflict, 1976.

Pridham, B. R., ed. *The Arab Gulf and the West*. Dover, NH: Croom Helm; Exeter: Centre for Arab Gulf Studies, University of Exeter, 1985.

Quandt, William B. "The Gulf War: Policy Options and Regional Implications." *American-Arab Affairs*, No. 9 (Summer 1984), pp. 1-7.

Ramazani, Rouhollah K. *The Persian Gulf and the Strait of Hormuz*. Alphen aan den Rijn: Sijthoff and Noordhoff, 1979.

Rizvi, Hasan-Askari. "Gulf Cooperation Council." *Pakistan Horizon*, Vol. 35, No. 2 (1982), pp. 29-38.

Robert, Rudiger. "Der Golfkooperationsrat: Die arabischen Golfstaaten auf der Suche nach Sicherheit und Stabilitat." *Orient*, Vol. 24, No. 2 (June 1983), pp. 235-59, 382-83.

Röhner, Edmund. *Wer bedroht die Golfregion?* Berlin: Dietz, 1981.

Rouček, Joseph Slabey, and Michael V. Belok. *United States and the Persian Gulf*. Malabar, FL: R. E. Krieger Pub. Co., 1985.

Sabah, Salem al-Jabir. *Les émirates du golfe: histoire d'un peuple*. Paris: Fayard, 1980.

Saleh, Samir. *Commercial Arbitration in the Arab Middle East*. London: Graham & Trotman, 1984.

Al-Salem, Faisal. "The United States and the Gulf: What Do the Arabs Want?" *Journal of South Asian and Middle Eastern Studies*, Vol. 6, No. 1 (Fall 1982), pp. 8-32.

Salem, M. Ania. "Gulf States Seek Cooperation in an Area of Conflict—Situation Reports." *South*, Vol. 8 (June 1981), pp. 26-29.

Sawyer, Herbert L. *Soviet Perception of the Oil Factor in U.S. Foreign Policy: The Middle East-Gulf Region.* Boulder, CO: Westview Press, 1983.

Sirriyeh, Hussein. *U.S. Policy in the Gulf 1968-1977: Aftermath of British Withdrawal.* London: Ithaca Press, 1984.

Sreedhar. "The GCC: How Viable Is It?" *Strategic Analysis*, Vol. 7, No. 11 (Feb. 1984), pp. 910-16.

Stork, Joe. "U.S. Targets Persian Gulf for Intervention." *MERIP Reports*, No. 85 (Feb. 1980), pp. 3-5.

"Study Casts Doubt on Integration." *Mideast Markets*, Vol. 10, No. 2 (Jan. 24, 1983), p. 3.

Tuson, Penelope. *The Records of the British Residency and Agencies in the Persian Gulf.* London: India Office Library and Records, 1979.

U.S. Congress. House. Committee on Foreign Affairs. *Developments in the Persian Gulf, June 1984.* 98th Cong., 2d sess. Washington, DC: GPO, 1984.

————. House. Committee on Foreign Affairs, Subcommittee on Near East and South Asia. *U.S. Interests in and Policy Toward the Persian Gulf, Hearings.* 92d Cong., 2d sess.; 93rd Cong., 1st sess.; 96th Cong., 2d sess.; 97th Cong., 1st sess. Washington, DC: GPO, 1972, 1973, 1980, 1981.

U.S. Defense Mapping Agency, Topographic Center. *Bahrain, Kuwait, Qatar, and United Arab Emirates: Official Standard Names Approved by the U.S. Board on Geographic Names.* Washington, DC: U.S. Defense Mapping Agency, 1976.

U.S. Library of Congress, Congressional Research Service. *The Gulf Cooperation Council*, Report No. 85-516F. Washington, DC: 1984.

————. *The Persian Gulf: Are We Committed?* Washington, DC, 1981.

————. *Western Vulnerability to a Disruption of Persian Gulf Oil Supplies: U.S. Interests and Options.* Washington, D.C., 1983.

Van Hollen, Christopher. "Don't Engulf the Gulf." *Foreign Affairs*, Vol. 59, No. 5 (Summer 1981), pp. 1064-78.

Veliotes, Nicholas A. *Statement before the European and Middle East Subcommittee of the House Foreign Affairs Committee and the Joint Economic Committee*, May 10, 1982.

Webman, Esther Souery. *The Gulf States: Middle East Contemporary Survey*, Vol. 6, 1981-1982. New York: Holmes & Meier, 1984.

Whittingham, Ken. "Gulf States (1): Six Nations Forge Ahead on Logical Path of Unity." *Strategic Digest*, Vol. 11, No. 9 (Sept. 1981).

Wingerter, Rex B. "The Gulf Cooperation Council and American Interests in the Gulf." *American-Arab Affairs*, No. 16 (Spring 1986), pp. 15-26.

Wilson, Desmond P. *The Persian Gulf and the National Interest.* Alexandria, VA: Center for Naval Analyses, 1982.

Wolfe, Ronald G., ed. *The United States, Arabia, and the Gulf.* Washington, DC: Georgetown University Center for Contemporary Arab Studies, 1980.
Yorke, Valerie. "Bid for Gulf Unity." *The World Today*, Vol. 37, Nos. 7-8 (July-Aug. 1981), pp. 246-49.
The Gulf in the 1980s. London: Royal Institute of International Affairs, 1980.
Zahlan, Rosemarie Said. *The Origins of the United Arab Emirates. A Political and Social History of the Trucial States.* London, 1978.

DOCUMENTATION

Charter, Cooperation Council for the Arab States of the Gulf, May 25, 1981. *American-Arab Affairs*, No. 7 (Winter 1983-84), pp. 157-76.
Cooperation Council for the Arab States of the Gulf. *Information Handbook.* Riyadh: Bahr Al-Olum Press, 1982.
The Unified Economic Agreement, Cooperation Council for the Arab States of the Gulf, June 8, 1981. *American-Arab Affairs*, No. 7 (Winter 1983-84), pp. 177-82.

INDEX

External policies, 80–81
Exxon, 49, 51

Fahd (king of Saudi Arabia), 153,
159, 161, 214
Fahd Plan, 40
Faisal, al-, Saud, 25, 150, 152, 153,
208
Fayez, Al-, Khaled, 67
Federation of Arab Emirates, 27
Fez Summit, 40
Fiqh, 208
Firqas, 186
First Chicago Corporation, 65
First National Bank of Chicago, 60,
63
Food security
memorandums, 246–247
Foreign exchange, 120
Foreign investment, 121
FRAB. *See* Banque Franco-Arabe
d'Investissements
Internationaux
France, 30, 44, 55, 177(n), 178,
178(n), 184, 189, 208, 213, 214
Franklin, Benjamin, 38
Freedoms, 32–33

Gadhafi, Moammar, 208, 213
Galadari, Abdul Whab, 63
GATT. *See* General Agreement on
Tariffs and Trade
GCC. *See* Gulf Cooperation
Council
GDP. *See* Gross Domestic Product
General Agreement on Tariffs and
Trade (GATT), 81
Geneva Convention (1927), 113
Geneva Protocol (1923), 113
GIC. *See* Gulf Investment
Corporation
GOIC. *See* Gulf Organization for
Industrial Consulting
Gorbachev, Mikhail, 163–166
Government contracting, 125–126
Great Britain, 22, 49, 53, 54, 55,
56, 141, 177, 184, 213
arms sales, 39

Bahrain and, 193, 206
federation and, 8, 28, 30
Kuwait and, 188, 189, 190
legal influence, 108–109, 112
military presence, 37, 39
Oman and, 29, 37, 39, 186, 191
Qatar and, 193
Saudi Arabia and, 29
sphere of influence, 8, 25, 28–29,
39, 44
Trucial States and, 8, 28
withdrawal of, 8–9, 10, 24, 26,
27, 28, 147, 169
"Greater federation," 24, 26–29
Greater Tunbs, 26, 28
Gromyko, Andrei, 157, 158, 161
Gross Domestic Product (GDP),
73–75, 90, 91(table)
GUFC. *See* Gulf United Fiberglass
Company
Gulbenkian Red Line Agreement,
49
Gulf Air, 31, 140
Gulf Aluminum Rolling Mill, 34,
139
Gulf Cooperation Council (GCC)
actions of, 133–141, 193–194,
194(n)
authority, 129
Charter, 32, 71, 72, 77, 82, 128,
128(n), 129–130, 132, 140, 172,
217–223
committees, 132–133
Common Agricultural Policy, 71,
78, 81
Common Objectives and Policies
for Development Plans, 71, 78,
81
Constitution, 10
credibility of, 13
defense role, 44–45
founding of, 10, 22, 156, 170
Industrial Regulations, 79
Ministerial Council, 130–131
objectives, 129, 172
organization, 11–12, 130–133
Organization for Measures and
Standards, 78